The Risks of Sunbathing Topless

and Other
Funny Stories from the Road

. . . .

EDITED BY KATE CHYNOWETH

SEAL PRESS

The Risks of Sunbathing Topless:
and Other Funny Stories from the Road

Copyright © 2005 by Kate Chynoweth

Published by Seal Press
An Imprint of Avalon Publishing Group, Incorporated
1400 65th Street, Suite 250
AVALON Emeryville, CA 94608
publishing group incorporated

ISBN 1-58005-141-3

9 8 7 6 5 4 3 2 1

Library of Congress Cataloging-in-Publication Data
Chynoweth, Kate.
The risks of sunbathing topless : and other funny stories from the road / by Kate Chynoweth.
p. cm.
ISBN 1-58005-141-3
1. Women travelers—Anecdotes. 2. Voyages and travels—Anecdotes. 3. Women travelers—
Humor. 4. Voyages and travels—Humor. I. Title.
G465.C5 2005
910.4'092—dc22
2004030250

Design by Gia Giasullo, Studio eg
Printed in Canada by Webcom
Distributed by Publishers Group West

For Leslie Miller, the best editor I know.

Table of Contents

· · · · · · ·

. . . . . .

Introduction

One of the many side effects of stumbling into freelance travel writing in my late twenties was that I pulled a lot of novice moves—and ended up with many humiliating stories as a result. But if my education in the black art of magazine and guidebook travel writing taught me to keep extra Tampax in my car, it also taught me to avoid mentioning all those unpleasant and boring truths. Thus, I learned to turn a horrific encounter on a weird island into a story about a pretty ferry ride; a near-death experience on a boat trip became a mental footnote in an article about a pleasant, white-sand beach.

Given this, it's probably not surprising that I yearned to write about the unvarnished truth, with all its freakish strangers, stained shirts, and missed connections. Writing about trips gone wrong is more fun—a pause, if you will, in the dizzyingly positive spin cycle.

Enter this book and my idea for the title—sunbathing topless—which, over the years, has become my own shorthand for unexpected embarrassments and humiliations, the type that only women can really understand.

This shorthand, of course, has a story behind it: Flash back to the summer of 1993, when I was traveling on the coast of southern France with one of my greatest high school pals, Matt. Our friendship, like almost all those shared at the cusp of adulthood, did not take itself too seriously. We goaded and teased each other relentlessly, finding our best laughs in mockery and repetition.

And what better target for mockery than when I opted to stay chastely covered at the beach in Nice? It was our first seaside encounter in France, on a stiflingly hot afternoon, and legions of deeply tanned, bare-breasted

Frenchwomen lined the beach. Matt waited barely five minutes after we parked on our towels to start haranguing me. Did I need a pep talk about my breasts? (No.) He adopted a concerned look and tone: He hoped I wasn't being so modest for his sake. (I wasn't.) Then why, he wanted to know—now that we'd conquered cliff diving, braved a nighttime skinny-dipping session with strangers, and overnighted at a house party near Amsterdam for three days straight—wouldn't I take off my top and treat those puppies to a little bit of sunshine?

I declared my reason, pointing to the cautionary tale visible in the form of the wrinkled, overripe-banana breasts on the older ladies at the beach. Matt looked at me skeptically and said he doubted a fatty liver would induce me to stop drinking. Good point.

In truth, I couldn't explain my prim behavior. I knew that going topless on this beach was perfectly safe; but for some reason, it didn't feel that way. Pointing my bare nipples straight up to the sun seemed, at the time, an invitation for harassment. And wasn't such self-preservation appropriate? After all, I'd already been flashed on the Paris Metro and felt a hand climb up under my skirt on an escalator—both of which I'd laughed off with Matt but felt deeply disturbed by—and for these encounters, I'd been fully clothed.

I was a woman, after all, and there were reasons to feel self-conscious—reasons that I couldn't explain to a guy. I rolled over onto my stomach and vowed not to take Matt's bait.

After a couple of days more on the sand with my top snugly tied, however, my own prudishness began to bore me. And finally, one day when the beach was slightly less crowded, I quickly rolled down my one-piece while Matt was swimming far out at sea. I squirmed out of the bathing suit while lying flat on my back to avoid drawing unwanted attention—although I felt certain that the glowing peaks of my never-before-sun-kissed chest made that nearly impossible.

For the first couple of minutes I lay rigid, waiting for someone to approach and chastise me. I glanced left and then right, as if expecting to see somebody familiar who might take a photograph for future blackmail. But eventually, the sun's soporific effect worked its magic, and I relaxed. It wasn't so bad, actually. In fact, it felt good.

I woke up abruptly to little flicks of cold water; Matt was flipping his mane of wet hair over my supine body. "I got lost on the beach," he crowed, "but I found my way back by your headlights! They're beaming!"

A few other American travelers nearby on their towels—liberated types who were tanning topless—glanced over, smirking. I must have blushed to the roots of my hair and the tips of my nipples.

This story—and Matt's punch line, which made him proud—was retold among our friends and acquaintances upon our return. It fits right in with my philosophy, never proven wrong yet, that men's "funny stories" are more often about other people's humiliation than their own.

Conversely, women, at least the ones I know, tend to relish the airing of a good, solid screwup. Maybe this is why I didn't really mind the recounting of the tale. Besides, what seemed funnier than Matt's punch line was that, after my first traumatic disrobing, I'd quickly acclimatized to topless life—and spent the subsequent weeks of our vacation running around topless on remote beaches in Greece.

So it was that, as I started work on the book, I reminisced about this bare-breasted encounter—and my many other embarrassments, large and small.

Fortunately, I turned up a surfeit of excellent stories from other women. Often, I had my fellow travel writers to thank—I recognized in the lurid, funny details of their essays a rebellion against the tyranny of postcard perfection that I myself had experienced. Many of them seemed as eager to share their tales of woe as I was eager to read them: Witness Paige Porter's humiliatingly public squeeze into a string bikini, or the near-incarceration of Lisa Taggart on an assignment to write about chorus frogs.

But I quickly realized also that it wasn't just travel writers who were dying to diverge from the pretty, predictable script and reveal their warts and bruises. It was also honeymooners, and journalists, and women taking tropical vacations alone. It turns out that everyone is eager to get the disasters off their chests—*especially* those former honeymooners, who sent in their submissions in spades: Essays herein by Marrit Ingman and Sarah Franklin show just how funny it can be when the ultimate escape devolves from its romantic intinerary.

Overall, I'm delighted with the essays and honored to report that none of them provide successful models for travel—although they do provide some excellent laughs. Ayun Halliday shares the results of climbing Mount Kilimanjaro with $14.99 worth of cheap gear from Sportmart and training by drinking beer and hand-rolling cigarettes. C. Lill Ahrens describes the translation problems that lead to the demise of her apartment kitchen in Seoul. In order to fund her trip, Kay Sexton takes on work as Rose the English Charmer in Germany's worst burlesque bar.

From Finland to Ecuador, from Cambodia to California, from New Zealand to Maui, these stories—unlike the majority of travel writing—are simply not predicated on notions of travel success: This is the antidote to the glossy brochure. But thank God we don't have the photos to prove it.

Kate Chynoweth
Seattle, Washington
November 2004

Roughly Translated

C. Lill Ahrens

• • • • • • • • • • • • • • • • • • • •

We swayed in unison, hip pressed to hip, thigh to quivering thigh. Limbs trembling, hands tingling, we rocked to a distant throbbing roar. I longed for release, ached for the finish, and clung to the strap on the jam-packed Seoul subway, wedged in with Mr. Chong.

The last thing I wanted this morning was to be on my own with Mr. Chong.

My first two days in Korea, my husband, Paul, had been with us. Mr. Chong, my husband's coworker in a Korean company, had helped us find and begin to furnish an apartment on the mountainous edge of Seoul. Mr. Chong was an excellent negotiator. So far he'd negotiated good deals on everything from forks to used furniture. There was still a lot to buy—pillows, lamps, a stove, etc.—and ready or not, we would be moving in tonight. But Paul had had to start work this morning, which left me to cope alone with the shopping list, a frazzled, jet-lagged brain, and Mr. Chong, who, for reasons known only to himself, had never spoken to me.

I clung to the pep talk Paul had given me: "Mr. Chong talks to me, hon. I'm sure he'll talk to you if he has to."

So far this morning, he hadn't had to. I'd stuck to him like a barnacle as he hustled from taxi to bus, bus to subway. Now he was still avoiding eye contact—not that difficult, really, since his eyes were level with my chin.

I could see his discomfort in the prickly line of flesh exposed by the part in his hair. I could feel it through his scratchy overcoat buttoned up to the neck. He was an engineer, after all, not a shopping guide. He was stuck with me, too.

The train roared around a bend; the passengers leaned as one through the curve, their hair a gleaming wave of ebony. The train itself sparkled inside, but the air caught in my throat. I knew the aroma was a by-product of the garlicky Korean diet, and that I'd get used to it eventually. Recalling that to Koreans, Americans smell like cheese, I began to breathe into the collar of my parka instead of on Mr. Chong.

He bought a newspaper from a newsboy squeezing through the crowd, folded it into a space-saving column-width strip, and began to read. Bleary-eyed, I passed the time trying to decipher the ads on the wall, wishing I knew Korean.

One ad pictured a woman strolling arm in arm with a curvaceous pillow taller than she was. The pillow had round black eyes, luxurious eyelashes, red lips, pink cheeks, buck teeth, and a blue bow tied around a single strand of hair that stuck straight up on top. A bed pillow! So far I'd seen lots of hard throw pillows in Seoul but not a single bed pillow on which to sleep. That ad might tell me where to buy them. It also gave me an opportunity to talk directly to Mr. Chong.

"Excuse me, Mr. Chong, what does that ad say?"

He glanced up to where I was pointing, then down again to his column-width newspaper.

"Mr. Chong?"

He brought his paper closer to his nose.

"That ad for pillows—please tell me what it says."

I was about to ask again when he mumbled something.

Aha! A crack in the ice. "I'm sorry," I said, "I didn't understand."

Staring fiercely at his paper he said, "O nee foe woe mon."

I pondered his cryptic message. At least it was a start. O nee foe woe mon. Oneefoewoemon. Oh! Only for women? Koreans had his-and-hers pillows?

"Excuse me again, Mr. Chong. Does that ad say where we can buy pillows?"

His cheeks turned maroon. "Not pillow!"

"We can't buy a pillow?"

"No! *That* not pillow!" He snapped open his paper like a wall between us.

Not pillow? I studied the ad again, squinting to see it better. Under the picture and Korean text was a small photo insert. The realization came in a slow hot flush. The woman's tall, round-eyed, pink-cheeked companion was a sanitary napkin.

MUTELY I SCUTTLED after Mr. Chong, up from the depths of the subway into cold winter sunshine, then into the shadows of an awninged alley lined with little shops. The shop windows displayed every kind of blender. The entire alley seemed devoted to blenders. Long tables piled high with blenders stood outside the shops, narrowing the passageway to about four feet.

A three-foot-wide pushcart trundled behind me, picking up speed. I ducked into a blender shop to let the cart pass, stepped out again, and was nearly run down by a motorcycle, its hot exhaust pipe passing inches from my shins.

Instead of waiting for me, Mr. Chong was already an alley ahead and not looking back. Struggling to catch up, I felt like a little kid tagging after her mean big brother—hurt, angry, indignant, and wishing he'd hold my hand.

I dogged him down an alley full of clocks, past an alley of musical computer chip doorbells ("*In your Easter bonnet . . .*"), turned right at an alley of boom boxes—I held my ears—turned left at the Alley of a Zillion Watches—"Hey, lady!" cried a vendor, "Rolex! Twenty dollar! Hey, lady!"—and started to run.

Out of breath, heart pounding, I caught up with Mr. Chong in the Alley of Telephones. He motioned me into a shop full of used phones and grunted—Mr. Chong's way, I surmised, of saying, "Please select a phone." I pointed to the nearest, a turquoise princess touch-tone. The clerk plugged it in. Mr. Chong punched in a phone number, barked into the receiver, and thrust it at me. Did he expect me to talk to the phone company?

But when I pressed the phone to my ear I heard, "Paul Ahrens here," my husband's beautiful bass voice, sounding at that moment like a benevolent god.

"It's me," I squeaked, strangling an unexpected sob. I told him that I guessed I was testing our phone.

"How's it going?" Paul asked. "Has Chong talked to you yet?"

"Sort of. I can't really talk about it now."

"I knew he would. Hang in there, hon. Love you."

Somewhat fortified, I hung up.

Mr. Chong haggled with the clerk, paid him from my envelope of *won*, Korean money, and must have made arrangements for delivery, because he left the shop without the phone. I sprinted after him to the Alley of Used TVs. He grunted at me to point to the one I wanted, haggled with the clerk, paid him, and we moved to the next alley, where he grunted, I pointed, he haggled and paid. Grunt, point, haggle, pay; grunt, point, haggle, pay—like a crude Korean conga. But once I got the rhythm of it, I had to admit this was the most efficient shopping I'd ever done.

We congaed up and down the narrow alleys, not even stopping for lunch until, in addition to the phone and TV, we had a used clock radio, two used lamps, and the biggest used refrigerator to be had in the Alley of Used

Refrigerators, four feet tall. I had almost risked speech at that point, to ask if there was an Alley of Used *Large* Refrigerators, but then noticed the freezer compartment was just big enough to hold a half-gallon of chocolate ice cream and let it go.

So it wasn't until we entered a used stove shop that I finally had to break our tacit pact of silence, for we were surrounded by stacks of what looked like stainless steel briefcases with two gas burners on the lid and control knobs where the clasps would be. Yuppie camp stoves?

I uttered my first word to Mr. Chong since the incident on the subway. "Oven?"

He grunted.

"I need a stove with an oven."

"No . . . oven," he said, and since I wasn't pointing, he picked up a stove, turned his back to me and started haggling with the clerk.

Thinking he might not understand the word, I dug out my English/Korean dictionary. It listed three different words for oven: *hwadok*, *kama*, and *sot*.

"Excuse me, Mr. Chong, I want a hwa dok."

He paused the negotiations long enough to say, "No *hwadok*," and turned his back to me again.

I tapped him on the shoulder. "Ka ma?"

Mr. Chong and the clerk stopped haggling to gaze at me thoughtfully. "You have chair," said Mr. Chong. They resumed haggling.

I was exhausted, suddenly weak with hunger, and Mr. Chong was taking my money out of my envelope to buy something I didn't want. I had one word left. "Mr. Chong!" I cried, "I want to buy a *sot!*"

The clerk clapped his hand on his mouth and shook with stifled giggles. Mr. Chong glared at me and hustled me out of the shop.

We stood silently in the gathering dusk, Mr. Chong with his hands in his pockets, rocking on his heels, looking at everything but me. He seemed to be at a loss as to how to proceed. I decided to start over on the oven problem—this time without using Korean.

I found an old receipt in my pocket, smoothed it out on my purse, and began to sketch a four-burner range with an open oven door. After a moment, Mr. Chong sidled closer to watch.

I drew a cake on the oven rack, then erased it, realizing it might cause confusion. I rendered the oven dark and empty inside, like my stomach. Tapping it with my pencil, I said, "Oven. I want a stove with an oven."

"Ah," he said, "no . . . used oven."

Aha! No *used* ovens. A different matter entirely. "*New* oven?"

He sighed, "New . . . expensive."

"Expensive okay!" Paul would agree it was worth the money. Feeling triumphant, I marched after Mr. Chong to New Oven Alley.

Identical cardboard cartons filled the shop. Only one model was on display. The clerk placed it in my arms as if awarding me a trophy. It looked just like the used stoves, only on the front of it, in between the control knobs, was a little drawer with a window in it.

Mr. Chong pulled out the drawer. "Oven," he said. It was just big enough for a toasted cheese sandwich.

"Very nice," I said, and handed the stove back to the clerk. It dawned on me that Koreans didn't bake much.

While Mr. Chong haggled with the clerk, I tried to think. Was the toaster oven worth the extra money? I could bake a potato in there, if I cut it in half first. Or a miniature pie, like I used to make in my Kenner Easy-Bake Oven . . . but where would I get the miniature pie tin? Wait a minute—what was I thinking? I rarely baked. In fact, ever since I'd outgrown my Easy-Bake Oven, I didn't even like to bake.

"Never mind." I said to Mr. Chong. "No oven. Used stove okay." And it occurred to me that the scene I'd caused over the used stove had been for naught. He rubbed his temples, gave a huge sigh, and marched me back to Used Stove Alley, giving wide berth to the first Used Stove Shop.

NIGHT FELL. The awnings lit up with strings of tiny lights. At the alley intersections, mysterious snacks sizzled and spit on crusted grills and crackled in black vats of oil. Mr. Chong grunted, which I translated to, "Please select a snack." Looking forward to a feast from the Kentucky Chicken outlet I'd seen near my apartment, I pointed to three bananas, enough to hold me for the long drive to the edge of Seoul.

Mr. Chong frowned at my choice, and for himself selected a flat, stiff squid. As the vendor passed it through a flame, the squid shriveled, tentacles writhing.

Mr. Chong handed me my envelope, now nearly empty of *won* but stuffed with receipts. Except for groceries, cleaning supplies, and the elusive pillows, I was finished shopping. But more important, Mr. Chong and I would soon be finished with each other. Tomorrow he would return to his life as an engineer. I didn't know who would feel more relieved.

I followed him to the delivery truck that was loaded with my purchases. We inventoried them and climbed up front with the driver, Mr. Chong courteously taking the middle. Here we were again, wedged hip to hip, thigh to vibrating thigh as the truck moaned through the gears, penetrating traffic.

Munching on my third banana, I suddenly felt grateful to Mr. Chong. He'd found me a home in this vast city, he'd helped me furnish it, and now he was taking me there to move me in. All this in three days, a feat I wouldn't have thought possible. I shouted over the engine, "Thank you for all your help, Mr. Chong! I love my apartment on the mountain! I will be happy there!"

His teeth gleamed in the dark. He was smiling? "You are very welcome!" he bellowed back. "But you still need to buy chicken! I will negotiate a very good deal for chicken!"

How did he know Paul and I were having chicken for dinner? Oh, Paul must have mentioned—wait a minute—Mr. Chong's English was excellent! That faker! I choked back a laugh. After all he'd put me through, why talk fluently now? Because it was no longer necessary? Because sitting down we were the same height? Or . . . because I'd said thank you? Maybe it was a gesture of friendship. A parting gift. Whatever the reason, the floodgates had opened, and he shouted nonstop. Parched for English, I leaned my head back and let it wash over me. He told me of the mountain village where he'd grown up, that he'd had to come to Seoul to make a living, that he missed the mountains back home. As he continued to shout, I fell asleep.

A COUPLE OF HOURS later, the driver killed the engine and I awoke, embarrassed to find I'd been drooling on Mr. Chong's shoulder. Climbing stiffly from the cab, we took deep breaths of the crisp mountain air. Paul must have heard us drive up, for he was waiting under the streetlight in front of our small apartment building. We all pitched in, and after a few trips up and down the stairs, alternately slipping our shoes off and on at our doorstep, Korean style, Paul and I were moved in. Standing in the entry, we said goodbye and thank you to the driver. Then a special thanks to Mr. Chong.

He bowed stiffly and marched out the door. "Chicken!" he called over his shoulder, his old stern self. "I will negotiate chicken!"

Dear Mr. Chong, still offering to help. I ran onto the landing in my socks and called to him as he hurried down the stairs, "Mr. Chong!"

He stopped at the bottom, turned, and looked up at me with a frown.

"Thank you so much, but don't bother about the chicken. Paul can do it." Smiling fondly, I waved goodbye.

He raised an eyebrow and returned a tentative wave. I wondered if he was as amazed as I that we'd become friends. I blinked back sudden tears, surprised to find I'd miss Mr. Chong. Like a newly hatched gosling, I'd imprinted.

Paul went for Kentucky Chicken, and I prepared for our first meal in our new home. First, the bleak overhead fluorescent had to go, so I shoved the kitchen table against the wall, set a lamp on the table, plugged in the lamp, and screwed in a negotiated light bulb. I turned it on and flicked off the fluorescent. The kitchen glowed with a cozy light, enhanced by warm yellow walls and white cabinetry.

I sank into a kitchen chair, giddy with exhaustion, relief, happiness, hunger—and enchantment, for it seemed I was living in a playhouse. My little refrigerator fit snug under the wall cupboard. My little stove sat upon its own little custom-fitted cupboard. Under the window, a little combination sink-and-counter unit stood on four little legs. It all looked so adorable, I wanted to cry. What was it with these tears? I needed food.

As if on cue, Paul bounded in, singing a bass aria from *The Mikado*, and dropped a soggy sack of Kentucky Chicken on the table. Before I could pounce on it, he crushed me in a hug. "Home!"

While I attacked the chicken, Paul told me about his day, his office, his private locker just for his shoes (with the toes folded up so they'd fit), and the executives' cafeteria, where he had enjoyed a huge, delicious Korean lunch.

I tossed a chicken bone aside and snatched another piece.

"My only problem," he continued, "is the sandals. They issued me the biggest ones they have, and they're much too short."

"I'll try to find you a bigger pair," I said between bites.

"Thanks, hon." He nibbled on a chicken breast. "Were you able to find pillows?"

I shook my head. "I'll stuff a couple t-shirts with clean underwear for now."

"Good solution."

A mound of greasy napkins later, my hunger appeased, I entertained him with my day. ". . . And then," I said, "I told him, 'I want to buy a *sot*,' and it was like I'd insulted him or something."

Paul took out his dictionary and flipped the pages to "oven." "Hmm. I think I see the problem. You rhymed *'sot'* with 'got.' According to the pronunciation table, it rhymes with 'goat.' What you said would be spelled s-a-t." He turned to the back half of his book, which was Korean-to-English. Mine didn't have that feature. He found *sat* and laughed. "It's a Korean wrestler's thigh band!"

I laughed too, though I didn't know what a wrestler's thigh band was, exactly, until I felt Paul shaking my shoulder: "Hold on! Hold on!" he said. "*Sat* has more than one meaning."

I blew my nose on a greasy napkin and wiped my eyes.

He was giving me a lopsided grin. "It also means 'crotch.'"

THE NEXT MORNING we breakfasted on leftover chicken and cups of hot water; then Paul left for work. More than anything I wanted to crawl back in bed for a well-deserved rest, but first I had to visit the corner grocery for food and household basics. Fortunately, that was something I could do without Mr. Chong. Now that I knew what I'd said to him, how could I ever face him again?

I had just finished dressing when I heard footsteps ascending my stairs, then a polite knock. A salesman? The landlord? Clutching my Berlitz, I opened the door.

Two men in business suits and a young woman in a black wool coat stood on my doorstep, smiling, bowing and talking at me in Korean. I returned their smiles and bows, wondering if they were a neighborhood welcoming committee. While I rifled the Berlitz for a welcoming phrase, they stepped inside, slipped off their shoes, and headed for the kitchen. I trotted after them, lit the fire under the kettle for tea, remembered I had no tea, and shut it off.

I found the word for "good morning," *annyonghashimnika*. While I sounded out the syllables, conscientiously flipping back and forth to the pronunciation guide, the men draped their suit coats over the kitchen chairs, and the woman kept talking and smiling at me as she took the silverware from the drawer under the stove, the dishes from the cupboard over the refrigerator, and stacked them on the table as if anticipating a meal.

If only I hadn't scarfed the last of the chicken.

The men inspected the now-empty wall cupboard, as if surprised it contained no food. I expected them to check the refrigerator next, but instead they rolled up their shirt sleeves, whipped claw hammers from their belt loops, and began to rip the cupboard off the wall. Shrieking nails drowned out my yelps. Bits of concrete wall splattered like shrapnel. Frantically I searched my Berlitz for an appropriate phrase like "Sorry, you have the wrong address" or "Is this a robbery?" while the woman chattered happily at me over the din.

As one man made for the door with my wall cupboard, the other man thrust my stove into my arms, kettle and all, and snatched the cupboard it had been sitting on. I balanced the stove on one arm, careful not to lose the kettle, and, using my free hand and teeth, flipped my Berlitz to the emergency section.

They stepped into their shoes. I found a phrase: "Stop or I'll scream."

I sounded it out—*Koo mahn too jee ah noo . . . . m . . . my on? . . . me oan? . . .* I checked the pronunciation table: *eow,* like a cat, *meown so ree rool chee . . .* —I wished I knew which syllables meant "stop" and "scream" so I could emphasize them— *. . . rool tee ee—.*

The door closed.

They were gone.

I stood unmoving, motes of concrete dust adrift before my eyes. Then, in lazy downward spirals, the dust settled on the dishes, on the kitchen table, on the suit coats draped over the kitchen chairs. . . . I blinked. The men had left their suit coats. They intended to return. Hope swelled.

Maybe they weren't taking my cupboards but replacing them. They could be coming back soon. Sure enough, I heard footsteps clicking up the stairs, my door opening. They padded into the kitchen, smiling and bowing. But empty-handed.

The kitchen sink slid easily out from under the wall-mounted faucets, because the drainpipe was just a hose stuck down a hole in the floor. I hadn't noticed that before. Like a corpse dragged from the scene of the crime, the sink oozed a murky trail across the vinyl and out the door.

The woman grabbed the suit coats and followed it out, waving at me gaily. The door closed.

All was quiet save for the slow *thip, thip, thip* of water on the floor under the faucet. I'd have to ask Paul to ask Mr. Chong to ask the landlord to fix that drip—wait a minute, I had no sink.

The empty sink corner had a greenish, fuzzy coating. Above the refrigerator, except for the jagged gray divots where the cupboard had been nailed, the wall shone bright white. I'd assumed the walls were painted yellow, but the color was apparently an accumulation of smoke and grease.

I moved to the kitchen window, chunks of wall crunching underfoot, just in time to see my kitchen disappear around the corner in the back of a pickup. It didn't look like they'd be returning it anytime soon.

I started for the bedroom to phone Paul but was pulled up short: The stove in my arms was still attached to the propane tank outside the kitchen window, the red rubber connector hose stretched taut. I took a calming breath, stepped back, placed the stove on the table. Then I dashed to the bedroom, called Paul at work, and told him the news.

"I know," he said.

"You *know*?" I collapsed to the sleeping mat.

"I was just about to call you. The landlord phoned my secretary, who asked me to tell you that people were coming to pick up the kitchen."

"But why?"

"It was for sale. That woman bought it."

"But—"

"It wasn't included in the rent, so it's all on the up and up. Kitchens are like furniture here. Fully portable. Isn't that interesting?"

I asked through clenched teeth, "Why didn't we buy it?"

"Mr. Chong says you told him not to negotiate, which surprised me. I thought you liked the kitchen."

"But I didn't! I mean, I didn't tell him not to negotiate the kitchen. It never came up."

"Hang on a minute, Mr. Chong wants to tell me something."

My face burned—Mr. Chong was right there? I cringed at the memory of my sanitary napkin and crotch faux pas.

Paul said, "Mr. Chong says he can help us get another one on Saturday."

"No. *Not* Mr.—"

"Hold on." Muffled voices, then Paul said, "Mr. Chong wants to talk to you."

"No! Not Mr.—"

Mr. Chong came on the line. "I am most very sorry. I thought you tell me 'do not bother.'"

I forced a light tone. "When was that, Mr. Chong?"

"Last night. After you move in. I say, 'I will negotiate chicken,' and—"

"*Chicken?*" I shut my eyes recalling the scene, and moaned softly, "Oh no. . . ."

"Oh yes!" he said. "I thought you say, 'Paul will do it.' My mistake. So sorry."

I didn't speak for a moment. I wanted to respond in a way that wouldn't make him feel worse than he already did. So I clamped my lips together while tears of laughter streamed down my cheeks.

When I could safely talk I said, "No, no, Mr. Chong. My mistake. I thought you meant the *other* chicken. For dinner? Kentucky Chicken."

Mr. Chong didn't answer.

"You know—the bird? *Bawk, bawk. . . .*"

Just heavy breathing on the line.

I flapped an elbow. *"Bawk bawk ba-CAWK?"*

Mr. Chong grunted. His way, I hoped, of laughing.

Kilimanjaro

Ayun Halliday

. . . .

My entire childhood, I was invariably the last one picked by peers charged with picking teams in gym class. This experience eventually metastasized into an uncharitable view of any physical exertion that couldn't be accomplished nude or, alternatively, drunk. Oh, I could work up a sweat waitressing, but it had become a point of honor to avoid any activity that might be considered "sporty." I preferred cultural pursuits, like lying on my side, eating Count Chocula straight from the box while reading e. e. cummings.

Needless to say, unless she's got a job at the Kibo Hotel, someone like me has no business at the foot of Mount Kilimanjaro. Preparing to make the dreaded climb, I found myself envying the maids who, unlike me, wouldn't have to take a single step up the mountain unless they wanted to. Presumably, I did want to. I'd been acting of my own free will when I signed up, adding an optional five-day Kili trek to the six-week safari that would take me through Tanzania, Rwanda, Kenya, and, not coincidentally, far from Chicago and the live-in boyfriend I'd come to view as a colossal drag.

I guess I reckoned that as long as one is ditching everything familiar to rough it on another continent, it would be foolish not to go whole hog. *No mountaineering experience necessary!* the brochure had promised. *Gradual ascent through four distinct biospheres. Suitable for visitors of all ages and abilities, even senior citizens and schoolchildren.*

This glossy reassurance, coupled with the knowledge that serious climbers dismissed the Kibo route as a mere bunny slope, was encouraging: Perhaps a phys-ed reject like myself did stand a slight chance of making it to the top.

Except. Rosalyn Carter hadn't. We'd missed her and Jimmy by just two weeks. The hotel staff still hadn't gotten around to taking down the welcome banner they'd swagged across the library in honor of the former First Couple's visit. Jimmy had reached the summit, the guy tending the hotel bar gossiped, but Rosalyn had succumbed to altitude sickness halfway up. Oh my god, I thought, downing another Tusker beer, what if that happened to me? How could it not? I got winded running for the bus.

My fellow climbers were much more fit. Strangers six weeks earlier when we boarded the truck that hauled us and our camping gear through the savannas of East Africa, we'd bonded through hardship: the rutted dirt roads, the packaged dehydrated curries, the jellied bowels, the constant engine trouble, the appalling lack of hygiene, the unstoppable German shutterbug who photographed our most private moments malaria even. . . . If we hadn't had much in common to start, we did now. It was almost like we'd gone through combat together. Our connection transcended boundaries of nationality and age, but could it withstand Kilimanjaro? In their civilian lives, my newfound buddies relished such alien pursuits as downhill skiing, ultimate Frisbee, jogging, spelunking, and watching ESPN. When they looked forward to the upcoming arduous trial, they did so without an overwhelming sense of dread and regret. How long until they started to regard me as deadwood?

"You fucking marshmallow," scoffed Bradford, one of two Midwestern frat boys who, to my amazement, had adopted me early on as a sort of lovably incompetent mascot. "Would you quit whining that you're not going to make it?"

"Okay," I consented, stuffing my cold-weather gear into a gunnysack to be handed over to the porters, who, thankfully, would also carry our food, cooking equipment, and bedrolls. "But seriously, you guys, I'm afraid it's going to be too hard, especially since I don't think I'm entirely recovered from that malaria."

"Dude, you're not the only one who had malaria," Bruce, the more rational of the two frat boys, pointed out. "I'm still running a fever."

"Yeah, and I'm shitting like a faucet," Bradford bragged. "So what?"

"But you guys are into hiking," I protested. "I'm not."

Bradford suspended his own gunnysack operation long enough to chuck a sour t-shirt at my head. "Will you shut up? Jesus, you're a lame-o."

"Don't worry, Lame-o. You'll make it," Bruce attempted to reassure me, "if we have to shove your ass every step of the way."

"Oh my god, Bruce, look!" Bradford squawked. "It's the giant sleeping bag!" Weakly flipping him the bird, I crammed the nylon albatross in on top of the bright orange parka I'd borrowed from my now-ex-live-in-boyfriend. My unwieldy sleeping bag had quickly become a running joke among my traveling companions. Their bags were all lean, mean, down-filled mummies. Squished into their matching stuff sacks, they were no bigger than two-liter soda bottles. Mine, on the other hand, was the sort of polyester-filled rectangular model a child might take to a slumber party. Because it was black, as opposed to ballerina patterned, I'd considered it rugged enough for Africa. Besides, it had been priced a good forty dollars below any of the mummy bags at Sportmart. Too late, I realized the psychic cost of that penny-pinching. It worried me that I'd gone for the el-cheapo option with regard to hiking boots, too. Not wanting to make myself look even more ridiculous by teaming clumpy, waffle-soled footwear with the brightly printed cotton kangas I'd been wearing like wraparound skirts, I'd resisted every opportunity to break them in earlier in the trip.

According to the literature, day one of the hike represented the easiest stretch, just three hours' climb from the national park where the hotel's Land Rover dropped us off at Mandara Hut, where we would spend the night. We posed for pictures before embarking upon the well-trod path snaking up through the thick vegetation at what struck me as a rather distressingly acute angle. In the photos from this session, my friends, all of whom harbored genuine enthusiasm for the challenge ahead, look excited but also a tad anxious, standing there in their multipocketed khaki shorts, their sensible footwear, and t-shirts that attested to prior recreational pursuits in the Great Outdoors. I, in contrast, sport butt-grazing secondhand gym shorts, olive-green Keds, and the expression of a professional daredevil, someone whose idea of fun involves Level Six white-water rapids. Under dangly beaded earrings and ridiculous wraparound sunglasses the size of front fenders, my smile is all toothy confidence. What can I say? I majored in theater.

At first, we marched along in a herd, making idle chatter, or rather, the others made idle chatter that I had difficulty hearing due to my own panting. I was wheezing like an elderly schnauzer, a fact not lost on Bradford, who imitated my labored breathing to the delight of the entire company.

"Quit picking on huh, Bridfuhd," tittered the young Australian Sandy, who, at twenty-two, was the baby of the group. "Or you'll be nixt!" I didn't know what this could mean, except that maybe Sandy was nursing a crush on one of the frat boys.

"What are you talking about?" Bradford protested, patting the top of my sweaty, ponytailed head. "Lame-o knows I'm just playing with her. Don't you, Lame-o?"

I tried to swat him but stumbled on a root, inadvertently woofing as I pitched headfirst over my ski pole.

Having kept the throttle on for the better part of an hour, my companions were visibly itching to pick up the pace. I told them it wouldn't bother me if they wanted to go on ahead. The path was so well tamped, it wasn't like I was going to lose my way. "I'll expect you to have lunch on the table by the time I get there," I rasped gaily as they sped away. Too bad for them. Bradford was going to miss a lot of good material. The higher I went, the less sure my footing became. The muddy slope was a mess of loose pebbles and tangled vines. In the places where recent heavy rains had washed away the existing trail, I dragged myself up on my knees, clinging to whatever plant life might offer purchase. My fingernails were caked with mud, and my glasses were badly in need of a defroster. Every now and then I'd hear a sprightly *slap slap slap* and a few seconds later, a porter bearing the gunnysacks of a descending group would appear, skipping down the mountain in flip-flops, apparently unbothered by the hundred or so pounds balanced atop his head. "*Jambo*," he would sing out in the tourist-friendly shorter version of the traditional Kiswahili greeting.

"*Jambo*," I'd croak, sides heaving, certain that in this moment I personified everything that was wrong with my sleeping bag.

"*Habari?*" the porter would inquire with rote concern.

"*Mizouri sana*," I'd lie, following social convention. Our exchange thus completed, the porter would continue on his nimble way, leaving me to contemplate how "very well, thank you" in his language sounded like "misery" in mine.

MY PALS WERE lounging on the lawn of the A-frame hut when I finally pulled up, accompanied by Elsie, the fair-minded Swiss citizen who had voluntarily doubled back to see if I had died. With plenty of time to kill before dinner, the frat boys talked me into a ten-minute lateral hike to a semi-scenic crater where we met some members of a Christian youth group, breaking for granola bars on their way down. Despite our ideological differences, I was heartened to note the physical similarities between their teenage bodies and my own flabby temple. Hoping to better assess my odds, I demanded to know if their entire party had made it to the top. "Ev'body but two," the taller one drawled in what was later revealed to be an Oklahoma accent.

"Got any pointers for those of us on our way up?"

The boys exchanged a glance.

"Well, whenever I found myself feeling discouraged," the short one suggested, "I just turned to the Lord and asked him for the strength to continue."

"And that worked?" Bruce asked, coaxing some caked mud from the tread of his boot with a stick.

The young believer nodded happily. "When I got to the top and saw that sun rising, the first thing I did was say, 'Thank you, Lord!'"

"And," his tall friend added, lowering his voice, "we were taking mountain medicine twice a day."

"Mountain medicine," we chorused, roused by the sudden turn the conversation had taken. "What's that?"

Sneaking a peek over their shoulders, the boys leaned in close. "They're these little white pills that help your lungs absorb more oxygen."

"Huh?"

"That's how come people get altitude sickness," the tall one announced. "Once the air thins out, the brain starts worrying that it isn't getting enough oxygen. That old brain says, 'That's it! I quit!' and to make sure the climber stops, the brain sends him this terrible headache."

This was beginning to sound very Old Testament, but adrift in the wilderness, I could see little profit in refusing to grab any straw that might help me reach the top.

"With mountain medicine, you're dealing with increased lung capacity," the short one continued. "So your brain's none the wiser. You know how there were two people in our group who decided to quit?" He paused for dramatic effect. "They were the only ones who weren't taking mountain medicine."

"They won't take aspirin, either," his friend clarified. "I told them God's not going to smite them over Bufferin."

"Shit, I wish we'd heard about this stuff earlier," Bradford muttered. My thoughts exactly. If I hadn't been trying to pass myself off as athletic, I'd have burst into tears.

The tall one hesitated, then ventured that they still had some left over. "I guess we don't need really need it anymore, seeing as how we're almost all the way down. . . ."

"We'd totally pay you for it," Bradford rushed to offer.

"No, it wouldn't be Christian to take money from you," the short one said with a frown. My heart sank. "But I guess it would be okay if we just gave you the bottle."

Praise God for victory.

WE TOOK OUR first dose after dinner. We had to be sly about it, because when we'd counted the virtuous Okies' stash, we'd realized that we only had enough medicine for the three of us, plus one more. After some deliberation, we'd settled on Sandy as the lucky fourth. Elsie had been a close runner-up, but we rationalized that a Swiss Miss like her wouldn't need synthetic assistance to get to the peak. Besides, the high moral standard to which she held herself might be a front for a dim view of illegal drugs procured from strangers. "You're *ibsolutely* sure it's safe?" Sandy whispered as we prepared to wash down our meds with hot Milo.

"No," Bruce said with a shrug, grimacing at the taste of the little white tablet.

"You guys," I hissed a couple of minutes later, holding my palms up for inspection. "Do you feel like you're losing all feeling in your fingertips?"

The others nodded, wide eyed. "Thy've gone all tingly," Sandy said in a tone that sounded more awed than alarmed.

"What are you all whispering about over there?" Canadian Carol demanded, her pale eyes suspicious.

"Nothing! Jesus! Why do you always assume there's some big secret?" Bradford overcompensated, palming the precious bottle.

"Bridfuhd was just remarking that his hinds have gone a bit numb," Sandy rushed to interject. "We were trying to remember if thit's a symptom."

"Of altitude sickness?" Carol's brow puckered thoughtfully as she fiddled with the flashlight she wore strapped to her forehead, like a miner. "I'm not 100 percent sure, so don't quote me, but you know, I think that *was* one of the symptoms listed in my World Health manual. You'd better take it easy, Bradford, or you won't make it."

"You're right," he declared, getting to his feet, uncharacteristically meek. A fifteen-year-old porter who seemed to regard the frat boys as the big kahunas offered him a toke from a fat joint as he passed. "No thanks, Simon, I need to preserve my strength. I'm going to bed."

"At seven o'clock?" Bruce wondered aloud. Simon laughed and ambled over to see if the other kahuna wanted a smoke. Bruce waved him away with necrotic fingers.

"God, can you imagine wanting to smoke that stuff up here?" I asked, my throat raw from the razor-sharp fresh air.

"Ayun," Canadian Carol chided. "You shouldn't smoke that stuff at all!"

WE RESUMED THE climb at six o'clock the next morning, following breakfast and "grace," the code name Bruce had invented so we could talk about mountain medicine in front of the others. The terrain made good on the brochure's promise by shifting from verdant jungle to Alpine moor in less than an hour. In a position of authority, Elsie decreed that our new surroundings did look something like Switzerland, though not nearly as much as the terraced hills of Rwanda had. We unzipped our packs to get cameras and sweaters. The brisk air, coupled with the mountain medicine, imbued me with the same purposefulness I used to experience in junior high school, on the day *Seventeen* magazine's fat back-to-school issue hit the stands. I cavorted in circles, singing that the hills were alive with the sound of music.

Then it started to rain. Before I could locate the head opening of my orange plastic poncho, the others surged ahead in a blur of sporty, water-repellent nylon.

"Wait up!" I cried, but they were gone. I felt like a kindergartner whose mommy forgot to pick her up at the bus stop. Shit. There was nothing to do but squish forward in my soaked tennies, hating them all. Bradford and Bruce. Ha! Thought they were so big, calling me Lame-o. I'd like to see them scan a sonnet for iambic pentameter! And Sandy, that ingrate. Had I known she'd ditch me at the first sign of precipitation, I would have voted to throw her share of mountain medicine down the hole of the filthy outhouse.

"Ooh, Breadfuhd," I simpered, attempting her accent. "Moy heends have gone all tingly!" As a reward for coming to fetch me the previous afternoon, Elsie alone escaped my wrath. Everyone else was in the doghouse: Canadian Carol, Timber and Tweedy, the married New Zealanders, even the porters and (to quote the opening theme of *Gilligan's Island)* "the rest." My childish poncho offered little defense from what could now be classified as a downpour. Long tendrils of wet hair plastered themselves to my steamed-up spectacles like kelp. It was the kind of day best spent indoors with a big bowl of popcorn and the works of Charlotte Brontë. Instead, I was slogging laboriously upward through Alpine-style meadows, nose running, teeth chattering, and lungs aching—despite the mountain medicine now coursing

27

through my veins. Not everyone from the truck had opted to climb Kilimanjaro. I could have followed their example and split for Nairobi or Mombasa or even the Seychelles. I could be drinking a Tusker beer or comparison shopping for Masai jewelry. Hell, I could be in Chicago with the pony-nosed guitar player who'd recently replaced the live-in boyfriend in my affections, but no. Having inexplicably chosen to climb Kilimanjaro, I now had to pay the piper by climbing Kilimanjaro.

"Sucks," I muttered aloud, for the hundredth time in twenty-four hours, no one around to hear me but whatever tiny creatures might be sheltering in the dripping foliage. Insects. Birds. Small mammals with short life spans and astounding lung capacity.

By the time I staggered up the steps of Horombo Hut, nearly six hours later, my fury had run its course. All I cared about was getting warm and dry, and, it turns out, I was in good company, since that was all anybody cared about. An unspoken honor system was in place regarding the potbellied stove, the uninsulated wooden structure's sole heat source. Each climber got a turn to hunker before the flames, waving the stick to which his or her sodden socks were tied. Etiquette dictated that this prime spot was to be vacated after no more than five minutes. "But my socks aren't dry," Canadian Carol whined when the rest of us accused her of lingering.

"Nobody's socks are dry," Bradford spat murderously.

"Come on, you guys, it's time to say 'grace,'" Bruce glowered, putting his arms around Sandy and me, hustling us toward a dark corner before Bradford could attempt to strangle Carol with one of her own rank rag wool socks.

After we'd downed our instant coffee, a couple of boiled potatoes, and the allotted portion of our illicit prescription, there was little to do but sculpt dice out of spilled candle wax before retiring to the sleeping loft, where rough-hewn, mattress-free box bunks were stacked three high. It was kind of like being in prison, except we were free to go outdoors at all hours, a privilege I exercised twice, once following the beam cast by the light strapped to Canadian Carol's head and once groping in the dark by myself, missing the final five rungs of the ladder and crashing to the cold wood floor (for one glorious moment, I thought I might have sprained my ankle). Both times I eschewed the horrors of the latrine to relieve myself on the packed earth near the front steps. The rain had stopped, and I paused, bare-assed, to take in the star-spangled majesty of the freezing night sky. "Okay, this is something you can't do in Chicago," I egged myself on. "This is pretty cool, right?"

Everyone who was taking mountain medicine awoke with full-blown head colds. "You don't reckon it's iltitude sickness, do you," Sandy snuffled as we choked down our morning dose with the oleo-smeared white bread that now constituted breakfast. The oatmeal was all used up, as was the Milo.

"Maybe you-know-what is destroying our immune systems," I suggested. "Maybe God is punishing us."

Bradford stepped onto the stoop to execute a maneuver he referred to as a "farmer blow."

"Oh, sick!" I heard him scream. "Somebody laid down a big puddle of liquid shit right at the bottom of the steps! It's frozen solid."

I braced myself, but apparently he was too disgusted to try to lay the blame I so richly deserved at my feet.

Bruce shouldered his day pack in stoic preparation for the trek across the vegetation-free zone the brochure had described as a "volcanic moonscape." This high up, there was no longer any pretense of sticking together, but he shook my hand on his way out. "Lame-o, good luck. If I don't see you at Kibo Hut, I'll see you in hell."

Unable to keep up with Sandy and Elsie, I crept along with Canadian Carol for a while. She wasn't bad company, in that her example served to make me feel somewhat less pathetic. At least I wasn't dropping to my knees to retch every five minutes. After an hour or so of these intermittent dry heaves, she curled into fetal position and started to cry. "I can't go forward," she sobbed.

"Uh, okay," I said, wondering if this meant she couldn't go backward, either. I had my orange plastic poncho but no idea what, in this lunar waste-land, I could tie it to to make a lean-to. I wasn't an astronaut, for Christ's sake. I wished Elsie hadn't gone on ahead of us. She'd have known what to do.

"I'm so disappointed," Carol hiccupped. "Ever since I can remember, I've wanted to climb Kilimanjar-har-o."

"I know. I know," I murmured mechanically as I rubbed her back, and I did, sort of. I mean, I never ever wanted to climb Kilimanjaro, but I'd recently admitted that a Broadway audience throwing roses at me seemed a long shot, at best. It's a bitter pill, having to swallow your dreams.

"I don't want you to think you have to stay here with me," she whimpered, as I blew on my hands, calculating. If I wanted, I could use Carol as my Get-Out-of-Kilimanjaro-Free card, accompany her back to Horombo Hut, improvise a bedpan until she felt better, and lie around in my big sleeping bag waiting for the others to wend their way back down. Assuming there was a way to retrieve my sleeping bag from the porter's gunnysack, that is. For all I knew, Simon had sprinted way ahead and was now passing the dutchie around the potbelly of Kibo Hut. Plus, what if I, despite my misgivings, was destined to make it all the way to the top? If so, it'd be a shame to pass up this once-in-a-lifetime opportunity to reach the summit, to squander a full quarter of the Christian youth group's stash, even if the situation ensured that my bailing out would be cloaked in a mantle of Samaritan-style honor. Would Carol usher me back down the mountain if I were the one stricken? Probably, but my friends sure wouldn't. Those guys wouldn't hesitate to look out for number one.

Just then, I heard boots crunching toward us across the volcanic pebbles. It sounded like someone eating a bowl of cereal. It was Timber and Tweedy, the married couple from New Zealand. Not having seen them at breakfast, I'd assumed they'd headed out at dawn, but no, they'd been passed out cold in their mummy bags. "Didn't git t'sleep till four o'clock," Timber explained. "People stomping around till all hours, up and down, going to the toilet, no respect. I'd swear this one idiot ictually fill down the ladduh."

"Good show," Tweedy snickered.

"Yih, he'll be bruised up good t'night," Timber yawned, bending over Carol's now-prostrate form. After some brief consultation, it was decided that Timber would run back down the trail to ask some porters they had passed for help. Tweedy would wait with Carol until Timber returned. I was to continue onward.

"Are you sure?" I asked.

"Get on with yuh," Tweedy replied pleasantly, stretching herself flat against a sun-warmed rock. "We'll kitsch you up."

"Be lucky to get there before sun-sit, the right you're going," Timber chuckled over his shoulder as he trotted back down the trail. "Lime-o!"

THE BROCHURE WAS right about that volcanic desert bearing a striking resemblance to the surface of the moon. What it failed to mention is that the surface of the moon is boring, boring, boring, especially if you're still subject to the laws of gravity. The substandard hiking boots that had replaced my olive Keds were like a metronome, pounding out a tedious rhythm in my brain that unfortunately morphed into a familiar song: "My bologna has a first name. . . ." The loop was short but endless. Over and over with Oscar Mayer. Increasingly desperate to get the damn ditty out of my head, I tried to recall a few snatches of Shakespeare. The furthest I got was "thou art thyself though not a Capulet" before my bologna reasserted itself. It was driving me mad. "Stop singing it," I threatened myself. "Stop it this second, or else!" Of course, without the song, there was little to divert me from the sensation that my lungs were turning to steel wool. Christ, what a trial. To this day, I cannot write the word "bologna" without experiencing a slight pinch in my upper respiratory tract. Whenever possible, I try to side-step the entire issue by spelling it "baloney."

MY COMPANIONS BROKE into applause when I crawled across the threshold of Kibo Hut. "I don't believe it," Bradford cried, clapping me on the back.

"I need to say . . . grace," I croaked, collapsing in a decidedly unsporty heap.

THE FINAL LEG of our upward journey commenced at midnight, when the porters roused us with exhortations to hurry, hurry, if we didn't hurry, we would miss the sunrise.

"Fuck the sunrise," Bruce muttered, yanking a polypropylene bandeau over his ears.

"You cannot miss sunrise, because as soon as sun rise, ice start to melt," Simon the pot-smoking fifteen-year-old porter retorted, herding us toward the door before I could tie my boots.

"We are not all ready," Elsie stonewalled, gesturing to the caterpillar-like shape of a still-occupied mummy bag. A hank of hair and a lifeless hand protruded from the opening. It was Tweedy.

"She's a bit off," Timber cheerfully informed us. "Iltitude sickness most likely. Says this is as far as she goes." I groaned in horror. My god, to make it through the rain and the bologna song and the unpleasant Brillo pad sensation in the lungs, only to crap out a few hours shy of the top. It was unimaginable, almost as bad as the vertical ascent I was facing. "Does innyone want her gloves?" Timber called. With a guilty glance at the lumpy outline of the no doubt toasty-warm Tweedy, I wadded my Sportmart clearance bin specials into the pocket of my coat and raised my hand.

We felt our way out into the utter darkness of a subzero night. A few other parties had already embarked, their porters' lanterns twinkling up the mountain like strings of Christmas lights. This was it. Last chance to dive back into the safe harbor of my much-maligned sleeping bag. There was no shame in it. I could tell friends back in Chicago that I'd overslept. "Man, these stupid frat boys I'd been hanging with swore that they'd wake me up when it was time to go!" It would be so easy to rewrite this moment. Instead, I took a step forward. Damn, it was dark. I couldn't even make out Elsie's parka, mere inches in front of me. Over my shoulder, Bruce's breath was labored. Not nearly as labored as mine, mind you, but it was gratifying to hear someone who windsurfed for fun wheezing away like Grandpa Joe. Oh fuck, wait. Had we remembered to say grace with dinner? No! That's why Bruce sounded like he was going to die! He wasn't getting enough oxygen in his lungs, and if he wasn't, I wasn't! I pitched forward onto Elsie's back. Bruce smacked into me. The whole damn line tumbled to the ground like quilted, down-padded dominos. The snow wasn't nearly as bad as I feared. It was warmer than the air, and soft, so soft. If not for the certainty that more climbers would be along shortly to step on my head, I'd have happily stayed where I was, maybe burrowed a bit deeper into the abundant white stuff. Swinging a homemade coffee-can lantern, Simon materialized to get us back in line.

I aimed my flashlight at his feet as he hoisted me up by the armpits. Boots. Good. Had he been revealed to be wearing flip-flops, I'd have had no choice but to slit my wrists. I was also pleased to discover that the Oscar Mayer song seemed to have left the building. Perhaps it was the sonically subtler crunch of the crusted snow, as compared to the more substantial volcanic pebbles or possibly the presence of my fellow man. The greater likelihood was that the physical stress of this insane undertaking was scooping out all extraneous thoughts, leaving my head as empty as a jack-o'-lantern's. The only thing left was an imperative to breathe, a tidbit gleaned from

Canadian Carol's World Health manual. According to the experts, every third step of the final ascent a climber should fully expand and contract her lungs. Oh my god, my lungs, my poor lungs. I'd subjected them to an unknown substance and then forgotten to give them their fix at Kibo Hut. Not to mention the fact that I'd devoted a lot of time over the last six weeks to rolling my own unfiltered cigarettes.

Oxygen. Must procure lots and lots of oxygen. With no regard for appearances, I snorted twin jets of the frosty element in through my nostrils, then let my mouth fall open to expel great gusts of carbon dioxide directly into an orthopedic-looking white polar-fleece dickey I'd hiked halfway up my face ($2.99, on sale at Sportmart).

The porters were convinced I was hyperventilating. "You are sick?" Simon asked, tugging on my sleeve. I couldn't answer because all breath was earmarked for my ludicrous breathing regimen.

"Sounds like she's . . . having a fuck . . . ing baby," Bradford gasped to no one in particular.

When the porters allowed us a five-minute pit stop, I was drenched with sweat. I had to remind myself not to chugalug too much water, partly because the bottle I was drinking from belonged to Elsie, and partly because I wasn't sure how one endowed with female equipment might modestly empty the contents of her bladder on the steep, slippery angle of a pitch-dark mountain whilst swaddled in numerous down-filled layers.

"Hiv we got much farther?" Sandy wheezed.

"Here is halfway to the top," Simon calculated.

That meant another, what, two, two and a half hours? Like driving from Indianapolis to Cincinnati, except vertically, without a car. We fell in line behind Simon like automatons. Eventually my yogic breathing became second nature, freeing me up to think about things like Siberian death marches and other mortifications of the flesh: a play I'd seen in college about Captain

Scott, a Victorian adventurer who'd taken days to die when a freak snow-storm waylaid his party, a plane crash in the Andes where the surviving passengers ate each other. That kind of thing.

All of a sudden I realized that I could see Elsie's back. It wasn't much to see, a broad expanse of navy blue nylon lurching from side to side like a dancing bear. But still, if I could see, it meant the sun was preparing to rise, which meant we were nearing the top. (Of course, this also meant that the ice cap was due to start its treacherous daily melting any second now, but why accentuate the negative?)

"When?" I grunted, expending far too much oxygen on the question.

"Soon," Simon laughed, pointing up. "Very soon."

A jagged peak poked up out of the gauzy, gathering light. I knew the fucker. I'd seen it from a distance while meandering across the volcanic surface of the moon. I'd even taken a break from the bologna song to snap its picture.

We soldiered on. Well, well, well. It looked like I was going to make it, even though I'd forgotten to say grace. Then, not five feet from the pinnacle, I decided I was close enough. To set foot on the top, the actual, pointy, stab-a-flag-in-it, Jimmy-Carter-was-here top, I'd have to haul myself straight up, seeking out crevices rock-climber-style, as Bradford and Elsie were already doing. And I really didn't want to do that. It just wasn't my cup of tea. Too much like climbing those stupid ropes in gym. What was five feet, after all? I had a beautiful view right here on this nice little plateau. Look, I was a theater major. It's not like I had anything to prove.

"Go, Lame-o," Bruce agitated, impatient to get moving.

"Here, Bruce, you go around me." I tried to get out of his way.

"Go!" He insisted, crowding closer, his down thumping against mine.

"Actually, Bruce, I'm cool staying right here. You go on ahead. It's okay. I feel satisfied that I've made it to the top."

"This isn't the top, though." He looked like he was fixing to punch me. "That's the top."

"I know, but I just feel done, you know? For me, this is as good as making it to the top."

He shook his head wearily. "God, you're a lame-o." With no further ado, he seized me by the buttocks and literally shoved my ass the final five feet, just as he had facetiously promised he would back when we were packing our gear at the Kibo Hotel. Before I could protest, he'd bulldozed me all the way to the peak. I knew it was the peak, because there was nowhere to step but down. I couldn't believe it.

"You see? You made it." Bruce rolled his eyes, took off his gloves, and rapped them lightly against the side of my head.

"I made it! I made it!" I did a little hornpipe.

"Way to go, Lame-o!" Bradford smiled, pumping his fist in the air.

"I made it! Oh my god, I made it!" I repeated.

Bruce raised his eyebrows and nodded, looking at me over the neck of his water bottle. Sandy gave me a stick of gum. Elsie took my camera and snapped a picture. Simon gave me a hug and asked if he could have my boots when we reached the bottom.

"I climbed it! I climbed this fucking mountain!" I flopped backward in the snow, my lungs swelling with what I can only describe as exhilaration made manifest by the dizzying knowledge that I'd never—ever—climb another one. God, what a good feeling.

Hamil's House of Fun

Kay Sexton

• •

I n our year of craziness, before we became responsible, Tony and I bought a fifteen-year-old red van from a builder, filled it with clothes, and set off. We'd both grown up on the Isle of Wight, off the central south coast of England, and we wanted to spread our wings before settling down for good.

We might have created an itinerary if we'd realized, upon setting out, that growing up on an island of just twenty by forty-two kilometers would hamper our ability to comprehend long distances. Mad idealists in search of new experiences we might be; organized we were not. Our trip planning consisted of perusing my high school atlas as we left Dover on the ferry for France, pointing out the place names that we recognized: Paris, Athens, Barcelona, St. Tropez, Madrid, Rome.

When we reached Germany, we'd been exploring Europe for nearly a year. However, unlike the chatty groups of travelers who shared the hostels with us—who seemed to know what they were doing and where they were going, and never seemed to lack funds—we journeyed alone. At the end of each day, we had no idea what we were going to do the next, and we took on odd jobs as we went along in order to replenish our bank accounts.

Sadly, for my new husband and provider, there were never any odd jobs that called upon his employment experience: He'd served an apprenticeship as a radar installer. There were, however, entirely too many that relied on my background as the daughter of a motel owner. So the poor lad had to go to museums or sit on the beach while I served dinners and cleaned hotel rooms to earn the cash for our next little hop across Europe.

Around Christmas, we started hearing rumors that many of the more organized travelers were heading for Hamburg, no doubt drawn by visions of holiday cheer, plentiful sausage, and cheap beer. We followed. Immediately, we checked into a youth hostel and discovered that although it was cheap, everything else in the city was expensive. Our finances would let us either stay in the hostel for a week and starve, or eat for three days and sleep in the van in the subzero weather. So we started to look for work—urgently. Thus far on our travels, we had discovered that we could cook, wait tables, wash up, chambermaid, courier, tend gardens, and decorate houses—so why did I end up dancing on a table at Hamil's House of Fun?

Simply put, we were too late. In early December, a great noisy wave of Australian and New Zealand students descended on major European cities. They got work—the good gigs came with accommodation—and sat tight until mid-January, when the holidays were over and it was cheap to start traveling again. Always behind the day's march, we arrived to discover that all the jobs had been taken, the youth hostels were closing for two weeks over Christmas, and the cheapest available hotel room cost more per night than we'd been spending on food for a week.

As usual, the youth hostel dining hall was full of old hands who had good advice, which made me wonder sometimes why they didn't take it themselves. This time around, the good advice was that Hamil always needed staff at his beer hall. A helpful volunteer rang Hamil's House of Fun for us, as we didn't speak any German yet, and told us that Hamil was looking for table dancers. Since Tony didn't quite fit table dancing specifications, it was left to me to apply for the job.

By this point, six months or so into our journey, I'd learned *not* to use my imagination. If the job was bad, thinking about it in advance did no good, and if it was great . . . well, I'd never had a great job while we were traveling. It couldn't be worse than picking sweet corn, I thought, or cleaning buckets of mussels to sell to rich travelers, or sewing up holes in fishing nets. I was wrong.

Hamil himself interviewed me at the House of Fun itself, which seemed to be a converted aircraft hangar on the outskirts of the city. He seemed to contain a lot of suppressed hostility and a very small English vocabulary. It was hard to judge what the place might be like filled with music, light, and customers, but Hamil's neckless shaven head, set on his short but solid body, along with his glaring eyes, made it hard to imagine him as a host filled with bonhomie and good cheer. Still, beer works wonders—I knew that from past experience.

"Dance," he said. Not sure if it was a command or a question, I nodded, feeling shaky.

"Now," he said.

Realizing he wouldn't wait, I tried to perform—of course, without the benefits of costume, lights, music, or crowd. In my head, I tried to hear something nice and upbeat with a sexy undertone: "Hound Dog" by Elvis Presley would have been ideal. I thought about the Folies-Bergère, with frilly-outfitted cancan dancers, and tried to achieve a few snazzy moves of my own. I hadn't actually seen any cancan dancers in Paris, because I'd spent most of my time pressing bellboy uniforms for a large hotel to earn money. Fortunately, I had a vivid imagination.

The one good thing was that there were no mirrors. I couldn't have got though this impromptu rehearsal if I'd been able to see myself, still in my ski cap, scarf, jacket, and boots, clutching my gloves in one hand, trying to bob around seductively and pretending to swirl a frothy cancan outfit around my skinny form. I felt completely daft.

There was a long silent pause when I faltered to a stop. Hamil glared at me. I imagined he was trying to work out why this bony British brunette with no sense of rhythm wanted to be a dancer. I was wondering about it myself.

"Six o'clock," he stated, and handed me a brown paper bag. Then he walked out of the warehouse, leaving me wondering if I'd heard him right.

I looked in the bag. It contained a black vinyl minidress, liberally embellished with straps, studs, and buckles; a pair of very high black stiletto boots; and a fuchsia Cleopatra-style wig. It seemed I had the job, but after seeing the gear, I wasn't so sure I wanted it.

The dress was very, very small. I had a vision of myself, drugged, driven across the city to a Reeperbahn brothel, and waking up in that ridiculous dress. Hamil could be a white slave trader, for all I knew about him.

"Y'alright?" A large Australian voice reached me through the gloom. "You got the job, then?" The man, who was nearly twice my height and weight, pointed to the bag in my hands.

I stared at him in surprise. Australians really do go everywhere.

"S'alright," he boomed. "Hamil's okay. He's just not a great talker. What's yer cossie, then?" "Mmm," I said. I wasn't sure what he was referring to and didn't want to offend him by acting unresponsive.

"Cossie, in the bag, what did he give yer? Betcha got the black job with the buckles on?" I nodded.

"Don't worry, you'll be fine. Great bunch of girls here."

He started to push the broom across the floor. "I'll tell Arla the Aborigine Beauty to look out for you." Business finished, I followed the route Hamil had taken to what I hoped would be a door to the outside world, rather than to a packing crate and and a one-way ticket to prostitution.

"By the way," the Australian called out after me. "You'll be Rose the English Charmer, all right?"

"Rose," Tony pondered when I told him. "Thistle, more like."

I pretended to hit him with my costume bag, which split open, spilling shoes, wig, and minuscule dress onto the snowy Hamburg street. I gathered it all up again; Tony was laughing too much to help. We agreed that Hamil was an odd character, but that the Australian sounded all right, and that the money was too good to pass up. I'd work one night at least, just to see what it was like.

"Think of the stories you'll be able to tell at dinner parties," he said.

It was a comforting prospect, imagining how all this would seem in twenty years' time, but then again, he wasn't the one who was going to have to get up and dance that night. I cringed inwardly.

Tony and I spent the day exploring the amazing mercantile heart of Hamburg. In the very center of the Speicherstadt, we wandered through the auction hall of the Coffee Market, once the capital of global coffee trade. Like a hundred other tourists, we stood under the three ancient but still-ticking clocks of the coffee stock exchanges that once graced New York, Rio, and Hamburg. The Coffee Market was cozy and well padded—rather like the local citizens—and at every point where the original timbers were exposed, a richly redolent odor of coffee could be detected by rubbing the wood until it released its ancient warm fragrance.

After exploring, we ordered Bockwurst, the ubiquitous German smoked sausages made of beef and pork, from a street stall. The Bockwurst was primo cheap food: Not only did it fill you up at a reasonable price and taste delicious, it warmed up our frozen fingers as we ate. We'd started the trip as vegetarians, but traveling teaches you not to be too fussy about food, and we'd quickly converted to the doctrine of "eat anything that isn't nailed down or too expensive."

We walked back to our room through a flurry of tiny snowflakes. Unlike the snowstorms we were used to in England, where snow pelted down heavily like frozen rain, these snow scatterings didn't seem at all sure that they wanted to settle. They traveled up, down, and sideways, whipped by strong winds into icy twisters that settled in every fold of clothing and flesh, and even blew up your nose. Fortunately, given the freezing weather, we still had a roof over our heads: The youth hostel management had grudgingly admitted that hardy souls with nowhere else to go would be allowed to stay in the annex over Christmas. The annex was an old school building with cold showers and no cooking facilities. Nonetheless, we were grateful to have a roof between us and the snow.

At six o'clock, Tony and I rolled up to Hamil's House of Fun in the van. I clutched my costume bag and a towel. (Like every reader of *A Hitchhiker's Guide to the Galaxy*, I had learned to never leave home without my towel.)

Tony slid out of the driver's seat to start his job for the night: counting all the entrances and exits, and then patroling the outside of the building all evening so that Hamil couldn't slide my tranquilized form out of a door and onto a small plane bound for the Orient. I was working from 6:00 PM until 2:00 AM, so Tony had a long, cold, and hopefully uneventful night ahead of him.

I waved goodbye to him casually. We were being British about this—no need for farewells; I was only going to work for a few hours, after all. But my knees were shaking as I walked through the back door.

The Australian showed me to the ladies' toilet and told me Arla (who, as it turned out, was his girlfriend) was already dancing. The women's toilet was surprisingly clean—I was to find out why later. As I started to get dressed, I realized I'd drastically underestimated how long it would take me to get into the costume: Doing up all the straps and buckles took forever. I considered leaving a few of them undone, but the thought of what might happen if an overenthusiastic punter grabbed hold of one of them encouraged me to persevere.

I walked to the bar entrance and peered through the gloom. It was like being back in the hostel, or in a barracks. Wooden tables with stools under them were lined up in military rows, with men sitting along each side. Waiters darted between the tables with fistfuls of overflowing beer steins. Hamil directed me to one end of a long trestle table lined with men clutching tankards. A statuesque blonde was already performing at the other end of it, and I observed her technique with interest. She stood as if rooted to the table and moved her body only from the hips up. A quick glance around the room showed me that all the dancers were performing in a similar fashion, two to a table. The drinkers watched stolidly.

The music—an uncompromising kind of heavy rock, with lots of long, screaming guitar solos—didn't help me relax. I clambered up and immediately discovered why the girls were virtually immobile: the tables were rickety and covered in spilt beer. I realized that one incautious move could lead to a fast slalom along the trestle top, ending with me, the beer mugs, and probably several slow-witted customers in a heap on the floor.

I locked my legs, waved my arms, and threw the blonde a tense smile. She returned the grimace and hissed, "Watch out for the waiters; they think it's a great joke to tickle the backs of your knees!" She sounded just like the Australian, only more miserable.

We gyrated for a while, and then I ventured, "Been doing this long?"

"Twenty-five minutes," she replied.

"I meant generally."

"Yeah. Twenty-five minutes."

We continued to sway like well-anchored seaweed in an underwater heavy-metal garden.

"Which one's Arla the Aborigine Beauty?" I asked.

"*I* am," she replied. "And when I get hold of that so-called boyfriend of mine, he's going to get more than a wet tea towel 'round his rear end!"

"Right," I said nervously.

"You met him earlier," she hissed. "He cleans this dump. After the last Arla walked out yesterday, he suggested I double our earning capacity by taking over her spot. He didn't mention that it was an endurance contest."

This was where I should have started guessing at my second miscalculation: that Hamil would give us rest breaks. Usually, go-go and cabaret dancers perform seven minutes on and at least fourteen off. As I was soon to discover, such humane protocol wasn't in practice here. At Hamil's you danced all night. Nonstop.

I eyed the blonde appraisingly. She was a large, fit woman, and I didn't fancy the Australian's chances of surviving the night when she did get hold of him.

We danced on.

Eventually she said, "Expert, are you?"

I thought about this for a while; there was no hurry, we were here for the long haul, and long conversational pauses helped conserve our energy. "No, I don't think I'd say that. Why?"

"Saw you brought a towel. Never thought of that myself, with the cold weather outside and all."

I took the hint and passed it to her. She wiped the sweat from all the areas not covered by her costume—in other words, from most of her body—and handed it back. I considered her outfit: chamois leather bikini and headband, suede boots, and a sheath knife strapped to her thigh. She had a necklace of shells around her neck.

"Is that what aborigines wear?" I asked.

"Dream on," she replied. I examined her again. From the crown of her glowing blond head to the tips of her pale pink toenails, she was about as much like an aborigine as a Barbie doll is like a real teenage girl. I smiled to myself. We made a great pair: Arla the Albino Aborigine and Rose the English Thistle.

By midnight, I felt like my knees would never bend again. The waiters did tickle the backs of your legs, and even worse, as Arla had suggested, they themselves were inclined to flick you on the rump with wet tea towels, an exquisitely painful experience that was loudly applauded by Hamil from behind the bar and received lukewarm smiles from the beer drinkers. I'd been gyrating for six hours straight and felt desperate.

That was when Hamil passed by. I hopped off my table to make a business proposition.

"Dance," he said, as soon as he saw me.

"You really ought to give us rest breaks, you know."

"Dance."

"You could be making a lot more money by giving the girls a break now and again."

"How?"

That was encouraging. I pressed on. "Well, look, if a girl has a break, she can go up to the bar, and one of the customers can buy her a drink—then you get the money for the drink, and the girl gets a chance to get her breath back. Champagne, for instance; everybody knows it's traditional for dancing girls to drink champagne."

Silence from Hamil.

"It doesn't have to be real champagne," I said in desperation, sharing a trick I had learned while working in a casino in Monte Carlo. "You can make up a champagne substitute by mixing half a cup of black tea and two drops of yellow food coloring with a gallon of lemonade. The girls get that to drink, and you charge as if it really was champagne. Big profit margin!" I added hopefully, in case he hadn't realized.

"I only sell beer. Dance!"

I got back on my table. "Where's Hamil from?" I asked Arla.

"Says he's a direct descendent of Attila the Hun," she muttered, as a drinker slopped foaming beer over her ankle.

It was the end of the night before I discovered the one good thing about Hamil's House of Fun: You got paid after every shift. Now I understood why the first Arla had left so suddenly—with no wages held back, nothing was to keep a sane girl from leaving at the end of any given session. A sane girl who didn't have to keep a roof over her head and her husband's, that is.

The fifty German marks that Hamil handed over seemed like small consolation for the fact that my knees refused to bend properly as I headed outside into the coldest night we'd had so far. My pink wig, which had been sliding sweatily around on my head in the steamy, beer-scented club, actually froze as I walked to the van. Tiny icicles formed on the end of each plastic strand. Tony was huddled in a sleeping bag, watching frost form on the windows. We were both too cold and grumpy to talk on our way back to the annex.

The next morning the van refused to start. She was old and gallant, but the subzero temperatures had defeated her; she would need an oil change and some tender loving care before she was fit to roll again. Until we could afford her treatment, we were stuck in Hamburg.

"We'll have to walk to Hamil's tonight," said Tony.

After the long night of table dancing, my legs felt as though they were going on strike in sympathy. But the thought of the Christmas markets spurred me on, and we headed straight for the Rathausmarkt in front of the town hall, where Glühwein, sugar-coated gingerbread, and roasted chestnuts made a heady start to our day.

The Alster River had frozen over already, and we took cones of sugared almonds and hot Bockwurst down to the banks to watch clever German children toe-looping and skimming around the lake. Tony looked almost tempted to have a go, but I pointed out that I must preserve my income-providing limbs from harm: If I fell on the ice we would be unable to pay for our annex room, let alone indulge all our newly discovered cravings for sausages, sugared nuts, and spiced wine.

That night, without a van to transport us, Tony walked me to work. We both felt depressed. The repair shop had said that lots of work was needed to put her right. I knew how she felt. I too wanted to go on strike. I too wanted to be back in the south of France, in the sun, traveling through resinous pine woods to a campsite where owls hooted overhead all night and a cheery campsite owner dispensed cheap red wine from his own vineyard in ten-liter containers. However, I didn't have a choice: It would take at least three nights' work to pay for the spare parts and labor that would put the van back on the road.

So, rather stiff-legged, we made our way to Hamil's. As we strolled through Hamburg's streets, choirs sang Christmas carols by candlelight from the steps of the churches we passed.

Arla didn't put in an appearance that night, so I had the table to myself. I did see her boyfriend, with a swollen upper lip that suggested Arla had a good right hook, but he avoided me all evening. I decided that to prevent another night of leg-cramping agony, I would walk slowly up and down the table as I "danced."

As for getting attention, it didn't matter what I did—the drinkers never seemed to raise their eyes from their beer, and the waiters only looked up to take aim with their tea towels. I could have spelled out rude messages in semaphore, and I don't think anybody except the other dancers would have noticed. There was a girl in a blond bubble wig and a Hawaiian skirt on the next table over, and just past her were a redhead in a leopard print catsuit and a dark girl in a tuxedo and top hat, dancing at each end of a table that looked even less stable than mine. From time to time we waved at each other, but it wasn't an environment for meaningful communication.

At around 10:00 PM, a plump and rather solemn-looking young woman appeared. She wore a mackintosh, and stared up at me with sad horror. "Rose?"

"Yup," I said. I understood now why the blond Arla from the night before had been so reticent with me; I felt that way now. Nothing this woman asked me was going to have an answer that she would enjoy.

"Um . . . I'm Arla. . . ." Her bottom lip was actually wobbling.

I hauled her up on the table and helped her bundle her coat into a small ball that we placed midway between us. She filled out the chamois costume rather more than her predecessor. In fact, if she'd moved at all rapidly, the costume would probably not have accompanied her very far. I made sure she understood the principle of dancing while not moving and then tuned out for a while. When I returned my attention to the new Arla, I noticed her lips moving. She was muttering to herself. I moved a little closer to listen.

"Lord, how many are my foes! How many rise up against me! But you are a shield around me, oh Lord; you bestow glory on me and lift up my head. To the Lord I cry aloud, and he answers me from his holy hill. I lie down and sleep; I wake again, because the Lord sustains me. I will not fear the tens of thousands drawn up against me on every side. Arise, oh Lord! Deliver me, oh my God! Strike all my enemies on the jaw; break the teeth of the wicked."

I suspected she wouldn't be back the following night. She wasn't.

The next Arla was a German student of physics, working her way home to Stuttgart. The following one was an Irish au pair, earning extra money during her holidays. The one after that was a Dutch girl, backpacking around Europe.

I lasted nine nights, beating the house record for Rose the English Charmer, whose previous incarnations had managed a maximum of four. Those nine nights of hell paid for our board and lodging until after Christmas and a complete rehaul of our lovely red house on wheels. As we rolled out of Hamburg, I hoped that my legs would recover from my nine nights of dancing as fast as the van had recovered from the cold.

Some months later, back in England, I received a letter, c/o Hamburg Youth Hostel, via Geneva Youth Hostel, via my bank. It had a picture of a beer stein on the front, filled with laughing girls in tiny costumes. Inside it said, "Greetings from Hamil's House of Fun," and underneath was a postscript in heavy, dark writing, which read, "One cup black coffee, six drops yellow food coloring, two drops red food coloring, one gallon water, one liter lemonade = beer. Always a job for you at Hamil's." I should have delighted in my victory, but I doubted that I'd done anyone any favors. No Hamil's girls were really smiling if they had to drink *that* concoction on their breaks.

I Could Do This in My Sleep

Karin Palmquist

· · · · · · · · · · · · · · · · · · · ·

"It's going to happen today for sure."

I had been saying the same thing to my editor every day for three weeks. I still didn't feel too sure, however, and nothing in my editor's voice suggested that he believed me.

For three weeks I had been hanging out in Jakarta, waiting for an interview with Abdurrahman Wahid, the president of Indonesia. I had spent countless days waiting at the president's office, only to hear another excuse for why he couldn't see me that day.

It wasn't that I was suffering that much. If you're going to be stuck somewhere for a few weeks, you might as well make it the Grand Hyatt in Jakarta. I was used to staying in places with communal showers, where if there was something dripping in the lobby it was rarely a tropical waterfall surrounded by huge gladiolus.

But my editor's impatience was registering, and I was aware that in the end, he expected me to *produce* something. Like a profile of the president of Indonesia.

And today, we had been told, it was going to happen.

My colleague Anil and I headed out the glass doors of the lobby and into a waiting cab.

We had spent a lot of time waiting together the past three weeks, and all in all I had found Anil from Bombay to be a very good chap. I had never used the word "chap" in my life before I met Anil, but Anil's very proper Indian-colonial take on English was rubbing off. Within a few days, a sentence like "I think I'll give that friendly chap from the embassy a tinkle" sounded like the right thing to say.

I checked my hair in the rearview mirror. It hadn't yet totally collapsed in the humidity, but it was only a question of time. Most of my body was covered, and only the tips of my shoes showed under my long skirt. I was suffocating wearing so much clothing in the tropical heat, but I wasn't going to blow my chance at interviewing the president of the world's largest Muslim nation by showing up in a mini. If I looked modest, Anil looked the opposite. He wore a business suit in a shiny material that gave off a better reflection than the rearview mirror, and rings with sparkling stones on every finger. I hadn't seen such a diverse collection of gems since my school trip to the National Geological Museum. But most noticeable of all were the sunglasses: cat-shaped, thick-rimmed shades that would have made Dame Edna jealous.

In the three weeks that we had been in Indonesia, there hadn't been much else to do than pick on Anil. But Anil was so incredibly correct in his behavior that it wasn't much fun in the long run. His wardrobe, however, totally intrigued me. How could such a proper man be such a flamboyant dresser?

Anil had the looks and the attitude of a Bollywood movie star, and he liked to make an appearance—preferably in a Mercedes. He refused to travel by *bajaj*, the ubiquitous moped rickshaws that spit out clouds of exhaust as they made their own traffic lanes in the tight space between bigger vehicles. And he always picked a cab according to the make of the car. I had grown up in Sweden, the land of Volvos and Saabs. I wanted to go in a rickshaw.

Sometimes, I had the suspicion that Anil had ended up in media for the glam factor, rather than out of some undying wish to tell the truth. He was flamboyant and worldly yet easy to embarrass. I made him blush for three weeks straight: It was as easy as faking an asthma attack in the elevator to get the Indonesians to put out their cigarettes. One wheezing breath first. Then another. And another. At this point Anil was beet red and darting out of the elevator on the wrong floor.

I couldn't figure him out. As he ran his hands over the fabrics at the markets in Glodok, Jakarta's Chinese district, comparing texture and shine, or haggled with street vendors over gaudy sculptures of horses in full gallop, I watched and wondered if Anil approved of his own life. He clearly craved more glamour than his arranged marriage and two adorable little daughters allowed.

On the day of the interview we'd been promised, we pulled up at the president's palace and went through the customary checks. Our bags were put through the machine. We had been through this routine many times before, and the guards in their short-sleeved gabardine business suits always seemed much more interested in us than in the lethal weapons that might be in our bags. A quick glance at us, and it was understandable why they were curious, with Anil in his pimp garb and me, six feet tall and pale, even by Swedish standards. In this security check, I felt like the tallest, blondest woman alive.

We were ushered into a waiting room, which felt like progress. On previous visits, we had waited in a room as big as a soccer field, with a spooky echo and a few couches lining one wall. It was so vast I had developed a severe case of agoraphobia.

This waiting room, however, was much more cozy, with gold-framed posters on the walls and plastic potted plants. I had the comforting feeling that we were moving closer to the goal. As we waited, I looked over my notes. Abdurrahman Wahid had come to power in the fall of 1999, edging out Megawati Sukarnoputri in the nation's first democratic presidential vote. After a tumultuous spring of racial riots that ended the rule of B. J. Habibie, Wahid, a Muslim scholar, seemed like the gentle man who could ease tensions between the different ethnic groups and unite the nation. Fifty-nine years old and almost blind, he had suffered two strokes. An hour passed. Two. A little nervous, I checked my hair. Then I checked again, like a nervous twitch.

"He's blind," Anil said.

Good point.

Another hour passed. Other visitors came and left. Japanese businessmen with black portfolios. Indonesian citizens in their best outfits. Then, finally, the chief of protocol came to get us.

"You have twenty minutes, no more. And don't deviate from the approved questions," the chief of protocol said. He was a curious little man with round, wire-rimmed glasses and a heavy Irish accent from his university days in Dublin. Here, just outside the office of the president of Indonesia, it seemed a bit out of place.

"Of course not," I said. I looked down at the list of bland inquiries that had passed inspection. My questions had been so watered down, they weren't even remotely interesting anymore. There might be people dying every day in the Moluccas in clashes between Christians and Muslims, and the province of Aceh might very well be trying to follow East Timor's example and secede from the nation, but why bother the president with such talk? Let's talk about happy things.

A light knock, and the chief of protocol opened the door to the president's office. After three weeks of waiting, we had finally made it to the inner sanctum. At first glance it was a bit disappointing. It was a large room with three pale walls and dark wood paneling covering the fourth wall. Fuchsia wall-to-wall carpeting clashed with gold brocade rococo chairs. It mystified me why a country with such beautiful textiles and woodwork would go for the faux-castle look in the most symbolic of all Indonesian buildings, the presidential palace.

A tiny little man in a brown batik-goes-psychedelic shirt and a little black cylinder hat sat behind an enormous desk at the far side of the room. When he heard us approach, he stood up and walked around the desk to greet us.

He was barely five feet tall, so short that his head came up to my lower rib cage. He looked incredibly frail. How could this man lead the world's fourth most populous nation? He should be in bed.

I had heard many stories about him from the local Indonesians. His people thought he had supernatural powers. Of course, I didn't believe any such talk, but I forced my thoughts to more neutral ground, just in case.

"I hope you excuse me," the president said, and reached for my hand. He stared straight into my navel with his blind eyes. "My feet were hurting, so I took off my shoes."

You're the president, you can do whatever you want, I thought, but said, "Of course, Mr. President."

We sat down, and the chief of protocol briefed him again on who we were and where we came from. The president nodded and said a few pleasant words about America and politely thanked us for coming all the way to Indonesia. So far so good.

I leaned forward in my chair and asked the first question.

"Mr. President, in the past, you have spoken out against religious extremism and in defense of ethnic and religious minorities. Sometimes your voice has echoed alone, against a chorus of less tolerant voices. How can the rights of minorities, like the ethnic Chinese minority, be safeguarded, and how can you prevent outbreaks of ethnic hatred, like the riots of May 1998?"

There was a long pause. The president's eyes were closed—nothing in his face let on that he had even heard me. After five years as a journalist, I've learned it's hard enough to make a connection with people you can look directly in the eye. Interviewing a blind man was a whole other ball game. Especially so, it seemed, if the blind man kept his eyes closed.

I started repeating the question.

"I heard you," the president said, but didn't make an attempt to answer.

Nervously, I looked at my watch. We had already wasted five minutes on pleasantries. I had only fifteen minutes left.

Finally, the president opened his eyes halfway and gave a two-word response to my question, denying any presence of ethnic tensions. Next.

Quietly wondering if the Chinese shop owners who'd been chased out of Jakarta's Chinatown in 1998 by angry mobs felt the same way, I moved on.

Second question, same response. A long pause before the president answered my question with a few abrupt words and a big yawn.

Then, by the third question, it happened. The president's chin fell to his chest, and he gave off a noise that sounded a whole lot like a snore. It couldn't be. He was the president; he couldn't fall asleep in the middle of the interview. I looked at the chief of protocol. He looked clearly nervous. Yep, the president was asleep all right. This was what I had waited for, for three long weeks? Three weeks of waiting, and all I get is abrupt answers to two questions before he falls asleep?

I wasn't used to being ignored. Well, at least not in Indonesia. Because of my height and my coloring, I got stared at wherever I went. More than that, people actually tried to pull my long, white-blond hair and touch my clothes. I actually ended up slapping a couple of people at the market. Slapping the locals probably wasn't correct travel etiquette, but it was getting a little too intimate. Then I read in my guidebook that for Indonesians, it is good luck to touch an "albino." Whether this is true or not, it made me feel better about the contact. I walked around with mental pictures of people landing jobs and winning the lottery after touching my magical hand. So how could it be that I had been grabbed and harassed by what felt like nearly all of Jakarta's nine million residents, but the one Indonesian whose attention I really wanted had just fallen asleep on me?

I cleared my throat. The chief of protocol cleared his throat. Anil coughed. The president didn't move.

Finally, the chief of protocol walked around the desk and gently touched the president's arm. Startled, the president sat up.

"Did you hear the one about the American and the Israeli?" said the president.

"Huh?"

"The American says to the Israeli, In our country it takes one week to get from one side of the country to the other by train. I know, the Israeli says, we have the same problems with trains in our country."

Nine minutes left and he's telling jokes?

"Mr. President," I pleaded. "About East Timor . . ."

The president was on a roll now. Two more jokes, shamelessly stolen from Art Buchwald. If he was going to tell jokes, he might as well come up with something original.

Just a few minutes left. What was I going to tell my editor? Did you hear the one about the American and the Israeli?

"Mr. President," I said. Without waiting for the punch line for the fourth joke, I went ahead with my question. "Ethnic and religious clashes have ripped countries from Yugoslavia to Rwanda apart. In the beginning, Indonesia had the opposition to colonial rule as a unifying cause. Indonesia has now been a sovereign state for fifty-five years, and colonialism is not a threat anymore. What will keep the country together now, as different regions, notably Aceh, call for independence, and religious tensions escalate in regions such as the Moluccas?"

The president looked grumpy. How dare I interrupt him like that? He went on to answer the question and went further than I had expected him to. It wasn't the most diplomatic answer, and it was just the answer I needed to save my story. Indonesia wasn't going to let go of Aceh, like it had let East Timor go, he explained. It didn't matter if the people of Aceh held a referendum in favor of secession; such a referendum had no legal bearing. And as far as East Timor went, Indonesia would set up its own military tribunal, and there was no need for the UN to get involved. Getting out this many words seemed to wake him up.

The chief of protocol twisted in his chair, looking much more nervous than he had when the president fell asleep. As the president paused, the chief of protocol broke in. "Your twenty minutes is up," he said in his Irish brogue and ushered us abruptly out of the room.

Just like that, my brush with fame and power was over. The president looked relieved. Anil and I were nothing but two bothersome flies, buzzing with questions, interrupting his nap. I'm not so sure he even remembered how we got there.

Adventure Pete

L. A. Miller

• •

Before taking to the road with Pete, I'd never traveled far with a dog. I still remembered when our curious family hound, Sabina, fell out of the Suburban on the highway. She'd rolled with it, waiting patiently in the middle of the road until my father realized the speck in the rearview was her, but still—in my childhood experience, dogs and cars didn't mix. As an adult, however, I found a certain clichéd road-trip mystique accompanies the idea of a lone driver with states to go before she sleeps, the whine of country music a fuzzy backdrop to the interstate, with a protective, silent companion by her side. In the end, I merged my history with my vision: Pete stayed in the car, but I wanted to *push* him out.

To back up, the only reason I got him in the first place was that my cat had died. Allow me to explain: This was no ordinary cat. Before succumbing to some freak neurological disorder, Sabby—short for Sábado—played soccer with crumpled pieces of paper. He fetched and he went on long walks with me. He liked to eat grapes and butter off the counter and would only drink from a running tap or a pint glass. In short, Sabby was more of a dog than most dogs. Certainly more of a dog than Pete turned out to be.

When I called my parents from L.A., where I was in graduate school, to sob that Sabby was gone, my father proffered the advice of one who not only had to routinely slaughter his pet calves as a youngster on the farm, but had always held the unenviable job of taking each of our family pets to be euthanized when its time came. "Get another cat as soon as possible," he said.

"But I don't *want* another cat," I sniffed. "Not some insipid, boring, cat-like cat."

"It's the only way," he insisted. "Trust me."

"Dad, I can't get another cat, because it won't be a cat like Sabby."

"Then get a dog."

I realize that people are generally divided into cat people and dog people, and never the twain shall meet. When I was growing up, however, we always had two dogs, two cats, and assorted snakes and lizards and gerbils and such (and which, in the end, the cats and dogs always ate). In short, I'd always embraced the whole animal kingdom. But all of my cats had been interesting, doglike, so maybe I really did fall into the dog camp after all. And for a year or so, I'd had my eye on beagles. Neither too big nor too small, medium-haired and smart, natural and inquisitive hunters, they seemed like the perfect breed. Before we were off the phone, my dad even offered to *buy* me the dog, which was both generous and necessary in my cash-poor situation.

Now I was financially equipped, as well as emotionally prepared: A dog had been in the works for a while. Six months prior, before I'd ever imagined Sabby's demise, I'd announced to my boyfriend in L.A., "I shall get a beagle, and I shall name him Pete." My boyfriend's lack of instant enthusiasm and list of reasons why dog ownership can be complicated was not the reason we were no longer together, but I can't say I've ever cottoned to someone killing my dreams, especially with cold reason and logic.

So, after shutting Sabby's used litter box in a cupboard (I couldn't bear to throw it away), I set off through the hazy smog and heat of a Los Angeles

April, clutching the address of the nearest beagle rescue I could find. I finally found the place deep in the Valley—a baying yard stuffed with waddling beagles too fat to be cute, submissive wetters that sprayed the chain-link as they licked my hands, beagles with too-short ears and rheumy eyes and docked tails. How to choose?

People who have never owned one cannot understand why there are so many beagles that need to be rescued, and why so many people who own beagles end up giving them up. The first public outcry came when it was revealed that beagles are the most common laboratory dogs; around that time, actress Kim Basinger freed hundreds of former test beagles near L.A. Given the wisdom that comes with hindsight, I can only say, based on her fervent need to set those dogs free, I *know* Kim Basinger has never owned a beagle.

Back then, of course, I was still smitten, fully ensnared by the beagle publicity machine. Back at the rescue, even faced with the factory seconds of the canine world, I was still giddy with the prospect of going home with my very own. Then, as I sat down on a bench in the yard to ponder my decision, a white blur ran over and leaped up beside me on the bench. He was snow white, with comely black spots and long, silky, fawn-colored ears. A perfect specimen. As I gazed into his soft eyes, he gently leaned over and licked my face. My angel!

In June, I would remember the heat of April with nostalgia, as first-stage smog alerts marked every morning's paper and the thermometer rose slowly toward the 100-degree mark. School and my teaching job over for the year, I was determined not to stay in this seventh level of poisoned hell for the summer. However, I quickly determined, no one else wanted to stay either, and the hordes I'd expected to clamor to sublet my cute bungalow on my palm-lined street never materialized. With rent still to pay, I did what any desperate twenty-something with nonexistent funds, a special-needs dog, and nowhere to go would do: I decided to work for my father.

It wouldn't be so bad, I reasoned. Pete would have a huge, fenced-in yard, and the boyfriend who had caused such a stir when staying at their house—because under their roof, no one who wasn't married slept together—was yesterday's news. My father would pay me a good wage, and I could go to Seattle every weekend and stay with friends I'd left only a year before. Not ideal. Not terrible, either.

Packing my car, I worried about the beagle peering at me from the window and barking. My few months of experience with Pete had taught me several things. One, beagles will eat *anything* and generally do not respect dog spaces and people spaces. For example, the idea of the floor being dog space, and the kitchen table being people space, simply cannot be absorbed.

I'd also learned that beagles cannot ever be left off-leash outdoors or tempted by open doors leading outside. The entire neighborhood now knew me and Pete, having helped as we played the fun game of Sprint After Escaped Beagle As He Runs Willy-Nilly Toward Busy Death Street. My angel was also special in that he turned out to have intense separation anxiety, which is how helpful Internet veterinarians described his insane and violent reactions to not having me by his side at all times. In short, he was Disney's version of Cujo.

Left to his own devices, he barked loudly, frantically, and insistently, destroyed anything within reach, and ate anything remotely edible. This included garbage, of course, along with used tissues, lipstick, antacids, and gum. Just a week after I got Pete, a dozen bagels mysteriously disappeared from the kitchen counter. Weeks later I had yet to find them, or the plastic bag that had contained them. I did find the jar of peanut butter, plastic lid torn off and shredded, contents eaten. Likewise, the whereabouts of my favorite shade of MAC was easier to trace—when I arrived home that day Pete sat calmly by the door. Only the bright lipstick adorning his white face, like that of a three-year-old playing dress-up, gave him away. I had to admit, his constitution was admirable, if annoying. Unlike Sabby, Pete did not fetch, or play soccer, and when we went on walks he pulled until the leash left marks on my palm. They did have something in common: Pete *loved* butter and ate it right off the counter, too.

I knew the road trip would be complicated by the fact that I had no air-conditioning in my car. This meant that under no circumstances could I leave Pete locked inside, even to take a potty break.

Because of this and Pete's general neurotic behavior, I decided to take my time with the drive. I'd break the trip up into three days, instead of the usual two I had done before. First, I arranged to stay at my ex-boyfriend's house, only about five hours away. For the second night, I secured a room in a Motel 6 near Weed (all Motel 6s accept dogs under forty pounds). Then I would drive the rest of the way, about ten hours more to Yakima, Washington—home sweet home.

THE DAY BEFORE I left, Pete and I paid a visit to the local pet emporium to stock up on supplies. As he rang up a collapsible water dish, individually bagged food, jaunty red dog panniers that I couldn't resist, and a special stuffed toy known to me and Pete as Fleece Man, the pierced hipster at the register gave me a look.

"You going hiking or something?"

"No, we're just taking a little road trip. Nothing that extreme," I explained.

"You have an SUV?"

I snorted. "A Sentra."

He put down my purchases and looked me in the eye. "And where is *he* going to travel?" he asked, gesturing toward the floor where Pete was straining toward some impulse buy. Jed, a.k.a. PetsMart Guy, went on to inform me that I was lacking necessary and responsible equipment: a dog harness/seat belt that would keep Pete lashed to the back seat and safe in case of a crash.

The helpful clerk vividly described the situation I would face if I opted out of the doggie seat belt. "*Man*, they go, like, *flying* out of the windshield doing, like, eighty," he said. "Like in those test-dummy commercials. You wouldn't be able to *peel* him off the road."

AFTER BUYING THE seat belt, I felt more optimistic about the trip. Just me and my dog, no responsibilities, no one to tell us what to do. Nothing but air and sky and blacktop, cigarettes and coffee and Fleece Man. And at least Pete would survive any crash.

I'd barely gotten out of the city limits when Pete started whining and scrabbling on the seat with his claws. Craning my head to see him strapped into his seat belt, I couldn't discern the cause of his alarm. "Do you have to go potty, Pete?"

He barked. So smart, just like Lassie! "Okay, okay. Shoot. Let me pull over, and I'll get out your leash."

For anyone who has never driven in Southern California, allow me to explain that a fundamental rule of the state is that under no circumstances may any driver dip below eighty miles an hour. No matter the posted speed limit, Danger Ahead signs, curves, on-ramps, exits, or accidents—like drinking water from the tap, it is simply not done. This meant that finding a place to pull over on the crowded interstate would be no easy feat. However, faced with either uncertain death or the certain stench of dog urine in an un-air-conditioned car, there was only one attractive option.

Finally, I found a patch where the shoulder seemed wide enough to accommodate us. Though I signaled for half a mile beforehand, honking and obscene hand gestures greeted my move to pull over. As cars and tractor trailers went screaming by, I clicked on Pete's leash, undid his seat belt, and pulled him out of the car. "Okay," I said. "Do your thing." Pete blinked in the bright sunlight and sniffed the tire, then pulled to go straight into the freeway. "No, no," I cautioned, pulling him back, "just go here." I waited. Pete waited too. Having freed himself from the constraints of the back seat, and that infernal dog seat belt, he was prepared for a stroll along I-5.

I'm embarrassed to say it took about five more false starts before the possible stench of dog urine paled in comparison to not making it out of the county before sundown. As a compromise, and because Jed at PetsMart would never know, I finally released Pete from his overpriced safety strap. I did so reluctantly, remembering taking the same trip just years before with Sabby.

Unlike dogs, as everyone knows, cats do not enjoy car travel. My vet had convinced me that Sabby would be much happier and easier to control should I provide him with some kitty Valium before we left California. He had mewed and yowled so piteously from his carrier that I had finally released him to sleep it off in the back seat. Moments after starting the car back up, I'd looked in the rearview mirror and screamed. My striped cat, legs stiff as though with rigor, was perched precariously in the back window, jaw slack and dangling, pupils dilated, a live version of Bill the Cat. Once he'd come to enough to vacate that perch, he'd spent the remainder of his time trying to hide under the brake pedal. The lesson gleaned from that trip— never release the animal from its tether—clearly had been obscured by the Southern California smog.

THUS FREED, PETE ate the emergency road snacks I'd packed and two cigarettes from an open pack, then chewed through the pocket of my jacket in the back seat, in which a stick of gum had melted a few weeks back, all without breaking a sweat. When he managed to get half of his body out a window cracked three inches, we narrowly avoided an oncoming car as I pulled Pete back in. Even so, we made it to Bakersfield in one piece.

To say it was an uncomfortable reunion with my ex-boyfriend would have been putting it mildly. Why either one of us thought this would be a good idea is beyond me. To say it was an uncomfortable reunion with my ex-boyfriend's mother . . . Well, she handled it remarkably well for a woman faced with hosting the hussy terror who had first dragged her baby two states away, dragged him back again full circle, and then deposited him in her living room, brokenhearted. For years I'd been like a daughter, but, well . . . things change. The tension was compounded by their dogs' reaction to Pete. While he happily canvassed the house, knocking over garbage cans and shredding tissues, the older of their dogs tried desperately to kill this pint-size intruder.

"It will be fine," my ex's mom politely reassured me through clenched teeth, dragging her aged golden retriever away. "I'll just lock him in the garage." As I smiled and apologized my way through "family" dinner, trying to obliquely remind them why they'd liked me so much only a few months before, their dog barked furiously through a door only a few feet away. Pete looked on, happily shedding white fur all over their blue fabric couch. Needless to say, we made it a short overnight visit, leaving at daybreak.

The long stretch of road between the farmland of the San Joaquin Valley and the mountains of Northern California is hot and dry and populated with relatively few amenities. After having availed myself of as many drive-through opportunities as I could, I realized that drive-through bathrooms have yet to come into vogue. Besides, we were running low on gas. The moment was upon me: I would have to face Pete and his separation anxiety. I pulled over at a gas station.

"Mommy, what's wrong with that dog?"

"Is it hurt? Is she hurting that dog?"

"Does that lady know the dog is barking?"

Oh yes, the lady knew. I didn't need the carful of kids at the next pump to tell me that the tiny terror locked inside my car was raising holy hell only inches from my face. I was getting good at the apologetic smile, though, this time directed toward the others filling their tanks and wondering whether perhaps I was pushing splinters of wood under the nails of that doe-eyed, defenseless beagle.

Tank finally filled, I faced my next dilemma. It was before noon but already hot enough to fry an egg, not to mention a dog's brain. And I felt certain that leaving Pete alone in the car to use the restroom would result in a call to Animal Control and/or slashed tires or, worse, a do-gooder who would inadvertently free him, unaware of his status as the state champion of Run Willy Nilly Toward Busy Death Freeway.

So I got back into the car and scattered a dozen dog bones over the passenger seat. "Look, Pete, treats!" I then rolled down the window slightly and dashed out of the car, running toward the bathrooms. He went berserk. I thought he might break the glass, he was scrabbling so hard against it. Thanks to the cracked window it was all quite audible, too. Back to the car for plan B.

The bathrooms had an outside entrance. This at least meant I wouldn't have to take Pete inside and try to convince the clerk he was a service dog. After putting on his leash, I lashed a pleased Pete to a sturdy bush out front. Before I walked through the bathroom door, Cujo was back, barking insistently and trying to chew through his leash.

I ducked inside. Damn. Three closed doors faced me. I ducked back out and crouched down next to Pete, shushing him like a toddler.

"Cute dog," said a woman as she walked past, right into the stall that had just been vacated while I talked down the patient. The station was busy—it was clear I couldn't babysit Pete outside if I ever wanted to wee. Inside again. Barking again. I waited impatiently, then nearly knocked over the woman exiting the next free stall. Once finally inside, I had barely pulled down my shorts before an "Oh! Oh! Get away!" issued from the doorway. As I think I've previously mentioned, when calm, Pete has much the same effect as a sleeping kitten. However, when his little "issue" rears its head, I suppose, to someone who doesn't like dogs, he might seem—well, just a tiny bit out of control. Dangerous seems pushing it, but again, I am a dog person. And the elderly woman trying to enter the rest room blocked by my angel clearly was not; neither was her daughter, who held her solicitously by the elbow, glowering at me as I emerged, zipping my shorts and trailing toilet paper. Now I had graduated from being the dog abuser at pump six to the grandma abuser outside of stall two, and judging from the reaction from onlookers, that offense carried a harsher penalty.

I spent the remainder of the trip to Weed drinking coffee and Cokes from Jack in the Box and speed-peeing at rest stops only—parked as far from other cars as I possibly could to limit Pete's auditory impact as he barked his tiny canine heart out in his overheated coffin.

THE MOTEL 6 in Weed seemed an air-conditioned, bark-free oasis to me, rather than a cinder-block dump with a drained pool off of I-5 in a town called, well, Weed. After taking Pete on a constitutional around the parking lot, I bolted us both inside the frigid room and leafed through the yellow pages for a restaurant that delivered. So much for my visions of the freewheeling-road-trip me with my trusty hound by my side; Pete and his neuroses had made me a prisoner of small, ugly spaces. I was tired and famished and really wanted a drink, in public, but delivery mu shu and HBO would have to do.

The knock came, and I jumped up, Pete to the door before I was. Holding him back by the collar, I opened the door to the delivery guy. "Cute dog," he said, as I held Pete back with my leg and took the food.

"Thanks." I looked over at the table where my wallet rested, then down at Pete sniffing the air wafting in from the parking lot. I hadn't thought to go to the door with my money. I looked at the delivery guy, a bad-skinned teen with a wispy moustache. I didn't want to lock him in my room with me while I got the money—that seemed a little too friendly. But I also didn't want to shut the door in his face; that didn't seem friendly at all. When he bent down to pet Pete, I saw my chance. "Could you just make sure he doesn't get out?"

I was digging out a twenty when I heard, "Oh god, I'm sorry. . . . " Nothing like a rousing game of Willy Nilly before dinner!

THE ONLY STRETCH of roadway more desolate than that leading to Weed might occur just after the Oregon border, headed into central Washington State on I-84. Unlike the coast, central Washington is not verdant—it is, in fact, a desert. But it is *my* desert, the desert where I grew up. *So close, so close.* I had to pee, again, and my legs were cramping from the brake and the clutch, but my parents' house was only an hour away—a rambling home with expanses of clean porcelain and iced drinks, an enormous fenced yard in which the menace could frolic and bark and bark and bark and who would care?

So lost I was in my dream, I barely noticed the car pull up uncomfortably close behind me. It was an innocuous red Taurus-style car, but hey, man, there was plenty of road here, why so close? Then the lights went on. Then the loud-speaker: *Pull over please.* A state trooper. Welcome to Washington.

Finally, Pete would earn his keep. Officer, he was just going *ballistic*, he's a rescue dog, you know. He has serious issues. He just jumped into my lap—I couldn't see the speedometer. He tried to crawl under the pedals—it's lucky I didn't die! No, I'm okay. Yeah, thanks, he is cute. That's why I chose him to rescue—it's so hard, though; do you know how many beagles are abandoned every year? Do you have pets, Officer? Do you know he was given up not once, but twice? (Unsurprisingly, this part was true.) As the officer strode up to the window, I poked at Pete. I pinched him, discreetly, then shook him. "Peee-eete. Pete. *Pete!*" He stayed curled up tightly in the passenger seat, nose tucked under his leg. Totally immobile. Perfectly quiet. Like a sleeping kitten.

"Outside the city limits back there, the limit drops to fifty-five. Did you see the sign?"

Sign? I didn't see the *city*.

"You were going eighty-seven. Technically, that's reckless driving, but I'll cut you a break." Here it comes, yes, thank you, he *is* a sweet dog. . . . "I'll put you down at eighty-four—"

"You know, you're lucky," the trooper said as he handed me the ticket, gesturing with his pen toward Pete. "You've got a well-behaved dog there."

Constipated in Palinuro

Judith Levin

• • • • • • • • • • • • • • • • • •

Laura said we should send up white smoke when the Event occurred, but that seemed both sacrilegious and imprecise. Our neighbors in the tiny Italian town of Palinuro weren't waiting for the election of a pope; they were waiting for me to move my bowels. This was not what I had come to Italy for; however, it is an unfortunate fact that I enjoy travel more than my digestive tract does. I have gotten Montezuma's Revenge in Key West, shellfish-induced stomach cramps from hell on beaches from Ocracoke to Oregon, and what can only be described as gastrointestinal vapors in New Orleans. Paris, Provence, or anywhere else that serves French food, I get knocked out flat; for me, sauce, foie gras, and excess don't mix.

So perhaps it's not surprising that on a recent trip to Italy with my partner, Laura, I got constipated, even though this should have been physiologically impossible given the amount of olive oil I consumed.

Our itinerary in Italy was simple: to stay for two months in Palinuro, a small farming and fishing village turned tourist resort located four hours south of Naples. The town itself was a showcase of ugly 1970s Italian architecture, festooned with inflatable alligators and Barbie water wings, but we'd rented one of four attached houses on the grounds of a large house on a hill. Although we could walk to our favorite *gelateria* in ten minutes, we were surrounded by pine forests, orchards, vineyards, and vegetable gardens. From our shared stone terrace we looked out across the Tyrrhenian Sea, stretching delft blue to the horizon, more beautiful even than the photographs the local travel agent had emailed us. We were supposed to be writing, albeit with excursions to the sea as often as possible.

I did do some writing. I also ended up with a valuable and unwanted cultural lesson: If you've got something wrong with your intestines, southern Italians will do anything for you.

Like their Greek ancestors, southern Italians believe they have a sacred obligation to a guest, who may be a god in disguise. What's more, they find the digestive process genuinely interesting—not in the spirit of some great-aunt who bores you silly with descriptions of heartburn, but rather as a logical extension of their love for that which we digest. Unlike in the States, where food usually brings talk of carbs or calories, southern Italians seem to focus on health lore—much of it ancient. Even the paper towels I bought on our first trip to the supermarket informed me that mint leaves aid digestion and ease asthma.

In addition to paper towels, we bought nearly everything else on offer: bread from the bakery, meat from the butcher, and wine from almost any-where, including the supermarket, where the owner's uncle made his own and sold it for one euro a liter. And we shopped with an ulterior motive: We wanted, in our two months in this town, to become part of the community. So, like the townspeople, we food-shopped daily and intensively.

Since we were living on a hill, surrounded by a tall fence, our immediate community was small but interesting. The signora from the Big House was still in Naples most of the time, but Sara, her Valkyrie of a daughter, was studying for a law exam in one of the other three apartments. Cipriano and Lucia, caretakers from the gods, and their daughter, Gabriella, made sure she didn't starve. Our only other neighbors, also Neopolitans, had introduced themselves the day they arrived by asking us to eat lunch with them. The invitation was delivered in typical southern Italian fashion: We didn't know each other's names, but when they saw me one afternoon sitting outside without a plate in front of me around lunch time, they invited me to come join them. I didn't—but that was how I ended up meeting Beatrice, the matriarch of the family, who later become one of my main sources for intestinal lore and advice.

At the end of each day, the whole group of us congregated on the terrace and talked politics, admired the view, and planned to murder the noisily mating cicadas—or at least take away their Viagra. The sky turned rose-gold at sunset, and the sharp heat softened. Wrapped in dusk and mosquito repellent, lubricated with glasses of red wine, we made friends easily.

Getting to know the townspeople would be harder. In late June, when we'd first arrived, they already had a look of panic, braced as they were for the weeks in August when money pours in but they are transformed from townspeople and neighbors to service-industry workers. "It's *chaos*," they say—pronounced in Italian CAH-ohs—and they don't much like it. Nor do they like the tourists who walk the streets, so often looking right through them as though they aren't there. In my experience, Italians never pass one another on the street without saying "good day," even to strangers, but in panic-stricken Palinuro we had to say it first to receive a quick hello and a relieved smile.

As New Yorkers we were, we realized quickly, anomalies. It wasn't American tourists who invaded Palinuro, but other Italians, especially the dreaded Neopolitans, whose reputation in Italy is a bit like that of New Yorkers in the American heartland: loud people who don't know how to behave. We felt delighted that we'd found a region of Italy where people not only weren't tired of Americans, but in some instances had never spoken to one. We'd come here to enjoy the laid-back, down-to-earth Italian life—*Under the Tuscan Sun* and that whole fantasy—only to discover that these Italians wanted to know what it meant to be New Yorkers. What did we think of the war in Iraq? Had we seen the Twin Towers fall, and how had New Yorkers adjusted to living with terrorism? Was New York like in the movies? Like *Sex and the City*? Would Laura please analyze the Italian newspapers' coverage of the upcoming presidential elections and explain wherein it was insufficient? Did we like their town?

So, eventually, the townspeople got to know us. They found us a little strange. *Imagine not knowing how to cook zucchini blossoms!* the produce lady seemed to be thinking as she explained the process—but we took shopkeepers' advice on what to buy and reported back minutely on the success or failure of our cooking attempts. Soon, one of the butchers—the one who looked like a slender philosophy professor, not the one who looked like a butcher—would say the Italian equivalent of "and where have *you* been?" if we didn't come by often enough. He started giving us free sausages. The man in our housewares store gave us a discount and encouraged us to return the following summer and rent *his* guest apartment. By the end of two weeks, everyone knew Laura's family had come from southern Italy, they knew we were staying in an apartment of those rich people from Naples, and they knew why we had come to Palinuro, of all places.

"How's the writing going?" someone would ask, looking doubtfully—or sardonically—at our suntans. "Or were you at the beach again?"

We felt relaxed. We even ate healthily, for a change: One afternoon, Lucia brought us a huge basket of produce from the garden. It looked like Peter Rabbit's fantasy, spilling over with baby celery and ripe tomatoes still hot from the sun. I'd never eaten freshly picked lettuce, and we surpassed all heretofore known records in salad-eating. We were so proud of ourselves.

Just as we were settling into a routine, my intestines took us out of it. Not just my usual Italian *stitichezza*—okay, I admit it, I always get constipated in Italy—but a night of violent cramps and vomiting, reminiscent of the symptoms I'd had some years earlier when I had had an intestinal blockage. That time, I'd wound up with staples down my front, a tube up my nose, and morphine-induced hallucinations in which I believed I was a rice pudding. (Baked. With raisins.) If possible, Laura hated the experience more than I did, and it had left us both the tiniest bit jumpy about my digestive tract.

The night the affliction came on, I didn't sleep at all and spent the long dark hours listening to distant disco music—bad Italian rock—and planning my funeral.

Laura emerged out in the morning and took one look at me. "What the hell?"

I shook my head, wondering if I should say out loud that it felt like my guts were dancing the bunny hop: *fine, fine*, OUCH, *fine, fine*, OUCH, *fine, fine, maybe-I'm-over-this*, DAMN.

As our neighbors stopped by to say good morning, Laura told them I was ill. She also told them my entire medical history, including the intestinal-blockage story and the saga of my hysterectomy, during which the surgeon had discovered unrelated problems and had removed my appendix and several feet of colon. Everyone was fascinated. Southern Italians love operations.

So far on our trip, I'd sometimes felt left out while Laura had long conversations—my Italian comprehension was good, but my ability to speak was lousy. But suddenly, and unfortunately, I'd just found a way to get all the attention I could have wanted. Medical advice poured in.

Most of the advice was dietary, with speculation as to causes for the illness running a close second. Gabriella, the caretakers' twenty-five-year-old daughter, was a graduate student in sociology, her father's assistant gardener, and a benevolent dictator. She gave me a strict list of items to avoid, including all foods categorized by her as "roughage," dairy products, and anything that ferments, including potatoes.

Beatrice, the woman from Naples who had invited me to lunch, showed up next. She showed us her scars, some of them from having had *her* intestines untangled. Beatrice blamed my illness on the big salad she'd seen us enjoying at lunch the day before. Her explanation—that the greens had clumped together and formed a dry ball of blockage, like hay, in my intestines—felt like a historic moment: No one had ever accused me of eating too much salad.

"You have to drink liters and liters of water," Beatrice said enthusiastically. "I want you to look like a water balloon." She puffed her cheeks out to show how full of water I should be. I tried not to look too amused in between my grimaces of pain. It was possible I'd eaten too much salad, but still: a dry ball?

Beatrice also recommended that I eat boiled chicken and a tiny variety of pasta—called pastina—cooked in *brodetto*, which is water previously boiled for an hour with a little oil, a tomato, and a basil leaf. She further specified that the pastina had to be the variety with a hole through it, I assumed to prevent the pasta from forming the "ball" of food she found so pernicious. Then she fed me a teaspoon of olive oil, brought me a glass of carrot juice, and patted me on my head, despite the fact that she was ten years my junior.

Gabriella returned then, armed with a long list of local doctors, including one that made house calls. ("Not a quack, Signora," she said firmly.) The addresses, office phone numbers, home numbers, and cell-phone numbers of all the doctors were also on the list. I was dazed—partly from pain and partly from having been given a doctor's home phone number.

A little while later, the signora from the Big House came by with good wishes and counter-orders. No local doctors for me. She had doctor friends back home in Naples. No, they weren't gastrointestinal specialists, but she'd called around anyway to check which ones weren't on vacation. She offered Laura her palazzo in the city as a place to stay if I needed surgery.

Beatrice arrived with more carrot juice and upped the ante: *She* had a GI specialist in Naples who could untangle intestines laparoscopically. This doctor had even been flown to Japan to do a special operation in which he inserted a gauge into the stomach of a person who was trying to lose weight. . . . The Italians really do love surgery stories.

Laura, who can't bear inaction when someone is in trouble, said she would head out to do the food shopping—à la advice from one and all—while I napped. By the time I woke up, she was back, bearing chicken, juice, and good wishes from a suspiciously large number of people. She hadn't just been doing the shopping, she'd been worrying aloud to everyone we knew. Our businesslike young travel agent had *patted* her, she said, and sent me kisses. And people had offered numerous other theories of causality, including the cold.

"What cold?" I asked.

It was ninety degrees out. Yet the cold was everywhere, it turned out. Cold seawater, cold ice cream, a swim when there was a cool breeze. One windy day we'd watched mutinous children sweat onshore while their frantic mamas forbade them to chill their tummies by getting wet. A chilled stomach was dangerous, and I was proof of it.

Besides advice, people sent help in that traditional Italian form: food. Our butcher had picked an especially soft chicken breast for me and thrown in a handful of herbs to boil it with. I unrolled the paper towels to look up basil and rosemary. Yes, just as I'd thought: Both are good for soothing the stomach.

The owner of "our" *alimentari* said I had to drink pear juice. Laura described how total strangers had weighed in, argued, and, in the end, agreed that pear juice was just the thing for a bad stomach. The owner had also picked a handful of perfect small potatoes for me from her storeroom. She said the fermentation theory was nonsense.

After lunch and afternoon naptime, people reappeared to check up on me. I seemed to be in a teaching hospital with continuous rounds. Doctor Beatrice and her intern teenagers came by in bikinis to blow kisses. The girls were learning what questions to ask someone with a stomach ailment. Then Cipriano leaned on our terrace table, his work clothes smelling of warm earth, and asked again if I was feeling better. "How are you? How are you?" Sara shouted, carrying fat law books from the main house to the apartment.

There's an Italian verb, *coccolare*, that means to cuddle and comfort, and I was on the receiving end of the verb—its direct object. These people had known me only a short time, yet they visited constantly, willing me better, telling me everything they knew that might help. I felt cosseted, amused, babied.

I also felt like a fool. I'm forty-eight and a New Yorker. For all my desire to be part of this small community, I was quickly discovering that I like the part of urban life that allows people to walk down the streets talking to themselves and not to others, and does not require that every passerby be greeted. I like privacy—for which there is no word in Italian. Instead, near-strangers were monitoring both ends of my alimentary tract more closely than when I was a hospital patient.

"Have you made caca yet?"

No.

"Is there still pain?"

Yes.

"Have you eaten all your soup?"

Yes.

"Do you understand that you can wake us at four in the morning if you need to?"

I did. I come from a city in which one telephones the apartment next door rather than knocking, to avoid any potential intrusiveness, but in Palinuro I could bang on someone's bedroom window.

The following morning, my intestinal drama was temporarily upstaged when the owner's slobbering airhead of an Airedale got loose in the vegetable garden and dug up whole rows of the lettuces and tomatoes that Cipriano spent his days tending. Gabriella hauled the terrier out of the way of her father's curses, kicked it indoors, and told the dog's owner to keep the animal locked up. Then, with the air of someone who'd had enough nonsense, not just from the dog, but in general, she took my collar with a firm hand as well: She announced that I was going to the doctor whether I wanted to or not.

I knew there was no use arguing. Everyone had come outside to find out what the barks and shouts were, and I was outnumbered. At an American hospital, I have the right to refuse treatment, to throw interns out of my room, and to make decisions as an individual. The price of being part of this community was that I was going to the doctor, and that was that.

Gabriella's doctor-who-made-house-calls was making them elsewhere, so she escorted us to the home base/walk-in clinic of a local ambulance company. Ambulances in Italy carry an MD, and our local branch was especially well staffed, since the summer population consisted of accident-prone out-of-towners who sit on sea urchins, pass other drivers on the blind curves of the twisty roads, and otherwise require a high level of maintenance. I had just become one of them.

Flanked by Gabriella and Laura, like a prisoner threatening to escape, I slunk through a dense cloud of cigarette smoke and into a treatment room lined with shelves of medical supplies. I was suddenly relieved to have been overruled. If the doctors thought I was a hypochondriac, I could blame Gabriella.

We all shook hands with a man in blue scrubs and a man in green scrubs as Gabriella made introductions. Laura established herself as my translator and recited my current symptoms and my long, sad intestinal history. We established that I was able to fart, which made them very happy.

Me too. It meant my intestines weren't completely blocked.

Lying on the examination table, I felt transported into an Italian TV knockoff of *E.R.* as the man in blue, who looked like a very sweet-faced, very young George Clooney, palpated my abdomen. My abdomen has been the object of many palpations, and I knew Palinuro George knew what he was doing. I also knew that I was not well. As he poked, he reported his findings to the tougher-looking man in green, who then jammed his fingers into my belly and concurred. Laura translated: I had hard, sore intestines, and the treatment required a *flebo* (IV) of antispasmodics and a shot of muscle relaxant. Okay?

Even English comes through as static when I'm scared.

Fine, fine, OUCH *damn, fine fine* OUCH *damn, fine fine*—

Laura and the men in scrubs were looking at me.

"Huh?" I said blankly.

More Italian. Laura translated: "Signora, with your medical history, we can try to relax that spastic colon, or we can send you to the hospital. Okay?"

In my panicky haze I had missed a key piece of information about the shot, but I was deftly rolled and speared in the butt before I even knew what was happening. Then the man in green took my arm to insert the IV, and suddenly, the scene became extremely familiar, as he began to behave like every medical expert does when they encounter my impossible-to-locate veins: He called his colleague, the man in blue. They smote their foreheads. They raised their hands above their heads in dismay. They wrapped my arms in rubber hoses and tapped on the inside of my elbows with increasing force, miming that I should pump my hands open and closed.

I pointed to the back of my right hand and yelled for my translator.

"Tell them to use a pediatric needle."

The *flebo* was supposed to take an hour, but with the miniature needle it would be more like three. So once they'd gotten it into place, I settled in for what I knew would be a long morning at the emergency clinic. I stared at the white ceiling, forbidden to move lest I dislodge the IV.

Laura had gone to fill prescriptions for me before the pharmacy closed for its four-hour lunch break and to take Gabriella home. Neither had wanted to leave me without a translator, but as it turned out, nothing needed translation. Periodically, someone would check my IV—and my spirits. "*Tutto bene*," they'd say reassuringly.

I was indeed all right, mostly because they made sure I was. They didn't want me worried, tense, or bored. For them, that translated to bad medicine, rudeness, or both. The IV was to relax my intestines, but they were responsible for the rest of me.

So we hung out. When a third doctor showed up to help deal with a workman who had staggered in holding a bloody rag to his head, he came over to meet me while he folded bandages.

"What is your name?" he asked carefully, showing off his English.

"She's Julie!" shouted the man in blue, swabbing off the head wound. My name doesn't exist in Italian, so people generally get it wrong.

"No: *Judy*," I said.

"Joo-dee? Joo-dee? Ah—like Judy Garland," he said, obviously pleased with himself. Then, in Italian: "You morons: Her name is *Judy!*"

I watched as the doctors sutured the workman's gory head wound, crooning "*shhhhh*" to him when he groaned in pain, like mothers soothing a hurt child. Southern Italy—home of the tough guys.

When I was last in the hospital, I swear I could tell the status of people passing in the hall by their footsteps. A head resident walked differently than an ordinary resident, and an attending doctor walked differently still. These guys in the ambulance emergency ward, they sounded like they were dancing, or in a well-choreographed comedy routine. It kept me right there with them. As walking down the street saying "good day" to everyone kept

Palinurans connected in a way that stampeding New Yorkers shouting into cell phones are not, the men in scrubs kept me present, disallowing me to sink into a private panic.

When Laura returned, I was relaxing and so were my insides. She and the man in blue settled down for an hour-long discussion in which they compared the virtues of the Italian and American medical systems. One of the virtues of the Italian system was that my treatment was free, a piece of information that brought Laura briefly to tears, especially since it was accompanied by a short speech about the right of all people to have good medical care.

The conversation inevitably turned to food and to what I should eat. If the spasms were "functional"—a diagnosis the doctor favored in that he believed they were a reaction to heat or to cold (*he* didn't believe that my salad had turned into a solid clump of hay)—he advised me to follow a strict diet and take my medication. If the causes were physiological—adhesions, for instance—such measures would not solve anything, and the problem would persist. If this was the case, he sternly ordered, I should return to see him the next morning.

We never would know precisely what had caused my spasms—and my GI doctor in New York gave me his best "you've got to be kidding" look when I eventually filled him in on the summer's drama—but the Italian doctor's shot and IV and antispasmodic suppositories eventually cured the pain. The white smoke went up a few days later, to general rejoicing.

Of course, it could be that the Italian doctor's culinary advice is what solved the problem. Certainly, the diet instructions he'd offered differed considerably from the typed lists I'd been handed in the past by hospital dietitians in New York City. But he seemed confident in his prescription: No coffee, tea, wine, or milk products of any kind. Chamomile tea would be good, he said. (When I divulged that chamomile tea makes me vomit, I seemed to be upsetting about 500 years of medical knowledge.) No roughage. Nothing fried. Boiled cod was the best protein to start with. Mysteriously, he recommended against chicken but permitted red meat, as long as it was cooked on a *piastra* made of *ghisa:* Laura and I had never heard of this, but the doctor assured us we would find the item in a housewares store for eight euros. He also specified that I should have a tomato cooked in water and olive oil with a little onion and some herbs poured over tiny pasta: *brodetto again.* He did not specify that the pasta had to have holes.

The Trail

Erica J. Green

. . . .

hen I first arrived at the University of Ghana, I immediately noticed the anthills. Thick mounds of red dirt. Rising eight feet, they weren't so much anthills as sand castles of dripping wet earth. They towered in empty fields and lay in wait by the classrooms, blocking walkways as if they were signposts or garbage cans set out by the university staff. The tallest one, at nine feet, stood beside the African dance center. Two hillocks flanked the doors to the library—the University of Ghana's answer to the lions outside the New York Public Library.

While some students found the hills beautiful and others barely noticed them, I did everything in my power to avoid them. But the stories—maybe fact, maybe lore—were inescapable, and these floated through my head as disembodied voices:

"These ten-foot-high anthills take only moments to build. The ants swarm and work furiously and erect the hills within ten minutes or less."

"One time, a kid poked a stick in the top, and within seconds, his whole body was covered in ants. I think they bit him so much, he was killed."

"The ants leave as quickly as they come. I've heard that when an anthill is evacuated, people around it have to evacuate, too. What happens is, suddenly hundreds of thousands of them pour out of the top and march down the street and begin assembling another hill. The earth just moves."

I WANTED TO ask someone what kind of ants they were—the big fat black ones, the long red ones, the tiny ones. But I didn't want anyone to know I was terrified of these minuscule monsters. After all, I was a California girl, a confident first-born child, and a classic overachiever. I was here to hike through lush rain forests, study African literature, and forge a unique path that would help unleash my creative spirit. I was not here to spend a year being afraid of small crawling creatures. It simply wasn't part of my grand plan for personal growth.

My roommate had her own ideas for living an ant-free life. When I first met Sister Mary, a Ga-speaking woman, she was hunched over an ironing board, pressing the wrinkles out of a pair of large white cotton underwear. With her broad smile, big arms, and buxom chest, clad in a shiny polyester dress, she looked like the ultimate caregiver. I wanted to sit down with her and learn about her favorite books or places to go on campus, but instead, I asked the obvious question.

"Are you really ironing your underwear?"

"Oh, yes, yes. It is important," Sister Mary replied. "This way, it is so hot, it kills the bugs."

She explained how ants could get into clothes and lay eggs too small to be seen. "They crawl into you if you don't iron," she said. "Into your body. Into your skin. But the iron is hot. It will kill the eggs. I iron every day, *paa*. And, it keeps my appearances up. It is important to look very nice, very professional for the school."

The awful thought of having to iron every day was immediately overshadowed by the appalling piece of information she had just revealed.

Ants in her pants?!

Let me say now: I hate ants. I always have. And the thought of ants crawling in my vagina is my ultimate fear. Yes, it's weird. But it's major. Let me take you back to the hot summer when I was six, and my grumpy Uncle Vinnie, who always pretended to saw off my arm—"sawing" far too hard for comfort—asked me if I had ants in my pants. My older cousins laughed, but I looked down at my bathing suit and shrieked. Conjuring up images of those tiny creatures getting under my suit and crawling into my most private parts was too much for my six-year-old mind to bear.

I was not a prudish child, not a squealer, but this horrific image brought it out in me. Despite the fact that, as a tomboy, I climbed the walnut tree in our front yard, stepped on my share of bees without flinching, and took a summer-camp class called Creepy Crawlers, ants were my weakness. As the years passed, the thought of ants in my pants became a growing and ever more bizarre personal phobia. I avoided sitting on the grass and, if required to, propped myself up on soccer balls or a folded sweatshirt to prevent contact, all the while checking frequently to ensure that the slight tickle on my leg was not the first sign of an army of hundreds attempting to invade.

The paranoia persisted through high school, and while I didn't share my strangely visceral fear with the first boy to get into my pants, any male who suggested getting busy on the grass was immediately refused. A few of my closest friends were privy to this personal fear. They were the ones who, when I turned twenty, were most shocked by my decision to travel to West Africa.

"That will be great. Scary. Amazing. You will really have yourself an adventure. But what about the ants?" said my friend Kate.

I didn't laugh, and silently reassured myself that I'd matured into a learned, accomplished woman. I was an adult, practically, with a mission to study African literature and to travel. I would hardly let those little crawling things get in my way.

And yet here I was, starting my year in Ghana with this, my biggest fear, obstructing my path to classes and staring at me right in the crotch.

Ant-proofing my life became my first priority. Sister Mary and I lived on campus in Legon Hall, Annex B, room 214. Our dorm was an eight-story, whitewashed building in front of a flat green field at the edge of campus. Built in the early '60s, it was constructed in Soviet-era style, with thick concrete blocks piled one on top of the other. Students hung over the rails of the open hallways talking to their neighbors or hanging their laundry out to dry. Paint chipped off the sides and front of the graying building. Chunks from the lobby ceiling hung precariously over the stairwell. The elevator looked like it hadn't run in years. In the bathrooms, the water rarely ran. Instead, one tap at the front of the building flowed sporadically. Here, small boys gathered to haul buckets of water atop their heads up to the students, who beckoned them with whistles and snaps. In the field behind the working spigot, a pile of trash frequently burned, topped by two slightly charred porcelain toilets.

As the head of the Pentecostal Union on campus and the top-ranked home-science student, Sister Mary took her religion and her duty to keep a clean home very seriously. Her room decorations spoke to her passions. The laminated poster over my bed (specially sealed to preserve it from ants) depicted hundreds of Africans gathered at a religious revival meeting with a banner proclaiming THE BLOOD OF JESUS CLEANSES US OF ALL SIN. On my wardrobe next to my bed was another poster, which read ONLY THE BLOOD OF JESUS WILL SET YOU FREE! A river of blood would be the first thing I saw when I opened my eyes each morning. And then there was the lighter, more cheery image over her bed of a single daffodil with a simple line at the bottom: A SHOUT OF VICTORY TO A WORLD IN DARKNESS: JESUS LIVES. I wondered if Jesus was supposed to be the daffodil.

The posters, like the items on her desk, were perfectly placed, lined up straight along the edge. She provided both our desks with a plastic drop cloth, cut precisely to the dimensions of the writing surface. Both were patterned with blue gingham and orange flowers, akin to something my grandmother might have purchased at Pic-N-Save in 1979. And on the balcony, she'd set up a table with one burner and the two buckets of water, our bathing and cleaning buckets—a perfect kitchen/bathroom space.

While appreciating the dedication she put into decorating this intimate room, I wondered how, as a nonreligious person who generally avoided plastic decor, I'd be able to spend a year staring at the blood of Jesus and the Pic-N-Save drop cloths. At the same time, I knew that the cleaner the room, the fewer the ants.

But this wasn't just Mary's home, and I had my own personal items to take into account. And I knew from Tom, another American student who had already lived in Ghana for three months and who hung all his toiletries in plastic baggies from a clothesline on his ceiling, that leaving my Walgreens stash lying about wasn't an option.

"Ants go looking for goop and gunk and food and all the good stuff I've got hung on my ceiling," he'd told me.

"Toothpaste and deodorant?" I balked.

"You'd be surprised. They'll swarm anything."

I blanched.

After vetoing the idea of hanging my toiletries like Christmas lights around the room for fear of Mary's disappointment, I decided to focus on the top shelf of my wardrobe. Armed with microwave-safe Saran Wrap, the best kind for ant resistance, I set up shop. I lined the shelf with the plastic wrap, which I'd heard was impenetrable to ants, and laid out all my goods:

Advil; Gyne-Lotrimin; toilet seat covers; Stridex pads; a box of tampons; Skin-So-Soft lotion that was supposed to ward off mosquitoes; a bottle of DEET; Lariam, the antimalarial pills; my toothbrush and toothpaste; a stick of deodorant; and two plastic baggies—one full of Baby Wipes, and the other full of Q-tips. Everything was in a container and sitting on the Saran Wrap. I figured this was safe.

It took only one day for me to find two black ants crawling on my toothbrush bristles, a few big black ants drowned and sticking to the side of the Skin-So-Soft lotion, and lots of little red ants crawling on the Baby Wipes bag. I was repulsed.

Sister Mary laughed while she swatted at the few stragglers and picked them off the sides of my toiletries. She sprayed an unmarked bottle, presumably poison, at the Baby Wipes bag.

"No worries in life, *paaa*." She laughed and squeezed my shoulder. I threw out my toothbrush. I gave Mary my bottle of Skin-So-Soft as a thank you. I couldn't bear to think of what would happen when and if I needed to open the tube of Gyne-Lotrimin. I walked up and down the ant-free stairwell of Annex B to calm down.

Later that day, I tried a new approach. Wrapping up all the items, I pinned up a mini-clothesline inside the closet and hung baggies from it. I hoped with all my might that no more ant-faced crawlers would find their way into my private things. "No worry in life," I told myself as I grabbed a black t-shirt and pulled it over my head.

After surviving the ants on my toothbrush incident, I decided to treat myself to a bowl of the Special K I'd bought the previous week at an American-size grocery store, forking over something close to ten dollars for it. Never mind that I had never liked cereal; it was a hard-to-find item and thus a luxury. I scooped the powdered milk into the bowl, added bottled water, and stirred until the liquid became a whitish color and the powder dissolved. Inadvertently, I spilled a long white drip down the front of my shirt. Knowing I was going into town later, I changed, throwing my dirty one on the floor and grabbing a clean one. By the time I returned to the cereal bowl, I was too late.

In the few seconds it had taken me to change my shirt, there had been an invasion. The bowl's rim swarmed with dozens of tiny red ants so small that I could hardly make out their individual forms; the blurred red mass was the size of a silver dollar, and the group seemed poised to attack me. I let out a blood-curdling scream. But with Mary gone at the moment, I was forced to handle the crisis. I found an old rag and used it like a glove to pick up the bowl. Sprinting to the edge, I hurled the whole bowl over the side of the building. Only after taking some deep breaths did I realize that the t-shirt I'd thrown on the floor was also teeming with the tiny red bodies. I kicked the shirt outside and changed my shoes. It took a good ten minutes with Baby Wipes before all signs of the incident were gone.

Eventually, I learned to eat my cereal while holding the bowl, never setting it down for a moment. If I did, it took just seconds for some small red or black creatures to show up doing the backstroke, and I'd have to make a run for the edge of the building.

OVER THE NEXT ten months in Ghana, my ant survival skills continued to improve. I learned to eat while holding my food, flatware, and utensils; to get to class avoiding the scary red monstrous hills all over campus; to suspend my toiletries from plastic baggies; and most important, to keep ants out of my Tampax. While some may not have thought I was a brave soul in the ant department, I knew where I stood. Besides, I had pushed myself in other ways. Traveling throughout the country with two girlfriends, I'd survived insane car trips through Togo while a civil war raged. I'd boogied in Ghanaian discos, eaten *fufu* with my fingers, and donned a gazelle mask while attending an elaborate hunting festival with the women from my dorm. Seeing the Niger River at sunrise, learning to speak a bit of Twi, walking through the miles of the Kumasi marketplace, spending a holiday with Sister Mary at her family's home outside of Accra, and sitting on Umbrella Rock above Boti Falls all made me feel like I'd become a seasoned traveler who felt at home here. And according to my scorecard, I was winning the battle between woman and ant.

When June rolled around and I had less than two months left in Ghana, I thought I was at the end of the race and over all the major hurdles. Taking the antimalarial pill Lariam religiously, I had staved off the dreaded disease, although many other Americans on campus, like so many Africans, had come down with it. It seemed as common as the flu.

There's one problem with Lariam, though: The longer you take it, the more intense the side effects become. This worried me, since the side effects sounded almost worse than the malaria I was trying to stave off: insane drug-dreams, hair loss, blurred vision, and an endless list of other minor ills. There was even a disclaimer in the box that mentioned that the long-term effects of the drug were as yet unknown. To me, this conjured up visions of an eleventh toe, premature baldness, blindness in my left eye, or excessive wart growth on my face. I took it every day anyway.

It was at the very end of the tenth month of taking Lariam when the side effects caught up with me. I found clumps of hair on my pillow in the morning. My vision blurred. I dreamt of human-size ants building a sand castle on the beach back home. With less than two months left, I tried to stay rational. But the hallucinations intensified, and my eyes played tricks with my mind. A pen sitting on my desk became a swarm of black ants; the daffodil in the poster became a yellow butterfly; the Muslim man walking his goats across the campus was my grandmother. One morning, after grabbing a handful of hair out of my head, I was unable to read the words on the Jesus poster.

That day, I went into town and bought chloroquine and paladrin from the clinic, older drugs not as effective as the toxic, wart-growing Lariam but gentler on the mind and body.

One Thursday, two weeks later, I felt groggy getting out of bed, and the humidity felt thicker than usual. But after a standing bowl of cereal (I was an expert now), I felt better and I headed to the Arts Center to buy some batiks I'd admired. I had the newly purchased fabric in hand when suddenly, my body ached and my head started to spin. I was dizzy and then cold. In another minute I was hot.

I wondered if this was it. The Big M. Another wave passed over me and I felt fine. I stood to go, then had to sit. A second wave of dizziness struck me. Focusing on putting one step in front of the other, clutching the batik, I eventually made it out of the market and into a waiting taxi.

Back in my room, Sister Mary felt my head and said it was a fever, probably malaria. In less than an hour, I was at the Nyaho Clinic with a positive reading.

"Yes," the doctor said. "It is malaria."

Maybe going blind in one eye would be better, I wondered. But it was too late now. My fever soared and my thoughts began to blur. In the hospital, I sometimes believed I was in my old apartment in Berkeley, or in Annex B, 214. I was put in a private room and administered an IV. I floated out of dreams to watch a trail of ants on the window just on the other side of the screen. Then I'd dream again, and the ants would be marching through the room and circling my bed.

A day passed, and Sister Mary came to visit. I was starting to feel better. She brought oranges for me, and I kept down the juice, finally past the point of dry-heaving over the side of my gurney.

The next day a nurse came by to check my temperature. She stuck a needle into the IV to inject it with a fluid she said would "help me get better." As she punctured the plastic bag, a few drops of the anti-dehydration fluids sprayed out of the IV. She taped the syringe in place and stopped the small leaking hole. I fell back asleep. Night came and I awoke, relieved to see that the trail of ants outside my window had moved.

In the morning, I woke to sunshine and more hallucinations: It was the usual nightmarish trail of small black ants, this time, crawling along my IV. I felt exhausted and achy and disappointed. I'd thought I was getting better, but the hallucinations seemed more vivid than ever.

Or perhaps it was real? The worst of the malaria was behind me, after all; it was day three, and I was on the mend. I faced the ants and stared, hoping to rid myself of the hellish vision. Then, the trail shifted. A few straggler ants moved in a different direction, and the rest followed. Suddenly, I started to suspect that the trail of ants was real: Worse, the line was moving toward the bed. One hung precariously from the top of the IV and fell onto my face. I swatted at it and missed.

Of course, I missed it. There was no ant.

I breathed a sigh of relief, grateful that I'd come to recognize the Lariam-induced hallucinations. The vision still made me feel wary, however; I watched another ant crawl onto my bed. Then two, then three. I reassured myself: I was in a hospital—as clean a place as it gets in Ghana.

I felt a tickle on my upper thigh.

That's when Sister Mary walked through the door holding a pile of oranges.

I saw her long green polyester dress, the beads of sweat on her upper lip, and I thought of her nicely pressed, oversize, ant-free underwear. The sunlight glowed behind her, and I'm almost certain I heard church music as she entered. She looked at me and smiled. "Ah, you are almost going home," she said.

Then she stopped short and stared at my bed. She shrieked and clicked her tongue. "Oh dear. Oh no," she said, the oranges tumbling to the floor when she startled, her arms raised as if calling to Jesus.

How to Travel with a Man

Kate Chynoweth

. . . .

ave spent his formative traveling time alone in South
America and prefers his trips to be unpredictable and, in
my opinion, distinctly uncomfortable. Before the two of us
met in graduate school, he'd spent six months trekking
alone from Bolivia to Patagonia, through remote mountain
ranges and valleys, humping his gear instead of a girlfriend. His diet had
been such that the occasional indulgence in *cuy* (guinea pig served on
a stick)—with its little eyes burnt out and its tiny teeth bared—seemed like
a gastronomical delight. The nights spent on the dirt floors of strangers' huts
in Peru, and the detention by the Bolivian army for taking photographs near
a military base, were part of his "authentic" experience. My own travel
preferences, formed in Europe in my early twenties, involved nightclubs,
shoe boutiques, and cocktail bars in cities like Paris, Biarritz, Barcelona,
and London. Even though this was ten years later, and the bar I visited most
often was of the olive variety at the nearby Whole Foods, I still wanted some
of the same things out of travel: a bit of glamour, a lot of comfort, and
some minor, preferably urban, excitement. Given these differences, Dave's

and my vacations tend to be a bit contentious—I want a place that calls for a little lip gloss; he inevitably gravitates toward tents and sleeping bags and fabrics that wick.

Yet when we started planning an excursion to southern Baja last spring, I imagined a more harmonious kind of trip. We'd both recently turned thirty-one, which I sort of pathetically believed meant that we'd magically *evolved.* Plus, a few recent excursions had showed hopeful signs of maturity: In the Gulf Islands, Dave had browsed art stalls with me and liked it; before that, I'd joined him for the toughest three-day trek of my life in Washington's Cascade Mountain Range and enjoyed myself. Besides, southern Baja was the perfect destination for our needs and desires. Todos Santos, an artsy little surf town on the Pacific near the Sierra de la Laguna mountain range, had beaches, hiking, *and* a luxury hotel or two. To the east, the city of La Paz, set on the Sea of Cortez, offered great snorkeling—an activity we both love outright. I couldn't control the optimistic and embarrassing visions of the two of us removing our snorkels to kiss passionately and cavort in the warm azure water, and returning tousled from the beach to gaze into one another's eyes while reclining beneath a romantic thatch-roofed *palapa* like the beautiful people in *Travel and Leisure.*

Halfway into our first day of vacation—and halfway into a grueling, fourteen-hour hike in the Sierra de la Laguna—I realized that my seductive magazine fantasy was not to be. What Dave had promised would be "just a day hike" entailed climbing four thousand painful vertical feet in the burning hot sun. The thrilling views of the ocean, when we reached our goal at a high ridge, did not outweigh the extreme hamstring pain and insistent rumblings in my stomach (we'd forgotten the lunch in the car). The most idyllic thing about the whole day was that it eventually ended; and as I limped into bed that night, I dreamed of indulging in the lazy beach time and relaxation we now so richly deserved. I'd lived through his vacation; now he would get a taste of mine.

Dave greeted the next day's session of sunset cocktails at a luxury hotel overlooking a palm-fringed bird estuary on the Pacific with a yawn.

"Don't tell me this isn't pleasant," I said, snuggling up close to him, sipping my potent gin and tonic and reveling in the sight of giant pelicans skimming the water.

"I'd rather buy some beer and find a nice sunset spot of our own than hang around at a *resort*," he said.

"Oh, god." I pulled away and gave him a good, long dose of what he calls "The Flutter," which is somewhere between a shocked blink and an eye-roll of disgust. "It's not like I brought you to *Sandals*."

"Hey, if you like clichés," he said, finishing off his beer, "I'll play the part." Using our favorite smug and smarmy voice, he said, "It's just, you know, I prefer an *authentic* experience."

I laughed but wished he was actually joking, not just pretending to be.

That night, over dinner at a fish taco stand that lacked chairs, tables, and virtually any sign of hygiene—his win, since I'd suggested the hotel cocktail hour—we decided it was time for a change of venue. So the next morning we loaded up the car, said goodbye to the hostess of our bed-and-breakfast and headed east to La Paz. Although we didn't discuss it, I still hoped that with snorkeling, at last, we'd both have fun. *Fun, easy*, like vacation is supposed to be.

Even while splitting town, we couldn't outrun our disagreement. While I wanted go with a snorkel outfitter who would guide us to the best spots and preferably provide a deluxe picnic lunch, Dave wanted to rent gear and explore alone—by public bus and by foot. Understanding his wishes did not prevent me from straying a few boozy steps off the *malecón* during our post-dinner stroll that evening and happily finding myself in a boat-excursion office with lurid color photographs in the window. A young, good-looking guy, who introduced himself as "the Captain," brought out a thick three-ring binder filled with stock nature photos. In addition to snapshots of tourists snorkeling with adorable sea lion pups, there were shots of magnificent whales and dolphins. By the time the Captain got to the blue whales, I was sold. They'd been my favorite animal as a kid, having replaced wooly mammoths in my affections as soon as I learned that they were longer than three school buses and, more importantly, not yet extinct. I'd been on numerous whale-watching cruises in the past with the promise of seeing my beloved blue whales, and all had been fruitless. Although I'd finally accepted that I'd never see a blue whale outside of the Discovery Channel, the Captain inspired a certain optimism. Plus, hope springs eternal, especially after you've been drinking strong margaritas out of softball-sized goblets.

I looked at Dave and said, "What do you think?"

His clear, blue-eyed gaze looked a touch manufactured, but I took him at his word when he said, "Sure."

By the time we left, we'd agreed to shell out a hundred dollars to snorkel with sea lion pups and potentially see blue whales.

BAJA WAS HAVING the coldest spring in years, and I shivered waiting for the van outside the hotel at 6:00 the next morning. I was relieved when we climbed into the heated vehicle, at least until the Captain—attired in a jaunty red windbreaker and wraparound shades—started driving like a drunk Nascar driver through streets better suited to accommodate mules than minivans.

At each screeching stop, new day trippers climbed aboard: two athletic Dutch ladies in their early forties and two snotty French girls who looked no more than seventeen. One of the Dutch women, a burly blond figure in bright blue athletic shorts, introduced herself with a face-splitting grin that showed the big gaps between her little corn teeth. The name she barked out sounded like "Binky." Dave and I nodded and smiled. The Frenchies kept to themselves; I tried to eavesdrop on them, but over the noise of the engine all I heard was that the ghostly pale, extremely thin one was named Marie. Her friend, short and round with pink cheeks, looked hearty and efficient, more like Marie's chaperone than her travel mate.

After speeding along twisty coastal roads for nearly an hour, we turned through a gate in a rusty chain-link fence and parked in the shadow of a dilapidated old hotel. We stepped out, blinking, into the bright morning light and went into the lobby to sign legal consent forms. I raised an eyebrow at Dave, feeling a little jittery about freeing the Captain from any responsibility given his outfit's obvious decrepitude, but he was too busy scribbling away his rights with a ballpoint pen to notice. I had the sinking feeling that our shabby surroundings buoyed his hopes for the day's potential "authenticity."

After we signed, the Captain led us down a paved ramp to a musty room by the dock filled with snorkels and flippers. While we looked for the right sizes, he said, "It's a little colder than usual, guys. Maybe you want wet suits?"

"How cold is the water?" Marie asked.

He shrugged. "Without one, people stay in the water for maybe ten minutes."

"How much do they cost?" asked Binky.

"It costs only a little bit more," he said.

It sounded like he was just trying to make an extra buck, and after sharing doubtful looks, the French duo opted not to rent them.

Dave and I shared a look that said, *We've come this far, we might as well,* and joined the Dutch women in trying on wet suits. The four of us mutually ignored the awkward disrobing, sucking noises, heavy breathing, and tugging that went with the territory.

Set up with the thick neoprene outfits and snorkel gear in net bags, the four of us strolled to meet the French girls at the dirty concrete dock festooned with empty beer cans—and joined them in surveying a fleet of decrepit *pangas,* small outboard fishing boats complete with peeling paint and dented sides. No sign of the shiny white boat I'd seen in pictures at the office the night before. Finally, after a long wait, we heard the roar of a loud motor and a large fishing boat as imposing and gleaming as the *pangas* were battered, nosed up to the dock. As we viewed our sleek ride, there was a seismic shift within our group. The Dutch duo became immediately more jolly. The French pair remained predictably blasé.

"Looks like it'll even have a loo," said Binky, flashing a crooked smile.

But just moments after we climbed cheerfully aboard, our good fortune reversed.

"Sorry, guys," the Captain said. "If we have eight, we take the big boat. If we have six, the smaller boat." He shrugged again, more elaborately. "We were waiting for these other two, but they just never find us. So we take the smaller boat."

He gestured to our replacement boat, a tiny, rusty, dented little *panga*, and I watched Marie's thin face fall into a surly expression that I felt sure mirrored my own displeasure. The boat's worn canvas canopy top flapped violently and looked like it might fly away with the stiff breeze.

Next to me, Binky crossed her thick arms, "Don't tell me we are taking *that*," she said. "I don't know if I can get even one leg in that boat."

I had my own worries, partly due to the giant cup of tea I'd gulped on the dock, which was drip-drip-dripping into my notoriously small bladder. But there was no time to make one more bathroom pit stop before climbing aboard. Now that he'd decided on the small boat, the Captain seemed eager to leave.

Dave took the change of plans in stride, literally, by stepping into the *panga* first and gallantly helping me and the others board. I realized that he was probably happy to be taking the shitty small boat—more "authentic." Meanwhile, I was starting to fear for our lives. The old man behind the wheel was none other than the one who I'd watched snoozing on the dock while we'd been waiting earlier; he now looked only slightly more awake.

Despite the uncomfortable seating, two abreast on hard, narrow benches, I felt relieved as we motored away from the decrepit harbor. Surely the day would improve. I felt even more hopeful after we chugged out past the mustard-colored headlands and saw our destination, the island of Espíritu Santo, shimmering in the distance as if covered with snow. This was where we'd find clear tropical water, the adorable sea lion pups, and possibly dolphins and whales.

The only problem was that the closer we got to our goal, the choppier the sea became; we bounced mercilessly up and down. The wind took its toll, too, and we all pulled extra jackets out of our packs. The French girls pulled out their beach towels to drape across their chilled legs, and we all followed suit, teeth chattering in the freezing wind. At the Captain's instruction, we scanned the horizon for aquatic life—but as thirty minutes ticked by, and then forty-five, we saw nothing. I shaded my eyes against the bright diamonds of light on the water, waiting for a sarcastic comment from Dave. I wouldn't resent it when it came, I decided. My choice of excursions was clearly a loser, and I had to concede that he'd been right—renting gear and exploring on our own would have been far better than this. I recalled my drunken optimism at the boat shop the night before and felt a shudder of guilt that I'd engineered this lame, overpriced trip.

Instead of holding it all against me, though, Dave chatted cheerfully with the two Dutch women about Fiji—and the critique I expected never came. I watched him affectionately, marveling at his patience and impressed by what I perceived as his positive attitude. (Later, he told me that at that moment he'd been thinking, *We're not gonna see shit out here* and *No critique needed, this shitty experience speaks for itself.*)

Finally, just at the point when I thought I'd have to ask the Captain to cut the engine so I could leap in the water to pee, we rounded a point on the island, and a tall column of dull whitish rocks came into view. Some other boats were already anchored nearby. The Captain maneuvered our tiny little *panga* between them and threw down the anchor.

"Here we are," he said. His manner was bored and practiced, like a trophy wife showing off her diamond for the billionth time.

I tried to see the place as a beautiful tropical paradise. Upon closer inspection, however, it became apparent that the rocks were white because they were covered with bird shit; I immediately wondered if the murky water was the result of shit of another kind—the obese sea lions draped across the rocks looked like they'd drop hefty loads.

Binky covered her nose and mouth with one hand and said, "It smells fucking disgusting." I was impressed with her English.

I scanned the choppy water. I didn't see any other snorkelers, but I could glimpse huge, shadowy sea lions cruising just below the surface.

"Merde," said Marie, shivering dramatically. Her chubbier friend responded soothingly in French.

The Captain's red windbreaker flapped in the cold breeze as he gave his usual tourist spiel. "Don't go after the babies," he said. "Wait for them to come to you." Then he pointed to the 1,200-pound males lounging on the barnacle- and bird shit–covered rocks. "Don't get closer than five meters. The mothers are big, too, but they won't bother you if you don't bother the pups."

Pondering this vague but threatening language, none of us made a move for our wet suits. Except for Dave. When I glanced over, he was efficiently grabbing his own back zipper and pulling it up. I glared. I hadn't minded earlier, on the boat ride, when his good spirits had buoyed my own, but now his enthusiasm was going to force me to jump into freezing, shit-clouded water with a bunch of overprotective sea lions.

"You don't have to go in," he said, generously, "if you don't want to."

In this moment I realized two things. First, this was supposed to be *my* day, and I wasn't having fun. Second, Dave *was.* I slumped over in defeat. This was final, irrefutable proof that we would simply never like the same things, that we'd never be that hip, happy, couple in *T&L.* I wondered how much worse things could get, realizing grimly that Dave seemed to get incrementally happier the further this outing careened off track.

The Captain's disappointment at our lack of initiative was palpable. "Hey, girls, don't worry," he almost pleaded. "They're playful, like puppy dogs. You'll have fun."

"Those ones look scary," I said, nudging Dave and pointing out a monster dad in full roar.

"Just remember: Don't go within five meters of the rocks," Dave said.

Meters? I opened my mouth to ask, but in that moment he secured his goggles, lifted his hand in a wave, and neatly flipped backward over the side of the boat.

How long was a meter? Three feet or three yards? Wait: How long was a yard?

Dave bounced back up in the water, grinning. Opening his mouth obscenely wide to insert his snorkel, he then slid beneath the surface, swimming away quickly. Seeing little choice but to follow, I grimly stepped into my wet suit and moved toward the edge of the boat. Marie's thin face tilted up and away as I let myself fall backward over the edge of the boat, trying to accomplish the same efficient flip that Dave had just executed. But my flipper caught on the way down, and my head slapped painfully into the side of the boat. Someone graciously freed my flipper, and I sank into the water with all the grace of a large bovine.

I strained to see something interesting, but the water was grayish-blue, instead of the clear aqua I'd envisioned, and the swirling particulate prevented much of a view. Unfortunately, nothing could obscure the giant, shadowy mammals shooting by like torpedoes. I could easily decipher the hulking forms of the mothers. The babies, to my horror, looked more like adult mastiffs than the cocker spaniel–size pups I'd been expecting.

I gave a few halfhearted kicks of my flippers and then stopped; swimming toward the sea lion colony seemed just plain wrong. I felt like the girl in the horror movie running into the basement to hide when everyone *knows* the killer is in the basement; that was me, heading innocently to a death by mauling. So I floated on the surface, staying remarkably still until one of the creatures emerged out of the murk, cruised just inches from my face, and made me panic. A true animal lover would surely have thrilled at this brush with nature, but I reared up out of the water like some frightened beast, breathing noisily through the snorkel. I spotted Dave's snorkel tube above the icy gray waves and started swimming toward him, repeating to myself, *There's safety in numbers.* When I got close enough, I patted him on the leg, but he swam away, spooked. Then he turned around and saw me and reached out to squeeze my hand—for my part, it was as passionate a reunion as if he'd just ridden in on a white horse.

He gestured to me to swim in front of him. But even though my arms pulled at the water and my legs churned, I had the odd sensation of not moving. I redoubled my efforts, and then suddenly shot away as if I'd been released from a slingshot. When I broke through the surface again, I could see only a tumult of thrashing white water where Dave had once been swimming. When the frenzy subsided a moment later, Dave swam up next to me.

"I don't want you to freak out," he said. "But those little bastards bite." He lifted up his forearm, which had two wide pink arcs trickling a thin line of blood that formed the shape of a large mouth. "Keep your hands in a fist and your arms close to your chest."

I suddenly felt like a bumper car with a dead engine, stuck in the middle of a rink filled with cruel, oversized preteens. I was at the mercy of these wild underwater dogs! Despite his bloodied arm, Dave looked cheerful. "A baby was biting on your flipper, and I tried to distract it by waving it away," he said. "Then it just went for me." He actually let out a delighted giggle.

A short distance from where we bobbed in the water, the water churned again. We heard yelling. In the middle of the foam, I made out Binky, yelling and raising her big arms up high up over her head.

Deciding how to react took me just one split second: I doggie-paddled as fast as possible in the opposite direction. (Later, Dave would reenact my frantic paddling and snorting with glee.) I swam ferociously, wriggling with my fists tight and my arms clasped across my body. I reached the boat and pounded against its metal flank until the Captain hauled me up over the side. Landing in an uncomfortable heap, I glanced around in a panic, as if killer sea lions were lurking here, too. But no. Our sleepy driver dozed, the boat rocked gently, and it didn't seem at all as if I'd just escaped a massacre.

"They bite," I said to nobody in particular.

The Captain smiled a wide, benevolent, don't-scare-the-other-kids sort of smile. "They're just playing," he said.

Marie gazed at me with new sympathy; the other was readying herself to dive into the water sans wet suit—but changed her mind quickly when Dave climbed aboard a minute later.

His injury looked even redder and more raw out of the water. Marie gasped, put her hand to her mouth. "Will you be okay?"

He nodded and gestured to the water, where the two Dutch women were swimming back toward the boat at top speed. "Let's just keep an eye on them and make sure they make it back," he said.

Marie looked about to swoon at his manliness. I rolled my eyes.

Binky was the first to come over the side, her chest heaving from the effort of the fast swim.

"Did they get you too?" asked Dave.

"Yeah, those fuckers bit me," said Binky. She displayed her injury; there were bloody bite marks on several fingers of her right hand.

"I can't *believe* this," I said.

Marie leaned over and handed me her dry towel. "Do you want this for your hair?" she asked.

I thanked her and towel-dried my soaking-wet hair, then struggled out of my wet suit. The Dutch women had already taken theirs off and put them aside. Nobody needed to state aloud that we were all out of these infested waters for good.

"Well, guys," said the Captain. "Usually we hang around here for a while more, another hour or so. Sound good?"

"Yeah, right," muttered Binky. She pulled up the collar on her windbreaker and jammed her injured hands further into her pockets. "Fucking beasts. I want to get out of here."

"Yeah," I said. "I want to go back."

A new camaraderie bloomed between us. At least we were suffering through hell together. Although when I glanced over at Dave, he was shucking off his jacket with a cheerful expression.

"Hey," he said, smiling. "Are you cold? Do you want this?"

I nodded, and he draped it over me. Wearing short sleeves, he clambered toward the back of the boat and started chatting with the Captain and the boat driver in halting Spanish.

I stared at him in confusion. He was clearly enjoying himself, and meanwhile, I was cold, hungry, annoyed, and worst of all, strained to the bursting point. Thanks to the freezing temperatures and my fear of mauling, I'd failed to pee in my wet suit while in the water. But just as I was gathering my courage to jump back into the sea, still roiling with vicious mammals, the Captain started to pull up the anchor. I sat back down with mixed emotions, horrified that I'd have to endure a challenging, choppy boat ride before getting to a bathroom yet delighted with the idea of getting off the dreadful vessel.

"Hey, guys, you want to go somewhere else?" asked the Captain. He finally seemed to be grasping our misery. "We know this beach, and I usually don't stop there, but I take you anyway," he said. "It has really good snorkeling."

Binky shouted, "Yes!"

The French duo nodded vigorously.

Everyone looked at me, including Dave, whose empathetic look communicated that if I wanted to go home, he'd support me. But, looking at Binky and Marie, I realized that I couldn't disappoint them—even though I privately doubted his promise was good, given his track record.

"Sure," I said.

We zoomed away, exchanging the smelly, shit-covered sea lion colony for the open sea, where we once again grimaced in pain as we bounced up and down on the benches. Dave and the others busily scanned the water for signs of aquatic life. I'd given up on the prospect of seeing whales or dolphins. I'd seen barnacle-crusted gray whales on a recent trip to Vancouver, and that would have to suffice. As for dolphins, well, I could always go home and rent *Flipper*. I picked listlessly at my fingernails.

Next to me, Dave sat up and pointed. "Are those boats out there?"

I followed his gaze out to where a dark, hulking shape wedged against the light horizon line. As if timed for our benefit, a huge plume of mist rose to what looked to be about a hundred feet as a whale's dark, endless back glided above the water.

"Probably gray whales," I said, still grouchy.

Dave turned around to the sleepy driver, his newfound friend José, and pointed them out. José responded in Spanish excitedly. It was the most animated I'd seen him all day.

"Blue whales," Dave translated. "He thinks they're blue whales."

Despite my black mood, I felt a growing excitement as José turned the boat around and headed for the whales; miraculously, they swam toward us. Within minutes, my childhood holy grail was in sight. Two enormous blue whales, bigger then I'd ever imagined they could be, were swimming just three hundred feet away from our boat. As their sleek forms curved above the water's surface, large islands pushing their way up from below, I fantasized about jumping on their backs: an overaged whale rider with frizzy, wind-blown hair.

Dave leaned over and kissed my cheek.

We all gasped as one of the whales sent another huge plume of spray through its blowhole, then started to disappear beneath the water, flipping its enormous tail on the way down. "You can see by the angle of the tail going down that he's not coming back up," said the Captain. Moments later, the second whale sank from view as well, giving one last flip of its magnificent tail. Its wake rocked the boat.

The peaceful encounter left us all quiet, awed, and nobody talked much as the boat nosed along the shoreline, eventually pulling into a cove with water so crystal clear that I could see each grain of sand on the ocean floor. I jumped off the boat onto the white, sandy beach and sprinted up a steep sand dune, where, surrounded by waving dune grass and overlooking the beach, and where everyone's bright towels looked like mosaic tiles on the white sand, I had the most tranquil and satisfying pee of my life.

Thrilled by the whale sighting and the sheer joy of emptying my bladder, I sprinted back down the dunes, taking huge leaps, plunging my feet into the hot white sand until I arrived breathlessly where Dave lay on his towel, his eyes closed peacefully.

"This is going to be *great* snorkeling," I said. I stepped onto his towel to protect my feet from the burning hot sand and nudged his shoulder gently with my big toe.

Rather than leaping up with enthusiasm, Dave just gave a contented little sigh and rolled over on his stomach. Shading his eyes, he looked over his shoulder and said sweetly, "Don't you want to lay on the beach?"

I stared at him in amazement. "You're kidding. You finally want to lay on the beach."

"I like laying on the beach," he said. "Sometimes."

I sat down next to him, and looked out to the shallows, where Binky lounged in her wet suit like a seal on steroids. She shouted, "It's really amazing. You have to come in!" Her wide smile nearly split her face in two as she beckoned to me.

I leaned over and kissed Dave and said, "I'll be snorkeling, honey."

He nodded sleepily.

Sitting in the chilly clear water, I pulled on my flippers, pondering the irony of the situation. Dave was finally enjoying the beach, and I was having an outdoor adventure of my own. Privately, I could even admit that I'd at least halfway liked the hike, if only to complain about it. We might not be that well-tanned, ingeniously happy couple frolicking in various states of hip undress from the magazines, but liking the same things wasn't impossible for us; it just couldn't be planned. I suctioned my mask onto my face, put in my snorkel, and slid below the surface into an underwater world of hushed Technicolor. The crystalline water gave me a bird's-eye view to far, far below; it felt like flying. Delicate needle-nosed fish tenderly navigated the coral, and a warty, luminous white sea snake retreated into its dark cave at my approach. Schools of tiny, brilliant tropical fish darted about me like butterflies. I felt a tap on my leg and looked behind me. It was Dave, his face hidden by the mask, reaching out to hold my hand.

A Useful and Comprehensive Travel Dictionary for Girls

Buzzy Jackson

• • • • • • • • • • • • • • • • • •

Australia (Oz) *n.* **1.** A country—or is it a continent? Get it straight before you go. Located in the Southern Hemisphere, which means that the seasons are backwards. People celebrate Christmas on the beach here, or perhaps the Aussies I knew just did that for my benefit. Before you leave the Northern Hemisphere, you will be advised that the toilet water flushes down in the opposite direction. It's your responsibility to express amazement and consternation at this fact; then when you arrive in Australia you will stare into the toilet bowl to witness this natural wonder and realize that you never noticed which way the water circulated in your toilet back home. Don't panic: You will be sufficiently freaked out by the sight of the night sky Down Under, with its *totally different and weird constellations*, most notably the Southern Cross. Although, as with your home toilet bowl, you never really learned the constellations above your house (all right, maybe the Big Dipper), you will look up at the sky and understand what it means to be twelve thousand miles from home. **2.** A large land mass in the Southern Hemisphere, sparsely populated by beer drinkers and emerging Hollywood starlets. **3.** Country of origin for the little-known game **netball** *(n.)*, also known as women's basketball, which differs from the original only in that it features: a) no running, b) no backboard, c) a smaller, more dainty, "lady-like" ball, and d) no fun. In fact, Australians did not actually invent netball, but they're pretty much the only ones still playing it. Netball tournaments should be avoided by the foreign visitor, unless one's host is a champion **net-baller** *(n.)*, and then, sorry, you're just gonna have to go.

B

Barcelona (don't believe the hype—no one there pronounces it Bar-THA-lona. Seriously.) *n.* **1.** The capital of Catalunya, period. Don't ever forget that. The people of Barcelona are totally serious about their identity as non-Spaniards; they are Catalán, they speak Catalán (and Spanish, though they won't admit it to you), and "Catalunya" is how you spell "Catalonia", the end. The fact that more people speak Manx Gaelic than Catalán does not interest them, and mentioning this fact, even in Catalán, will not help you find the directions to the Gaudí cathedral you read about in your guidebook. If you must communicate, speak French. They think it's funny. **2.** A large city in northeastern Spain, known for its art nouveau architecture and its **tapas** *(n. pl.)*, small plates of food served at bars that are the protoypes for American tapas restaurants, which, if you've ever been to one, you already know are the biggest rip-offs in the history of food service. Twelve bucks for a saucerful of olives? Thanks, Barcelona!

C

Canadian highways (is it really necessary to spell this one out?) *n.* **1.** Where to begin? The maze of interprovincial thoroughfares is as vast as the permafrost tundras that make up the majority of this northern country's landhold-ings. Wait, that's so not true! The joke is that there is only *one* road that goes across Canada—just one. It's called the Trans-Canada Highway. It's cool because you can't really get lost on this road. Just take it east or west, and you'll get to the other coast eventually. Good old Canada.

D

Dudes (guys) *n.* **1.** Did you think you left them behind when you got on the plane at O'Hare? No way, dude! Dude, that species of American male, recognizable by its long, baggy shorts, baseball cap, and flip-flops, can be found throughout the world, particularly in warm-weather locales such as Phuket, Goa, Biarritz, Jamaica, and Fiji. Dudes congregate wherever beer, marijuana, and young women are found (in that order, and never separately). They typically travel in group formation; if you forget the names of the two dudes you just met, simply refer to one as "Abercrombie" and the other "Fitch," and it'll all work out fine.

E

Expensive (ouch) *adj.* **1.** What your trip will undoubtedly be, no matter how fortunate the exchange rate, particularly if you're headed to Europe. In fact, the exchange rate for Americans just keeps getting worse, or at least it seems like it when you try to figure out how much, exactly, 150 euros are worth. Too much to spend on dinner? Or not enough to get you to the ferry? And what happened to that good-looking dude on the Swiss franc?

It's worth noting that politically, most of the rest of the world (Tony Blair excluded) hates Americans now. So perhaps it's just better to think of the cost of your trip to Europe as one giant example of trickle-down economics. Sigh.

F

Female (chick, bird, Sheila, chica, mademoiselle, etc.) *n.* **1.** Just like in your regular life, when you travel, your gender will be constantly reinforced through quaint local practices such as whistling (North America), hissing (Spain, Latin America), catcalling (Italy, Russia, Baltic States), or frottage and/or genital exposure (France). To avoid such behavior, consider such destinations as the North Pole, Antarctica, or Pluto.

G

Girlfriend (romantic or platonic, either one is acceptable) *n.* **1.** The person with whom you should travel, if only for moral support in the face of global provocations from men; *see also* **female. 2.** The person who will watch your backpack while you go to the bathroom, speaks the languages you don't, and wears roughly the same size clothing, so you can occasionally change your look even though you only brought three shirts, one pair of pants, and one skirt. A true girlfriend not only loans you her clothes but assures you that, no question about it, that ensemble you're wearing—the pilled black sweater, those wrinkled, musty pants, and those stinky orange sneakers—is not only appropriate for a night at La Scala (somehow your girlfriend scored you rush tickets), it is de rigueur. Or whatever the phrase is in Italian. Helps if you wear the same shoe size and don't mind sharing. **3.** Will end up with the cute guy/girl you were eyeing in that bar in San Miguel de Allende, despite how totally obvious it is that you were the one who saw him/her first. And yes, she's doing it in the clothes she borrowed from you. So much for the orange sneakers.

H

Haole (Howl-ee) *n.* **1.** Derogatory term used by native Hawaiians against white-skinned nonlocals. Let me be clear: A lot of Hawaiians are paid to pretend they like you. Those who call you haole, therefore, are not getting paid enough. Aloha!

Hawai'i (Ha-wa-eeeee) *n*. **1.** Exactly what you think it's going to be like. **2.** The opposite of what you think it's going to be like. You know the drill: white beaches, palm trees, coconuts, alcoholic Slurpee drinks. Think again. The thing the travel agents never tell you is that people actually live there. They're called Hawaiians. And no, they don't like you, they're just paid to pretend they do; *see also* **Haole.** Hawaiians are a lot like other Americans. They drive SUVs. They annoy their neighbors with loud music. They take too long in the grocery checkout line. Mostly because everything in the grocery store is so damn expensive. Orange juice: six dollars a gallon? Forget orange juice. Eat like the Hawaiians do: Spam, Coke, and more Spam.

I

Inconvenient (ah-noy-ing) *adj*. **1.** Having sex while camping/staying in a crowded youth hostel or anywhere far from a clean water source for post-coital hygiene maintenance. Or is it just me? Bring Handi-Wipes.

J

Jew (member of the tribe) *n*. **1.** The original world travelers! Once found throughout the Mediterranean, Africa, and Europe, now found mainly in Manhattan, Burbank, and Israel. Look for signs of Jewish settlement throughout Eastern Europe, Spain, France, and Germany—wherever Christianity is sold. *Mazel tov!*

K

King (king) *n*. **1.** What some foreign countries have instead of presidents or prime ministers, though they're usually just benign figureheads responsible for supplying the local gossip rags with scandals and fashion photos. And keeping the game of polo alive. There's a funny story behind this one. See, back in the old days, leaders of nations (*kings*) were chosen not by popular vote but by bloodline and, occasionally, coups d'etat. You couldn't be the ruler of a country unless, like, your dad had been the ruler before you, or unless some ruling governmental body appointed you as such. Can you imagine what a backward, corrupt system that was? Whew! Thank goodness for good ol' fashioned American democracy! Kings—hah!

Krona (kro-nah) *n. pl.* **-ner** (Denmark), **-nur** (Iceland), **-nor** (Norway, Sweden) **1.** Cool-looking money with pictures of queens and poets on it belonging to cool-looking people like Björk. **2.** One of these is worth about twenty U.S. dollars; *see also* **Expensive. 3.** A thousand kroner will buy you an open-faced herring sandwich in a plaza café in Stockholm's Old Town. It sounds expensive, but hey—that's the price you pay (literally) for enjoying the good life, Scandinavian style. Ask anyone and they'll tell you: Scandinavia has the highest standard of living in the world, and it doesn't come cheap. What's that? They also have the highest suicide rate? Well, how would you like to pay twenty bucks for an open-faced herring sandwich? And by the way, no amount of kroner will persuade them to a) remove the herring or b) give you another piece of friggin' bread for the top of your sandwich.

L

Lesbos (lez-bose) *n.* **1.** Place where lesbianism was invented—no, popularized—no, mythologized—wait, ah, yes—commodified. **2.** Home of ancient Greek poet Sappho, namesake of Edina's daughter on *Absolutely Fabulous.* **3.** Popular tourist destination for homosexual women and lecherous, voyeuristic dudes; *see also* **Dude.**

M

Meltdown (oh, fuck it) *n.* **1.** What happens, eventually, at least once on every trip. **2.** The result of traveling with one's family or friends *(see also* **Girlfriend**), usually at the end of a long day in one car with three maps. **3.** The inevitable consequence of striving for cheerful agreeability when spending 24/7 with a friend who, let's face it, wasn't very good at making decisions about where to eat back in your boring hometown, much less in the middle of Budapest, where neither of you can read a menu. Now you're starving, and she's unsure as to whether the dumplings are truly vegetarian—hey! it's time for a meltdown. If she was so serious about the vegetarian thing, she should have gone to India. Alone. **4.** Emotional fatigue, often experienced just after disembarking from a train/bus in a foreign country, watching it disappear around the bend, and realizing you have no wallet/food/water/idea where in the hell you are on this godforsaken planet, goddamnit. Why did you ever leave home?

N

Nesting impulse (but I wanted the *pleated* bedskirt!) *n.* **1.** Something you do not possess if you are a serious traveler. **2.** *alt.* A feeling that will be brought on by travel, most often after schlepping a thirty-five-pound bag through airports, hotel lobbies, and Customs lines. **3.** A sense of rootedness and a desire to stay in one place that usually affects women nine to six months before childbirth and persists for approximately twelve months afterward, until an alarm goes off in her head and she realizes: Oh, shit, how am I ever going to get back to that groovy yoga retreat in Bali with this cute little screaming, crawling, wriggling baby attached to me at the breast? *(See definition* **2.** *re.* **schlepping,** *above.)*

O

Out-of-state plates (well, looky thar, Bubba) *n.* **1.** Your passport to rural harassment in the United States of America, particularly acute when the license plates in question denote vehicle registration from California. Common consequences include a) obscene hand gestures (Montana, Idaho, any other favorite spot for second-home ownership by Californians), b) increased likelihood of police ticketing for minor infractions (Nevada, Colorado, Arizona), c) increased encounters with unbelievably slooow drivers (everywhere but California, Massachusetts, and New York) who incite you to express your frustration by running those yellow lights, tailgating, and otherwise demonstrating the finer arts of road rage (yellow means "slow down," or so they would have you believe).

P

Passport photo ("it's fine, no one will see it") *n.* **1.** Yes, they will. The single image by which you will be recognized throughout the world. And, with the advent of digital imaging technology and enhanced global security measures, a portrait that will live on in Interpol and INS computer servers forever, preserving the squinting, double-chinned, lazy-eyed you as a series of ones and zeroes long after you and your progeny are dead and forgotten. **2.** *Obs. n.* The last visual link to a young woman who was once so innocent, so hopeful, so debt- and herpes-free.

Q

Questions (how you say . . . ?) *n.* **1.** To request clarification on local customs when you travel, as well as to get directions, and also to annoy your companions, who would rather just "go with the flow," whatever that means, even though they have no fucking clue where they're going or why they're going there. And it's so totally typical of them to ignore the one request you've made on this trip, even though your mom's family is *from* here and you think it might be worthwhile to check out the local museum, you know, for the sake of education, which is what they'll never appreciate anyway. **2.** The things you should have asked before you made the hotel reservation. As in, the bathroom is shared with how many others, exactly? And how far away is Machu Picchu/San Marco Square/Angkor Wat from the hotel?

R

Revolución (Marxismo; or *la gente unida, jamás será vencida . . .*) *n.* **1.** The idiomatically correct name for that large mob of remarkably excited-looking people storming toward you down the picturesque cobblestone *avenida.* They want justice/fair wages/governmental transparency/respect for basic human rights and—so do you! But the funny thing is, they think you, in your Puma sneakers, Patagonia windbreaker, cashmere scarf, and Donna Karan sunglasses, are a stinking capitalist pig. It's weird, I know, but trust me: Run. They won't be interested in the fact that you went to that Amnesty International concert at the L.A. Coliseum twelve years ago, even though you cried when Peter Gabriel sang "Biko." Just run.

S

Smoke pot/hashish (insert internationally recognized hand signal à la Cheech 'n' Chong here) *v.* **1.** Although illegal and/or officially frowned upon on worldwide (except, famously, in Amsterdam), this activity guarantees a speedy entrée into the bohemian underworld of all—and I mean all—towns and cities around the globe. By smoking pot or, as is more common in Europe and Asia, hashish, you will be exposed to the world of local commerce (often conducted under bridges, in alleyways, and other off-the-beaten-track hot spots) as well as a host of colorful characters who would otherwise be shooed away from your resort hotel like so many malarial mosquitoes. Remember the motto: Smoke pot—make a friend—go to jail—it's the law! **2.** An activity best performed immediately before crossing an international border, such as the Midnight Run Customs Pavilion in Ceuta, Morocco. Smoking all the pot or hashish you possess before entering the pavilion ensures that a) you are no longer carrying any illegal drugs on your person, as far as you can remember, right? and b) you can endure the normally slow, boring process of baggage and passport inspection with an entertaining sense of abject paranoia and dread. Some pot-smokers in this situation have also been know to renew their relationships with a higher power, usually in the form of promises of enduring fealty in exchange for a safe return home to Mom—alive.

T

Time Bandits (like Monty Python with a bigger budget) *n.* **1.** 1981 film directed by Terry Gilliam depicting a form of travel you will never achieve: not over oceans or across borders, but through time. Still, if you've ever had to cancel a trip because you realized you couldn't get the time off work or lost your credit line, you could do worse than ordering some pizza and beer and watching the Criterion Collection *Time Bandits* DVD. John Cleese is really funny in it, and Sean Connery, who, as we all know, is a sexist jerk in real life, looks totally hot playing Agamemnon in a skirt. Oh, come on, we all know that sometimes sexist jerks are hot. And did I mention the skirt?

U

Underwear (never "panties." Never.) *n.* **1.** You will always wish you'd brought more. No matter what they say, washing them out in the sink of the Sleep-Inn Youth Hostel in Rotterdam will not result in that clean, fresh, springtime feeling that one can only truly achieve through modern high-spin laundry technology. No, your **undies** *(slang, pl.)*, once snowy white and soft as kittens, will soon be dishrag-gray tatters of pilled cotton and maxed-out elastic, resulting in bulging, binding diaperlike garments that will give you the silhouette of a fishwife. **2.** In developing countries they will be appallingly dowdy—high waisted and low legged—and cost nothing; in Italy, France, and Spain they will be overtly, absurdly "sexy"—crotchless and crusted with scratchy lace—and beyond your budget. **3.** Reliable sources report that in Japan, businessmen buy used schoolgirls' underwear from vending machines. Your mission? Go to Japan and find out if this is true. (Report back for volume two of this book.)

V

Vacuum (nowheresville) *n.* **1.** A concept referring to a geographical site that appears to be hermetically sealed off from the rest of the world. I know what you're thinking: *I'm from there.* But trust me, travel will expose you to the surprising truth that vacuums—cultural, political, culinary, and other-wise—exist all over the globe, even in countries that once sounded glam-orous to you when you first saw them in your big brother's atlas. You'll stumble across quaint little vacuumlike towns in Eastern Europe, where peo-ple still believe that Mickey Mouse is the governor of California. Tiny vil-lages in Central America, where the idea that a woman of thirty would be single and childless by choice is regarded as the height of comedy. Entire cities in Africa in which the only soup on the menu is palm fat soup. And just for you, the special visitor: extra fat! Or how about our old pal Spain, which got around to legalizing the practice of Judaism in . . . (wait for it) 1992! Only half a millennium after the Inquisition! Yes, vacuums exist all over, not just in your hometown, where people are still shaking their heads over that whole lambada scandal. **2.** A cleaning device that you dread using while at home but one you'll wish for when faced with a filthy hotel room or train cabin. You will also attempt to use a vacuum cleaner on your shredded, reeking backpack/suitcase upon your return home. Don't bother—the smell of three-month-old gruyère and stale baguette macerated in a stew of dirty undies (*see* **Underwear**), spilled Kronenberg, and a squashed tube of antifungal cream will never leave your belongings. Burn them.

ധ

While you were out (you should have been here) *n.* **1.** Title phrase of innumerable little pink pieces of note paper inscribed with passive-aggressive messages from your self-martyring coworkers while you were on your trip and left in a heap, or else violently impaled upon a stick, on your desk, and either way a visual reminder of the dues you will be expected to pay for saving up your measly two weeks of vacation and leaving during the worst heat wave of the year. **2.** The period of time in which you realized how much your job truly blows and during which you decide never to return there again.

X

Xanax (zan-ax) *n.* **1.** What your mother/father/significant other needs a prescription for before you go talking about your plan to hitchhike through Kyrgyzstan (4 mg is good). **2.** What you will need a prescription for if you are forced to endure one more trip to your cousin Michelle's to see her perform in *Up with People!* Remember: Domestic travel also has its dangers.

⅄

Your wits about you ("It's no laughing matter, missy") *n.* **1.** What your mother correctly told you to keep. Have you? Are you? Will you?

Z

Zappa, Frank (superfreak) *n.* **1.** Homegrown American genius rock star of special interest to world travelers because of his incredible popularity everywhere except in the United States. Former Czechoslovakian President Vaclav Havel, a self-professed "Zappaphile," appointed Zappa Special Ambassador to the West on Trade, Culture, and Tourism in 1990. The supersquare U.S. State Department, under the command of George Bush Sr., pressured Havel to reconsider, and unfortunately, he did. Nevertheless, the prepared American traveler to the Czech Republic will prepare herself by memorizing a broad repertoire of Zappa songs—don't bother with "Valley Girl," which was Zappa's only American hit (but ignored by the rest of the globe); instead study up on "Help, I'm a Rock," "Theme from Burnt Weenie Sandwich," and "Prelude to the Afternoon of a Sexually Aroused Gas Mask," among other favorites. By demonstrating your knowledge of the Zappa oeuvre, you will distinguish yourself from 99 percent of your fellow Americans—you know, the ones you don't want to be confused with in the first place. You've seen 'em: the pleated shorts, the big white sneakers, the Christmas sweaters, the no-habla-nadas (*see also* **Dudes**). As Zappa himself said of those folks, "America Drinks and Goes Home." Be the one American in your youth hostel to show the locals you know a different way: You'll drink and stay there. To quote another Zappa song: "What Ever Happened to All the Fun in the World?" Leave home and find out.

Tri Training in Russia

Mara Vorhees

• • • • • • • • • • • • • • • • • • •

A ccompanying my husband on a four-month stint in Saint Petersburg, Russia was an enticing prospect. It was 2003, the city's tercentenary, and a big, blowout birthday bash was taking place. The exquisite baroque buildings were receiving fresh coats of paint, and special events were scheduled throughout the year. I anticipated exploring the endless art collection in the Hermitage, watching nimble ballerinas dance in *Swan Lake*, and finally finishing *War and Peace*.

We had spent enough time in Russia in years past that I was familiar with the country's shortcomings in climate and cuisine. But this time, living in Russia would present additional challenges. I vowed the trip would not disrupt my goals for the year—one of which was to test my stamina, raise money for a good cause, and bond with fellow women in an all-female sprint triathlon back home in Boston.

That is how I found myself getting ready to train for a triathlon amid the imperial grandeur, socialist grit, and nouveau glitz of Russia's second capital. I knew it wouldn't be easy. Physical fitness is not exactly a priority in Russia, where beer is considered a breakfast drink and a pint of sour cream sits atop every entrée. Exercise is exclusively reserved for Olympic athletes, sportsmen, and soldiers. Not women. Somebody running on the street is invariably trying to catch a bus.

Just when I needed to immerse myself in Swim! Bike! Run! I found myself in the workout underworld, the antithesis of Wellville. But I was determined. The triathlon was mere weeks after our return from Saint Petersburg, and I had my heart set on racing.

MY FIRST STOP was the public swimming pool, located just outside the imposing walls of the Peter and Paul Fortress, the site where Peter the Great founded his new capital three hundred years ago. The sun glinted off the gold spire of the cathedral, the most majestic building inside the fortress. I tromped across the snow-covered grounds, where Peter himself was posing for photos in full regalia.

Nearby, a small crowd had gathered on the banks of the Neva River. Of course the river was frozen solid, except for a twelve-square-meter pool formed by a large hole in the ice. The crowd watched a gangly teenager as he stripped down to his shorts and plunged into the ice bath. He emerged from the frigid waters and stood proudly with his arms above his head in the sign for victory. Here was the newest member of the local Walrus Club, a group of hearty souls who exhort the health benefits of taking a daily dip. Many of the ice swimmers, known as *morzhi,* or walruses, have been paying regular visits to this spot for twenty years.

Thankfully, this frigid pool was not the one I was looking for. I pulled my fur-lined coat tighter around my shivering body and continued on my way to the more conventional eight-lane, twenty-five-meter indoor facility across the street. Entry into the swimming pool required a doctor's written permission, which could be obtained from the pool's resident MD after a physical examination. Having heard more than a few horror stories about germ-filled Russian medical facilities, I entered the doctor's office with trepidation.

Behind the desk sat the platinum-blond, white-smocked doctor, busily filling out forms. "Ahem," I said, as I carefully cased the room for used syringes. "I'm here for a physical."

"I know," she replied, reaching for a blank form. "Name? Birthday?" She duly recorded my replies. The doctor glanced up and briefly looked me up and down, jotting a note on the form. "Sixty rubles," she announced, handing me a *spravka*, or permission slip.

"That's all?" I asked, relieved but puzzled. "Shouldn't I even take off my coat?"

"Why? Are you ill?" The money was quickly deposited in her smock.

"Not at all," I hastened to answer and retreated out the door.

One legacy of the Soviet period is that older women in frumpy uniforms are stationed in all public facilities to shush, scold, and tell people *nyet*. The pool's babushka was different only in that she sported a hot-pink tracksuit to go with the standard-issue cold stare. She enforced a seemingly infinite and ever-changing list of rules.

One of the most important required everyone to take a soapy shower *without* a bathing suit before entering the pool. Bold signs emphasizing this rule were posted everywhere, and the point was evidently made. The shower room hosted a perpetual performance of splashing suds, flailing limbs, swinging breasts, and bouncing buttocks.

The irony was that once you actually made it past all these rules and into the swimming pool, chaos reigned. Standard activities in the lanes included old folks practicing water aerobics, girls gathering mid-lane to gossip, and teenagers diving on your head. On a day that I finally had a lane to myself, the surly babushka in pink interrupted my workout by splashing a kickboard in my face. "Lane one is open," she barked, pointing to a lane already full of two heavyset ladies and an elderly man.

I looked longingly at the other near-empty lanes. "Only lane one?"

"Only one!" she snarled, and turned to yell at somebody else. Russian service sector workers are notorious for their short tempers and rude remarks. I reflected, as I resumed my swim in the crowded lane, that the public pool is probably the one place where Pinky can exert such authority and others must comply. Such hostile behavior, I thought, is a weapon of the weak.

Eventually, I figured out that the most effective response was not to cower in fear or to yell back. Rather, a smile and a nod are so unexpected, the perpetrator usually can't help but respond in kind. Which does not mean she stopped yelling at me. During my time at the Russian pool, I discovered a whole slew of activities that get you in trouble: wearing shoes in the locker room, entering the pool area without a bathing cap, swimming too fast near the lady with the broken foot, and so on.

After one workout, I was sitting on the edge of the pool when I saw Pinky headed my way. "Don't sit there, young lady," she reprimanded. I smiled weakly, clueless as to what I might be doing wrong. "Don't you want to have children someday? That cold concrete will make you infertile!" Perhaps not scientifically sound, but at least the rule had a reason—for once!

But Pinky and her rigid rules were remnants of old Russia. New Russia is a whole different beast, as I discovered when a friend invited me to check out the private sports club where he was a member. Angry babushkas were not welcome here. Instead, we were greeted by smiling, trim young women who seemed genuinely happy to see us. They tried to accommodate every request. And they never yelled.

The female members of the gym tended to be well-manicured women who got lots of calls on their cell phones: Russia's beautiful people. Their hair looked better in aerobics class than mine did at my wedding. The locker room resembled a Victoria's Secret catalog shoot: matching lacy bra and panties seemed to be a prerequisite for club membership.

Planet Fitness had all the features of Bally's or Gold's Gym: shiny weight machines, treadmills with heart rate monitors, spinning classes, Pilates, towel service, juice bar, Jacuzzis . . . and a hefty hundred-dollar-a-month price tag. That's a lot of cabbage in a country where the average salary is a meager three hundred dollars per month. Most important for my purposes, Planet Fitness had a fully equipped cardio room, complete with stationary bikes. My swimming training was going reasonably well, but this was a triathlon, after all. And how else—when the city was buried in snow—could I bust a move on a bike?

Saint Petersburg's river was frozen solid. The wide path along the riverbank, an attractive biking trail in other seasons, was now hidden under several feet of windswept snow. The embankment was deserted, except for the occasional dog walker, hidden by fur coat and hat. Yet here I was, pedaling a sixty-minute endurance course, protected by a thick pane of glass that blocked out the howling wind and bitter cold.

On the day we visited Planet Fitness, my friend and I had the cardio room to ourselves, save a jacked trainer assisting a young woman on a Stairmaster. A dozen bikes were lined up like racers awaiting the start gun. The sun shone through the giant windows overlooking the Neva River, and the chrome on the bikes glistened in the bright winter light. Outside, icebreakers cut a path through the frozen river and glided past the ironclad battleship *Aurora*, whose mutinous sailors had started a revolution in 1917. Inside, the room pulsated to a techno beat. I admired the view from my perch atop my stationary bike and anticipated a long soak in the Jacuzzi.

After a while, my friend went to the weight room and left me to pedal it out against the blinking red dot on my bike's digital display. The muscle-bound trainer seized the opportunity and came over to chat me up.

"Can I please to meet with you?" I was never sure how to respond to this ubiquitous pickup line. "You are foreign lady, no?"

I smiled. "You are Russian, yes?"

He was not discouraged. "I know you are foreign because I see your shoes," he explained, pointing out that we were both wearing New Balance sneakers. He was clearly impressed, as the brand was a rare find in Russia. "I buy them on Regent Street in London," he boasted. "One hundred pounds."

"Mine are factory outlet seconds from Boston," I shot back. "Half price." Muscles frowned. In new Russia, price is a direct indicator of desirability, so he was unimpressed with my bargain-hunting skills. My fit friend quickly returned his attentions to his trainee. I made a mental note of this effective strategy for deterring unwanted attention from Russian men and pedaled on.

In April, the snow finally began to melt. Local residents emerged from tiny apartments, populating the local parks and gardens and squares when it was still too cold to be comfortable. Art lovers meandered through the Mikhailovsky Gardens, admiring the handsome facade of the Russian Museum. Mars Field, traditionally the military parade grounds, became parade grounds for flirty young girls and nervy boys. The lime trees in the formal Summer Gardens began to bud, adding a touch of green to the fountains and pavilions that had been bare for months. I longed to take my exercise outdoors, but the thaw was a gradual process. Like an archaeological excavation, each day uncovered a new layer of the winter's history: sleds that were left outside during a storm in February, vodka bottles thrown out after the New Year's celebrations, gloves that had been lost since December. The ground was finally visible by the month's end, so I decided to lace up my running shoes and take them for a spin in Tauride Gardens.

Catherine the Great had built the fabulous baroque palace for Grigori Potemkin, a famed general and one of her many lovers. Once the romping grounds of the czarina, the palace gardens had since become—in true Soviet style—a park for the people. I thought the tree-lined dirt paths crisscrossing the landscaped park and circling a picturesque pond would make an ideal setting for my triathlon training.

It is an understatement to say that a runner on the street or in the park is an unfamiliar sight in Russia. Even the act of wearing running shorts is bound to attract stares—ironic in this country where women in midsummer wear little more than lacy undergarments and a pair of heels. A German friend had recounted tales of her jogging adventures in Saint Petersburg. When she ran past some teenage boys sitting on a park bench drinking beer, they were so amused that they chased after her, poking and taunting. Finally they could not keep up with her, so they just threw their empty bottles at her. My friend was so distraught that she ran straight home. With this harrowing tale in mind, I arrived at Tauride Gardens in my spandex tights and running shoes, prepared but wary.

A sign on the gate declared that the park was closed for *prosushka*, or "a thorough drying out." How appropriate, I thought; this whole country needs a *prosushka*. But I could see a few folks wandering around inside, most of them pushing baby strollers or, yes, drinking beer.

A park worker sat lackadaisically near the gate and opened it to allow patrons to exit. He would not let me enter. "The park is closed."

"How did all these people get inside if the park is closed?" I questioned.

"They went in through the entrance on Paradnaya Street," he said matter of factly, pointing across the way. Another group of people left, and he locked the gate behind them.

"The park is closed, but the other entrance is open?" He did not seem to notice the inherent contradiction.

I trotted a half mile down the sidewalk and around the corner to see for myself. Sure enough, mothers with children, teenagers with beers, workers with tools—everybody was walking freely in and out of the park. I established a jogging route around the perimeter of the park. I picked up my pace as I ran past ungainly groups of teenage boys clustered on the benches. But they just strummed their guitars and sang their raucous songs, having a ball and paying me no heed. I was also wary of the workers, who could at any moment tire of all these people interfering with their work on the park and expel us. But they also ignored me, concentrating on laying sod and planting flowers. Kids climbed on the playground while their mothers observed. Artists captured in watercolor the palace's reflection in the pond. Lovers embraced underneath the trees. The sun shone down on the people and— despite their defiance of the posted *prosushka*—dried out their park.

After a week or two, emboldened by my success, I took to the streets. I dodged the jovial youths spilling out of sidewalk cafes and wizened women selling produce from their stalls. They stared, but they got out of my way. I cruised past czars' grandiose palaces, Lenin's revolutionary haunts, and Dostoevski's inspiring canals, exploring Saint Petersburg by sneaker.

AT THE END of my time in Russia, I was pleased with my training progress. The wrath of the swimming pool babushka had abated as I established my place as a regular in the lanes. My sprints around the city increased in number, so I was confident I could outrun any drunken teenager or angry worker. I would have liked to spend more time at Planet Fitness on the bikes and in the whirlpool, but my friend was out of free guest passes, and I felt fortunate even for my brief stint as one of the beautiful people.

During my last week in Russia, I paid a final visit to the swimming pool. I was wistful as I watched the kids competing in breath-holding contests and women doing sidestroke. I spent a few minutes stretching, partly hoping they would leave the lane, partly hoping, for old time's sake, that they would not. Out of the corner of my eye, I noticed my nemesis, the steely-eyed babushka, heading my way. I wondered what crime I might be guilty of. "What are you doing?" she queried. I explained in the most pleasant voice I could muster that I needed to stretch before commencing my workout.

Her face softened. "You are a sportswoman?" Intrigued, she started questioning me about what kinds of workouts I did and what I was training for. She wanted to know all about the triathlon circuit—who organized such events and who competed. This cold, scary woman who had been the source of nightmares became warm, friendly, and downright enthusiastic about my triathlon prospects.

Before I knew it, she was yelling at the old folks and young kids in lane two. "This lane is closed now," she bellowed. "Move into another lane." The swimmers looked around in confusion but crowded into the other lanes without protest.

The babushka turned to me and smiled. "Lane two is yours."

Worry Warts

Lisa Taggart

• • • • • • • • • • • • • • • • • • • •

y mother taught me when I was a child that no matter how bad things are, there's always something worse looming that you forgot to worry about. This is how her line of thinking goes: When I was hired as a staff travel writer for a glossy lifestyle magazine six years ago, she gave me a congratulatory gift package: three dozen individually wrapped sanitary toilet seat covers, a two-in-one tool that would cut through my seat belt and break my windshield in case I drove into a river, and an under-the-door security alarm for hotel rooms with the most ear-shattering buzzer I've ever experienced.

The take-away message is simply that if I could anticipate every possible disaster, my life would be cupcakes. Unfortunately, even after decades of training, this is impossible. Still, I try: When I had to spend a week driving up the California coast to the Oregon state line, through what could be described as the West Coast's own *Deliverance* territory, I got my first cell phone and called my husband every few hours. When, at a cheap motel in Salinas, the cleaning guy—significantly, the fellow who had keys to my room—looked me up and down as I was unloading my luggage and said suggestively, "You look nice," I promptly reloaded my car and drove to a different motel.

Often, when I meet someone and say I work as a travel writer, the person will say, "Oooh, what a great job!" No one understands the disastrous possibilities lurking in every day and the energy required to fight them off. Poor little travel writer—they don't want to hear it. But I'm telling you, all this worrying wears a girl out.

Even when I set out to interview a frog counter in San Francisco, fifty miles north of my home, I gave my husband the man's name, address, and phone number. Especially since I was meeting the man alone, at his apartment, at dusk in a funky section of the city where I didn't even know people lived. And also especially since, as far as I could tell, counting frogs was this man's full-time occupation. Nice—someone's gotta keep track of those little guys, right?—but still odd. Worrisome.

It turns out that the reason I didn't know anyone lived in the falling-down warehouses along the dead-end streets in this industrial section by the highway is because nobody does. Not legally, at least.

"We're squatters," said Frog Guy, after he'd securely locked his aging German shepherd in his even older truck as I remained at a safe distance because the dog "doesn't like visitors." He continued, "The landlord looks the other way of zoning laws. He likes the rent checks."

The warehouse/loft space, whose front door was a sliding garage-style device, was one of a dozen in the corrugated aluminum building, next to a dusty gravel parking lot and a weedy chain link fence bordering a dump area at the edge of the green, still arm of Islais Creek. The view was of a huge gantry crane, several other warehouses, and the highway off-ramp.

Frog Guy had bobbed, straight gray hair and was missing two teeth in front. He had on jeans and a flannel shirt. He offered me coffee. I love coffee. I drink a lot of it. It was late in the day, and I was a little sleepy from the traffic-laden fifty-mile drive I'd made to get there. But right away my worrywart buttons clicked as he disappeared up a ladder to the "kitchen." When he returned with a clear glass mug, I sniffed and sipped carefully, wondering if my java expertise was good enough to detect the presence of the date-rape drug—or some other trippy, froggy hallucinogen. I kept drinking; the coffee tasted fine. Better than that, actually; it was Peet's.

Frog Guy knew a lot about frogs and other water-loving creatures. He was a volunteer for the National Wildlife Federation. He also had all kinds of cutting-edge electronic equipment he used to record frog calls and images of the wildlife in his neighborhood park, trying to save it before transit agencies like Caltrans and Muni, and other urban conspirators tore it down.

"Right here are the only populations of Pacific chorus frogs on this side of the city," Frog Guy told me. "Islais Creek, which comes from an underground reservoir, used to run three and a half miles, and there were huge colonies of them. You could hear thousands of them every spring. But Muni filled in the last creek outlets to build a maintenance yard. Almost all the frogs are gone now."

He was angry at the mayor, and all major transportation officials, and most construction companies in the city. I was getting to really like Frog Guy. He was fighting the good fight. I wouldn't be able to quote much of his anti-authority rant in my 150-word column for my mainstream magazine, but at least I could get the word out about the endangered frogs— helping to rally suburban readers to his cause in my own way. It was the kind of thing that made me feel like my job could be part of the solution, despite the fact that I work for the world's largest media conglomerate. And I was glad Frog Guy was here, looking out for the frogs that everybody else was trampling over. Plus, as far as I could tell, he hadn't poisoned me. Another point in his favor.

The sun was starting to set, and Frog Guy got excited. "It's time to go," he said. Out front of his place, we walked past the parking area and climbed around a falling-down section of chain-link fence. There were chest-high clumps of ragweed and wild fennel, a sea gull eyeing us from a hunk of wood at the water's edge, and several tires half-buried in the mud. The sky had turned a bright pink, and suddenly there was a croak, then another, coming from the bushes against the chain-link fence. Then we were surrounded by dozens of croaking voices. I realized that we were standing smack in the middle of the "park" Frog Guy had been talking about for the last hour.

The frogs—Frog Guy estimated there were a few dozen of them—sounded exactly like this: *Ribbibbit. Ribbibbit. Rrrrhhh, ribbibbit ribbibbit.* "They're movie-star frogs," Frog Guy whispered. "They're the voices you hear in every movie soundtrack. Because they have such a classic croak."

"That's so cool!" I said enthusiastically, clapping my hands. I said it too loudly, too enthusiastically. The frogs stopped. Absolute silence reigned. I looked at Frog Guy. He shook his head.

"They're very sensitive to movement," he said sadly. We stood there a few more moments, totally still. But I'd ruined it. "They won't start again until we leave."

We climbed back over the fence to the gravel parking area. I felt bad. "Thanks," I said. "That was really very interesting." I held out my hand.

"There is one more frog spot," Frog Guy said. "It's just up the hill."

"Oh?"

"But you have to promise not to write about it. It's a complete secret. I don't want anyone to know. It could ruin it for the frogs."

The first ten minutes with Frog Guy had turned up more than enough material for my column. Still, I'd already ruined it for the first round of frogs, and he seemed so excited about the secret place. "It's only a half mile away. We'll be back in fifteen minutes," he said.

"All right." I replied. He grinned and skipped back to his place to get his recording equipment.

We had to take my car, of course, because Killer, the aging female shepherd, was still locked in Frog Guy's truck. She gave me a morose, I-may-be-old-but-I-could-still-take-you glare as we drove off. Frog Guy seemed a little uncertain as he gave me directions—past the highway, up the hill, down a dead-end street, no, wait, turn around, and then, oh, there!—until he pointed me into the parking lot of a drab, long, gray warehouse building.

We stopped by the front door, near the two other cars in the lot, on the short side of the rectangular building. A small sign by the entrance said RING BELL, which Frog Guy did. "This guy I know, Frank, works here. He's the only other one who knows about the frogs." No one answered, though we could see through the little windows that a light was on in the building. Frog Guy knocked, too; no answer.

We wandered into the hip-high weeds by the car but didn't hear anything. "Let's go around," Frog Guy said. "There're more frogs there." He hopped into my car, so I got in, too, though I wasn't sure where he meant. He pointed me around to the other side of the building, on the back side, farthest from the entrance. But I thought it was odd; we'd driven around a lot that would have taken a minute to walk across.

Frog Guy was so excited he leapt out of the car, leaving his door open, and tiptoed into the brush. He turned back and held his hand out by his ear, the universal signal for "listen, but quietly!" and turned on his recording equipment. I stood by the car, immobile, not wanting to interrupt this time. The hillside had been cut into to build the parking lot, and a large seep down the dirt cliff was edged with dark, mossy stuff, ending in clumps of weeds at the base. It was from here that the frog sounds were coming. The sky was an uncharacteristic clear deep blue, and the frogs were calling like crazy, croaking in deep, theatrical voices, a percussive, rough-edged symphony in the soft night.

It lasted maybe two minutes. The Frog Guy might've scared them this time. Or maybe they were just done for the night. "Got it!" shouted Frog Guy, grinning hugely. He pumped his fist in the air.

I started up the car, relieved that I was done and a little sad that I wouldn't be able to write about this part of the frog population, and Frog Guy's quirkiness, for my very short article. And I was sad for all the endangered frogs of the city; basically, to sum up my interview, they were doomed.

We drove around the side of the building. But something was wrong. The lot was dark and quiet. The light was off inside the warehouse. And the two cars were gone. And the gate was shut. I drove up closer, my headlights beaming through the chain link fence into the empty street out front. The gate was locked. We got out of the car to gaze up at the spirals of razor wire edging the fence top. Frog Guy checked the padlock holding the heavy chain at the gate.

We looked at each other.

"How'd that happen?" I asked.

Frog Guy looked panicked for a moment. Then his face lit up. "I'll call Frank," he said. He pulled out his cell phone.

Thank God for cell phones, I thought.

"Shoot," Frog Guy said, fumbling with his phone. "What's Frank's last name?"

"I don't know," I said. Unnecessarily.

I walked over to the warehouse building and knocked on the door, loudly. I pounded on it, rang the bell. But the building had the dark, quiet feel of empty warehouses everywhere.

"Industrial Warehouse Business Corporation," said a sign on the building's front. "San Francisco. For information, call (415) 555-1234."

I pulled out my cell phone, thanking Providence for them again, and dialed. The number rang in my one ear. And in the other, I could hear ringing on the other side of the empty warehouse door. It rang, and rang, and rang, until a recorded voice came on to inform me of IWBC's business hours.

It wasn't a good moment. I didn't know what to do. I didn't have a lock-picking kit in my car so I could break into the warehouse and get the keys to the gate. I didn't have bolt cutters or even wire cutters to slice through the fence. What good were my sanitary toilet seat covers now?

Fog was rolling in off the bay, softening and blurring the night sky. The street in front of us, a dead end, was empty. In this section of the city, in a warehouse below a massive, boarded-up housing project, I could imagine there might not be any traffic for the rest of the night.

I called my husband, Jim, who was an hour's drive away. "I'm stuck."

"Stuck? Stuck where? What do you mean, stuck?"

I explained.

"Are you okay? Is that guy with you? Is he crazy?" Jim asked.

"Sort of," I said.

"Look! Hey! Hey, over here!" Frog Guy was shouting.

"If you're in danger, say . . . 'frogs,'" Jim said.

"Hey! Over here! Help! We're stuck!" Frog Guy jumped up and down, waving his arms. The warehouse property to our right ended in a deep ditch, and across from this, another warehouse site began. In that parking lot, a young woman was getting out of her car. "We're locked in! Help! Can you call someone to get us out?" Frog Guy yelled.

"No, I'm fine," I told Jim. "I just don't know how I'm going to get out of here."

The woman turned and shouted something at us, lifting her arm in the air, then scurried into her building.

Jim offered to call our friends who lived in San Francisco on the other side of the hill to see if they had any bolt cutters. "He's an architect," Jim reasoned. "So he might . . . I'll call you back."

"What did the lady in the parking lot say?" Frog Guy asked as I hung up. I shrugged. "Maybe she didn't understand us," I said.

Frog Guy thought he'd call his neighbor and have him look up Frank's phone number. But his neighbor wasn't home. Frog Guy started calling all of the squatters in his building, but apparently they were all out for the night.

Jim called back to say our architect pal didn't have any bolt cutters. "I think you should call the police," he said.

"I think we should call the police," I told Frog Guy, "or we're going to end up sleeping here." Frog Guy nodded.

"How can I help you?" said the solicitous voice at San Francisco police dispatch.

"Yes, I need some help," I said. I realized I should have thought a little ahead about what I was going to say. "I'm stuck in a parking lot at the Industrial Warehouse Business Corporation. I'm locked in."

"Okay," he said. "How did you get there?"

"It was open when I drove in. The people who work here went home for the night, and the gate is locked. And there's razor wire. And I can't get out." I said. "I'm with a . . . friend."

"Do you work there?"

"No."

"Does your friend?"

"No."

"Where is this warehouse, exactly?"

"I, uh, I'm not sure . . . Hold on one second."

"Where are we?" I asked Frog Guy. He squinted up his eyes, then shrugged. "Twenty-third Street?" he said. "I think."

I had an inspired moment and dug around in the back seat until I found the Soviet-issue binoculars that had been in my car for about two years—a gift from my mother when, on a road trip with me, she'd discovered them, marked half off, in a dusty general store in the Sacramento Delta. "You never know when you might need these," she'd said. Yet again, my mom was right. I handed them to Frog Guy.

"My associate is working on determining our location," I told the dispatcher.

"All right. Well, what were you doing on the property?"

"We were here to count—"

"Don't tell them about the frogs!" shouted Frog Guy in my ear. "It's a secret!"

"Just figure out where we are," I hissed at him. Frog Guy peered through the binoculars at the street sign a hundred yards away.

"I, uh . . ." I am a terrible liar. "I'm a journalist, and, uh, I was interviewing a, uh, wildlife specialist."

I heard a disbelieving "hunh" on the other end of the line.

"We were doing a wildlife survey behind the warehouse."

The Frog Guy gave me a wide-eyed, angry look. "Did you figure out where we are yet?" I barked.

"Yes?" said the man on the phone. "I'm not sure I understand."

I gave up. "Frogs! All right? We were counting frogs," I said. "There's a large population of Pacific chorus frogs behind the warehouse here, and we were counting them." Frog Guy looked crushed. I added, "It's, um, kind of a secret population, sir."

The "sir" thing just popped out. I've never "sirred" anyone in my life, but talking to a police dispatcher, it just felt right.

"All right. Let me get this down. You were counting secret frogs at a warehouse whose location you're not sure of. Neither one of you works there, but you're locked in the parking lot. And now you want us to come get you out."

"Yes, that's right," I said.

"Twenty-third and South Dakota!" Frog Guy yelled in my ear. "We're at Twenty-third and South Dakota!"

"Did you hear that? Sir? We're at Twenty-third and South Dakota Streets."

"Yes, I heard that." He sighed. "I'll send a car. You're lucky it's a slow night."

It really didn't take that long for the patrol car to pull up at the gate. We had the binoculars. We watched the moon rise. Three officers got out, two middle-aged, tough-looking women, doing that swagger walk that I suppose is related to the vests and gear they have to wear. And behind them, a young, skinny Asian guy; he looked, at best, twenty-two years old. He approached the gate, and the two women loomed behind him, like backup singers waiting for their turn.

"Can you explain to me what you're doing here?" Officer Skinny said, his face cross-hatched by the chain link. He spoke in a falsely deep voice, a tone he created by keeping his chin tucked in.

"We were counting frogs," I said. I had decided full disclosure was essential to us getting out of there. "There's a large population of Pacific chorus frogs behind this building. They're the frogs that you hear in the movies; they make this classic *ribbit, ribbit* sound. It sounds like, *ribbibbit, ribbibbit, rrrrhhh, ribbibbit, ribbibbit,*" I said. "Officer," I added.

He stared at me. I babbled on. "I'm a journalist, my name's Lisa. Hi." I gave him a friendly grin, like we were meeting at a party. I think I might have even waved through the fence. "And this fellow here, he counts frogs," I said. I said this all in a voice that indicated that I, for one, thought this was entirely reasonable.

The skinny officer didn't blink. "And how did you get on this property?"

"We drove in," I pointed to my car.

"I see. And you work here?"

I shook my head.

"Does he?" the officer asked. I shook my head again.

"Neither of you do?"

"No, sir."

"So you're trespassing."

"Um, well . . ." I stammered. Even with his too-big hat, Officer Skinny still managed to be intimidating. It was slowly dawning on me that I might be in trouble. "Yes? We are?"

"I know Frank!" Frog Guy shouted at my side. "Frank is my friend! Frank works here, and he said we could count the frogs. He said I could come on the property anytime." Frog Guy's voice was high and shrill. He'd been shifting his weight foot to foot and opening and closing his mouth nervously. Now he clutched at the chain-link fence. Frog Guy, I should have realized by his alternative lifestyle and anti-authority stance, was not very comfortable with the police.

"Who is Frank?" asked the officer. Meanwhile, the two women cops kept their distance, alternately staring at the razor wire and glancing at each other.

"Frank works for Industrial Warehouse Business Corporation," I offered. I pointed to their sign.

"If I could just get his number," Frog Guy moaned, "Frank would tell you it's okay that we're here."

But of course I was thinking, actually, it's not that okay that we're here. I didn't want to be there anymore. Not at all. "Do you think we could cut the fence?" I asked. "Do you guys have any tools in your car that would cut through this?"

Officer Skinny frowned at me. "The police will not break into private property. They will not do this, not even to get citizens off of private property on which they are trespassing."

"So, what do you think we should do?" I asked. He glared at me and then turned back to Frog Guy.

I hadn't anticipated for a second that the police might suspect me of something criminal. Did they think that Frog Guy and I were completing a drug deal, turned around to find the gate locked, and decided to call the police as an exit strategy? It even seemed possible that they might make me spend the night here and then arrest me in the morning. I wondered if I could take comp time at work if I had to spend the night in jail.

"If I could just get Frank's number. My friend should be home really soon, and he'll get my address book. Or you could go to my house. . . ." Frog Guy's voice had the high keen of the desperate. And then I thought, what if the police find out he's living illegally and he loses his housing over this?

The women were as silent as the chicks in a ZZ Top video.

"So it's a slow night, I hear," I tried. "Or you probably wouldn't be messing with this." One of them gave me a slight nod. "Or maybe this happens all the time? People get carried away counting frogs and lock themselves into parking lots?" I tried to laugh, exhaling half a nervous breath in a weak little tremble. They said nothing.

"I don't remember his last name," Frog Guy was saying. He clutched at his hair.

I was cold and hungry, and I wanted to get the hell out of there. "I don't really know him," I blurted out to the women. "I just met him for this interview. I was only going to do a four-paragraph story on frogs. I don't even know if I have space for a quote."

"Where is your house, exactly?" Officer Skinny was saying, obviously confused by the obscure address Frog Guy was shouting at him. Frog Guy's face was white.

One of the women glanced at them, then took a step forward toward me, leaning into the fence. I could see that she was younger than I'd guessed; probably she was my age. She tossed her head toward Officer Skinny. "He's in training," she whispered. "We're just letting him figure this out." She flashed me a quick conspiratorial half-grin and then stepped back, parallel with her partner again.

"Okay." I nodded. Maybe it would be all right. The officer-in-training was just playing tough.

"Hello! Hello! Hey!" Two people came running over to the driveway. It was the girl from across the parking lot earlier, and with a tall, good-looking man. "Sorry I took so long," she said. "I had to go find Ethan." She pointed at the guy. "He says there's a hole in the fence. Good thing he works late," she laughed, smiling at the befuddled officers.

Ethan looked around at the officers and at me and at Frog Guy. "Whoa, so you called the police," he said. He kind of shrugged and walked along the fence, toward Frogland. "They've been having lots of break-ins here," Ethan said. "The owners said they were getting this fixed tomorrow." He walked about fifteen feet past the driveway and stopped. "Here." He pointed, then stepped through the huge hole himself, to my and Frog Guy's side. I wanted to hug him.

I didn't bother to be embarrassed that we hadn't checked the fence for holes before calling the police. There was too much else that was already humiliating about the night. Officer Skinny made a show of helping me and Frog Guy through the fence after I'd reparked my car in the lot and left a note, correctly guessing that the next morning it would be shockingly easy and very anticlimactic to walk into the open lot and drive away, no questions asked. I called our architect friend in Potrero Hill, and he agreed to let me sleep on their couch.

The officers, smiling now, milled around for a while after they copied down information from our IDs. Officer Skinny warmed up, shook Frog Guy's hand, and offered to give him a ride. "So what kind of journalism do you do?" asked the friendly woman officer. I handed her my card. "I'm a travel writer."

"Oh!" she said, exhaling. "I love that magazine. What a wonderful job!"

In Search of Sami

Ann Lombardi

• • • • • • • • • • • • • • • • • • • •

I admit I was an odd kid. While other girls at St. Thomas More Elementary School prayed for their very own snorting, galloping National Velvet for Christmas, I fantasized about owning a pet reindeer. Of course, part of my aloofness to horses stemmed from tumbling off a pony headfirst into a pile of pony poop in third grade during Ellen Vogt's birthday party. But my passion for reindeer also had another source: my fourth grade World Geography class.

It started the day Sister Grace Maria unfolded a faded map and announced that we'd be learning about a region in northern Europe beyond the Arctic Circle of Norway, Sweden, and Finland. She described a snowy, isolated place populated by the Sami reindeer herders of the Arctic north. "These peaceful reindeer people belong to one of the oldest cultures in the world," the Sister intoned, beginning a slide show that depicted men wearing red and blue woolen outfits and standing in reindeer-fur boots on the frozen tundra. "Since 1500 AD, the Sami have worked as reindeer-herding nomads. They use these trusty animals to pull their loaded sleds. They drink reindeer milk, eat reindeer meat, and make tents and clothing from reindeer skins. The Sami even use reindeer tendons for sewing, and they carve reindeer antlers for tools. The warm reindeer fur is ideal for Sami winter boots."

I was only half listening. Instead, I was already scheming to get my very own pet reindeer. My father took the pragmatic approach. He gently tried to convince me our backyard in Atlanta, Georgia, couldn't produce enough lichen and moss to meet the basic food needs of a reindeer. Dad also pointed out that our scorching summer weather might not be a reindeer's climate of choice. Unconvinced, I resorted to several evenings of unproductive sulking in my room after supper.

One Friday night, Dad called me into the living room for a surprise. I remained unimpressed after I opened his package and found inside a brown, hard stub. "It's a real carved reindeer antler," he said. His tone of voice was calm, but I could tell from his smiling eyes that this was something special. "It came all the way from Finnish Lapland. Your great aunt brought it back from a tour she took to Europe long ago."

Although a live reindeer to go with the antler never materialized, the souvenir solidified my unlikely passion, and as the years marched on, I still held fast to the fantasy of seeing the creatures in the flesh. Perhaps this explains why, forty years later, two weeks before Christmas, I was headed to Finnish Lapland. In the decades since my father had indulged me with the Sami-carved reindeer antler, I had become a travel agent (after failing to marry into money to fund my wanderlust) and a world traveler. I had frolicked with ballistic dolphins in the Caribbean, toured back streets of Moscow with a black marketer, come in dead last in the Berlin marathon, and flirted with North Korean soldiers in the DMZ I had fought for my life in the Acapulco undertow, punched out horny Italians on overnight trains, shared sleeping quarters with a grunting boar in the Swiss Alps, and been tear gassed in curlers outside a Seoul beauty salon. I had romped in volcanic hot springs with a naked Icelandic guy, crashed overnight on an

Amsterdam jail floor, been rescued from quicksand by a French tractor, and munched on roasted guinea pigs in Ecuador. But there was still a void in my life as a globetrotter: I had yet to take that dream vacation to Finland's reindeer country.

As I bubble-wrapped the treasured antler and tucked it away in my carry-on bag, my brother Pat implored, "Come join us at the beach like last year, Ann. Normal folks don't head for Lapland in the dead of winter."

"Beware of hypothermia," my well-meaning neighbor chimed in.

What did they know?

Leaving friends and family behind, I sped off to the airport. After sprinting down the crowded concourse to the waiting aircraft, I reached the departure gate and high-fived the dapper European executive behind me. Before you could say "Santa Claus," I was winging my way across the ocean to a winter fantasy land at the edge of the Arctic Circle: Lapland!

To visions of furry reindeer, brightly clad Sami, and salmon-pink winter skies, I drifted off to sleep for most of the ten-hour trip, jolting awake when the plane landed with an icy thud in Helsinki. I fished around for my mittens, grabbed my backpack, and scooted to my connecting flight to Rovaniemi, the capital of Finnish Lapland.

Feeling nothing short of triumphant, I arrived at my hotel—a mere stone's throw from the Arctic Circle, where reindeer reign supreme—and sauntered up to the hotel reception desk. A pink-cheeked clerk named Henna greeted me with a curtsy.

I inquired breathlessly whether the curtsy was a traditional Sami custom. Henna shook her head and explained that she wasn't Sami, but this disappointment was tempered when she offered to take the whole day off to introduce me to the "real Lapland."

It turned out I needed a guide for an authentic experience. At the bigger hotels in town, organized snowmobile trips carried tourists to reindeer camps, where most of the people wearing Sami clothes were actually regular Finns dressed in costume.

"Those reindeer excursions are arranged by the tourist office," said Henna. "But if you can ski, I will lead you to a secret place where there are no other tourists. You do ski, right?" she asked.

"We don't get much snow in Georgia," I answered, clearing my throat. "But yes, I ski."

At this point, I felt I'd say anything to encourage Henna to take me to see the real Sami, not the tourist version.

There was an uneasy silence.

"Well, I guess if you can walk, you should be able to cross-country ski. Let's go look for Sami reindeer!" said Henna. With our fur-covered rucksacks and long, skinny skis in tow, we ventured out into the snowy woods. Piercing rays of sunshine ricocheted off the bright landscape and temporarily blinded my jet-lagged eyes.

"You'd better get out your sunglasses right away," Henna advised.

Glistening fir trees in thick white coats dotted the winding trails.

"Incredible!" I gasped, enthralled by the winter paradise.

"Time to put on our skis," Henna called out. Miraculously, my middle-aged body stayed vertical as I wrestled with my gear.

"Not bad for a Southerner," I marveled out loud.

Then Henna tapped me on the shoulder. "Ann, you have your skis on backwards." I promptly fell flat on my face.

Muscular men with tight buns and 1 percent body fat zoomed past me in silver, skintight ski togs. "Some of these cross-country skiers are Finnish Olympians," proclaimed Henna proudly.

By that time, I didn't care. I had lost all feeling in my feet and legs. My nostrils were making funny crinkling noises, like the sound ice cubes make when you pour lemonade over them. "Cover your face with your scarf so you won't get so cold," Henna said. It was too late. My wool muffler had iced up and was now stuck to my bottom lip.

For crying out loud, why hadn't I bothered to study Mrs. Messner's Girl Scout first-aid book on warning signs of frostbite? I was having major trouble breathing, so I gave my muffler a tug to make way for more fresh air and in the process, ripped a chunk of skin off my lip. I didn't dare lick my injured mouth for fear the subzero temperatures would weld my lips together in just a matter of seconds.

"Come on!" yelled Henna, a full hundred yards ahead of me. "We are almost ready to cross the Arctic Circle." Pumping my fists wildly in the frigid air, I shouted with renewed vigor. I felt the spirit of Sir Edmund Hillary at the summit of Mount Everest. But then, we were back on the trail again, slogging for what seemed like several more hours. Finally we skidded to a stop, just short of a huge herd of startled reindeer.

The animals had gigantic antlers, something I didn't remember from my grade school slide show. I couldn't help but picture the dozens of sorry tourists lying gored and crumpled on the streets of Pamplona, Spain, after the annual running of the bulls. Just in case the reindeer were mounting a surprise attack, I glanced around nervously in search of an escape route, but the hundreds of brown eyes that followed our every move made a getaway seem unlikely.

Henna and I carefully glided our way to a hut, a tall tepee covered with beige reindeer hides. Thick gray smoke was billowing from its open top, lingering over the tent like a feathery wreath of clouds. The tiny athletic man who emerged from the reindeer hut was straight out of my fantasies, complete with a chiseled, ruddy face, blond hair, and high cheekbones. He sported a red woolen shirt underneath an embroidered blue tunic with reindeer-skin knickers and a bouncy skirt trimmed in red, yellow, and blue braid. Knee-high fur boots curled up at the tip of his toes, and on his head sat a floppy blue cap with four long points and a wide scarlet headband. He looked like a cross between an Arctic Keebler Elf and a court jester in winter wear. I took a deep gulp of the bone-chilling air to commemorate this life-defining moment: my first live encounter with a Sami reindeer herdsman. Here I was, face to face with the man who held down the job I'd coveted since grade school. How could I ever be content again back at the office?

"Rrrrooovarsen silia sil la laaaaa," the Sami called in a deep voice. He motioned for me to come forward. "What's he saying?" I whispered to Henna. "I think he wants you to try out his reindeer sled," she said with a wink. I popped out of those skis like I had a beehive in my britches and vaulted excitedly onto the sled. Unfortunately, it was designed for someone four-feet-ten. I made the best of it anyway, trying to ignore the fact that my cramped knees came precariously close to an intimate part of the reindeer's anatomy.

Before fear could take over, I grabbed the reins and yanked sharply.

The critter took off like its tail was on fire. *"Noro roto naaaara haliayaa!"* bellowed my new Sami friend from the sidelines. *"Haliayaaaa!"*

In an instant, we were racing.

I could hear Henna screaming something at me, and my own voice yelling "Ssstttoooooopp!" My whole life flashed before me, along with snow and sky.

The joyride came to a sudden halt when we rammed into a mammoth snowdrift. The impact of the crash sent me flying smack into a mound of only partially frozen reindeer muffins. Henna and the Sami cackled hysterically, slapping each other on the back as they doubled over in laughter. "That was super!" laughed Henna, her face crimson red.

Pride still intact, I calmly brushed off my shoulders and my backside. Though my performance was less than stellar, I was sure that with a little more practice, I'd be a natural behind the reindeer reins. And besides, what are a few aches and pains to live out a lifelong dream! It had been more than worth it. Bidding farewell to the herd and my dear Sami pal, I blew them a kiss. Then I snapped my skis back on and rejoined Henna on the trails. For a long stretch, the only sound besides my heavy breathing was the *crunch, crunch, crunch* of our waxed skis against the icy snow.

Six hours later, I emerged from the frigid forest, wobbly-kneed and bruised yet victorious. We trudged back to the hotel, where we chugged down steaming cups of hot black coffee. Henna disappeared into the back office. Minutes later she reappeared with an official-looking Lapp Reindeer Driving License that she had whipped up on the computer in my honor.

I thanked her profusely and headed back to the safety of my room. Flinging off my stiff clothing and my ice-encrusted backpack, I buried myself in my thick fleece bathrobe. Then I collapsed on the bed for a hard-earned catnap. Thirty minutes later, I made a shivering beeline for the hotel sauna.

Ahhh, the sauna, a quintessential Finnish ritual. I could hardly wait to take in the raw pleasure of it all. I opened the heavy door and peered inside the cedar-lined room. Three buxom blond beauties were lounging buck naked on long wooden benches at the front of the heated chamber. I instantly felt fat and badly claustrophobic. The air was incredibly thick and hot, and the room quite small and dark. I quickly shut the door and debated what to do. Sucking in tightly, I stripped in a nanosecond and sprinted into the chamber. Then I slithered to a far corner of the bench, so as not to intrude, and tried to talk myself down from the heights of my fear.

A few minutes later, one of the girls jumped up without warning, reached into a bucket, and pitched a scoop of water onto the wood-burning stove, creating a sizzling plume of steam. Unable to contain myself any longer and afraid I would pass out before I could escape, I yelled, "I'm trapped!" The trio of slender beauties snatched up their towels and left in a huff, scowling at me for disturbing their inner peace. I finally stopped hyperventilating and felt a relaxing calm spread over my limp body. With this sense of well-being, I decided there was no way in hell any Finn was going to trick me into rolling in the snow or plunging into an icy lake to wrap up my "authentic" sauna experience.

While I was daydreaming in the buff about the day's remarkable conquests, there came a loud rap on the door of the steamy sauna cubicle. The door opened, and a beefy, red-faced woman in a white uniform marched right up to me. I noticed she was carrying a bundle of unusually long twigs. I also observed that her forearms were bigger than George Foreman's.

"You want I beat you?" she smiled. Surely I had misunderstood. "You want I beat you?" she repeated. "Finns think very good for circulation." I was certainly not into flagellation at this stage of my life. I was still recovering from the brutal massage I had endured in Budapest a year earlier. Besides, my wiped-out body had taken enough beating today. "*Kiitos*, but no thanks," I said in my best broken Finnish. "My blood is circulating just swell."

That evening after my sauna, I enjoyed a scrumptious meal of savory salmon with Arctic cloudberry sauce and roasted potatoes in the cozy hotel restaurant. As I gazed out the window at the twinkling Arctic stars, I started plotting how to bring my Sami reindeer home to Georgia where he belonged.

Bigger Than France

Spike Gillespie

• •

L ast September, Beth, my then-publicist at the University of
Texas Press, emailed me a note regarding my ardent premarket-
ing moves to promote my about-to-be-released second book,
*Surrender (But Don't Give Yourself Away): Old Cars, Found Hope,
and Other Cheap Tricks*. Beth peevishly advised, "Your enthusi-
asm is essential to the success of the book, but try to *rein yourself in*. . . ."

When pressed, she also admitted to having sent out only four review
copies, though months prior, on her request, I'd given her dozens of personal
journalist contacts at publications ranging from feminist zines to the *New
York Times*. She explained the book was "just regional," and I needed to stop
aiming for a national audience.

Her attitude hardly shocked me. I'd already learned about book marketing back in 1999. On a visit to Simon & Schuster on the cusp of my first
book's publication, I sadly noted that, despite my imagined reception,
the Rockettes failed to materialize and high-kick down a golden spiral stair-
case, clutching and thrusting my galleys to and fro their bosoms.

The only publicity the S&S marketing folks got me before dropping the
book entirely was an appearance on an episode of Judith Regan's cable TV

book show, where I, a single mother, was pitted against an "expert" who claimed that children not raised by in-house biological fathers were bound to become drug-addicted criminals and eventual tenants of hell. On air, I asked if he was a Christian. Of course he was. So I pointed out that Jesus wasn't raised by *his* biological father, nearly prompting an apoplectic fit on the part of my assigned nemesis.

Despite the training from Simon & Schuster's publicity department and Beth's pessimistic attitude, I find myself scheming ways to promote my book. My most brilliant plan comes to me while swimming manic laps at the Y. As I swim I wonder, "Where can I get me a wedding dress?" Ecstatic at my own cleverness, I set to work implementing my scheme against the wishes of Beth, who informs me I am causing her unnecessary sweat, though my plan in no way involves her assistance.

At my book release party, I marry my career at the local independent bookstore. My first typewriter, which is around thirty years old, stands in as my career. I wear a huge poufy white wedding dress. And as my best friend gives me away, my thirteen-year-old son and his friend play "Foxy Lady" on their electric guitars. Around a hundred and fifty people show up, buy piles of books, and bolster my belief that I can move units, to hell with Beth's prognostication.

A few days after my nuptials, I call my friend Dan, father of three, who served as my pretend wedding celebrant. Dan's just had surgery, and I want to know if, during his recuperation, he and his wife need any help. Dan, voice slow and thick with painkillers, tells me there's just one thing I can do for him: Take a tour of Texas public libraries to promote my book.

I do not, at the moment, mull over this suggestion looking for obvious flaws, such as the fact that people don't go to libraries to buy books; they go for free books. Nor do I take a long hard look at a map of Texas, a state where you regularly see this bumper sticker: TEXAS: BIGGER THAN FRANCE.

Instead, I go straight to a website listing the hundreds of Texas libraries, contemplate the royalty possibilities if each ordered just one copy, and fantasize about readings with impatient lines of author-lovers forming to purchase my book and demand personalized inscriptions.

And then, very slowly, until I nearly go blind, I cut and paste more than seven hundred individual email addresses from the librarian database into my address book. In a bulk mailing I mention my career highlights. I speak of my sincere desire to reach a broad Texas audience. I include a heartbreaking essay about my older sister's high school boyfriend, the football star upon whom I had a crush, who died in a horrible car wreck at nineteen. And I offer to give a free reading in exchange for a chance to sell my book.

The return on these notes is about 1 percent. Initially I believe this to be a sorry response. Eight months, two cars, and several thousand miles later, I'm seeing the silver lining in not having been bombarded with requests for visits. It didn't take very long at all into my journey for foresight to tell me that the whole trip, if it would ever be funny at all, would only be funny in retrospect.

Stop one: West Texas. Having been invited to chaperone a trip of German high school exchange students in search of the archetypal Wild West right around the time my book is released, I make the brilliant plan to make this trip double as the first leg of the book tour. The first stop is actually not a library but the annex of a small independent bookstore in Alpine, Texas, population six thousandish.

I spend the day of the reading a couple of hours outside of Alpine, hiking Emory Peak, a particularly grueling stretch in Big Bend National Forest, outpaced by all except those German students who stop to chain-smoke their way up the trail. Then, worn out and aching, I abandon my charges post-hike to their church-style van and the other adults. I solo-drive our auxiliary vehicle, the Saturn wagon, across the desert, watching a purple sunset and imagining how easy it would be to drive off the road and die, with no one to find you for days.

I also entertain detailed impure thoughts about another one of the chaperones, a twenty-three-year-old Eagle Scout and recent college grad with a disarming grin. As strains of "Mrs. Robinson" fill my head, a very large bird decides this to be an excellent moment to commit suicide into my windshield, which, along with the rest of the vehicle, is moving at about ninety miles an hour.

The jolt brings me back to reality. I locate Alpine but, despite its small size, cannot find my precise destination. I stop at a gas station for directions. As I get back into the car, I hear a small, vaguely familiar noise. Unable to pinpoint the significance of this sound, I forget about it and focus on locating the bookstore. Destination located, I burst inside to face an audience of roughly nine octogenarians.

At which point the source of the noise I heard as I sat down in my car dawns on me. "Hello!" I shout. "My name is Spike. I think I might have ripped my pants a little." I turn so that my butt is facing the audience and I look over my shoulder, attempting to assess the damage.

The pants, perhaps snagged earlier in the day when I sat on a rock, are, in fact, torn from near the waistband to well past the edge of my left buttock, which is flapping in the wind. Luckily, the guy in the very front row is legally blind. He is also a member of the Mock Family, a now-defunct outfit of classical guitarists, he and his wife tell me later, and they then proceed to detail their musical adventures of days gone by.

This becomes a theme for the tour. I visit one town or another to tell my story and find those in attendance eager to share their own. Perhaps this is because I am a memoirist, and the form invites others to whip out their best versions of their own life tales. Or it could be, as a psychic once suggested, that I have a pointy aura, which compels people, even total strangers, to tell me their entire life stories.

The following day, I read at a speck of a library in another mote of a West Texas town, Marfa, population 2,100, famous for mysterious lights that flash in the night sky. There are perhaps seven in attendance, among them Doc Edwards, seventy-eight, who can't hear too well but who has a most pleasing firm and calloused handshake and a ready smile.

Doc, too, is a memoirist. He's published a collection of his tales of being the local veterinarian for fifty years. I pick up a copy of it that night when I give a reading at the Marfa Book Company, which Doc also attends. His book is called *Up to My Armpits,* and he gladly signs it for me. Except for one large group that walks out mid-reading (turns out it was the German students, impatient for dinner and unable to decipher my American humor), the evening goes well.

Another friendly senior is particularly attentive in the front row, smiling appreciatively at me. Later, Lynn, the store owner, explains that Celia recently learned she would soon be completely blind. Her reaction is to see as many things as she can before permanent darkness falls. And so she takes adventures, setting off for the Galápagos Islands for some turtle-watching and, much closer to home, up to the nearby, world-renowned McDonald Observatory to take in the then-very-close planet Mars through an über-powerful telescope.

Both a cynic and a romantic, I love coming across the Celias of the world, hearing of their profound grace under tremendous pressure. That she has made time on her to-do list to come observe me read registers deeply.

Mat with one T schedules me for two readings at the Brownwood Library, 146 miles north. He emails me details using military time and insists I take the scenic route, for which he furnishes specific instructions.

My car, old enough to vote and go to war, dies two nights before. Undeterred, I come up with a plan B.

Fronted $1,500 by an ex-boyfriend, the day before the reading I hastily purchase a '93 Toyota Corolla with 186,000 miles on it from a woman so retentive I suspect she changed the oil every weekend. While this does bode well for continued engine longevity, it also means dealing with a paranoid lunatic who refuses to sign the title over to me until we appear at the tax office together.

Which precludes my attending my first reading at the Brownwood Library, set for 0900 hours. I email Mat with the bad news, and he responds that they'll find a way to make do without me leading story hour. *Story hour?* I apparently have overlooked this part of the deal and wonder, when Mat scheduled me for story time, if he'd been hoping I would entertain the kiddies by reading from my essay collection a selection about my abusive father, or perhaps, my drinking problem.

I do manage to procure the new automobile title in time to make the reading scheduled for 1800 hours, for which precisely no one shows up. Mat, an undercooked and doughy man, visibly though not specifically off kilter in an unnerving way, looks across his desk at me when I ask his advice on dealing with the missing audience. "Maybe you should just go stand in the middle of the room and start reading," he offers humorlessly "and see if a crowd gathers."

The audience in Lake Dallas—round trip: five hundred miles, books sold: fewer than ten—increases by a significant percentage when the librarian's husband arrives.

Next, I convince my old college roommate to drive with me to a January gig in the oxymoronically named Mount Pleasant—620 miles round trip. Paula and I have been on countless previous disastrous journeys, both real and metaphorical, beginning with assisting her father in the early '80s with his Rich Folk Florida canoe tours.

Together we've braved the Okeechobee, bleeding and tamponless, and fended off tandem nicotine fits after accidentally dropping our last carton of generic cigarettes into the Itchetucknee. We traded boats for a car in the summer of '88, traversing North America from Tampa to Vancouver Island, stopping to buy gas, beer, crap, and once, a couple of tattoos at the Sunset Strip Tattoo Parlor in Hollywood.

This newest jaunt, then, two decades into our adventures, is a delightful trip down bad memory lane. Whereas the more faint of heart might have stopped when the rain came at the windshield so hard and fast as to emulate space travel on the *Enterprise*, we experienced road-trippers continue to hydroplane our way to our destination. Unable to find our hotel, we call for directions, and I make the teenage clerk stay on the line until I see the sun on the Comfort Inn sign rising before us on the dark, wet highway. Attempting to check in, we are informed our reservation is nowhere in the system and no rooms are available.

Onward to the Best Western, clearly the Mount Pleasant epicenter on a Friday night. A group of urban cowpeople stumble out of the hotel bar and across the sticky carpeting, their loud hick accents piercing my eardrums as one woman threatens permanent bodily harm to another who—fortunately or not, depending on your perspective—does not appear to be present.

Paula and I never thought we'd see in our lifetimes the inside of a room to match the Crank 'N' Skank motel we'd crashed in in New Orleans sixteen years prior. This hotel, then, underscores the old adage "never say never."

The turnout for my event, held in a basement deep in the bowels of the Mount Pleasant library, features about half a dozen citizens. I've offered to do a free poetry workshop in addition to my reading. We start with an exercise to reveal where you come from, not in a physical sense but more who you are. Without scanning the material ahead of time, I randomly select, for the purpose of an example, a poem from an anthology put together by some teens I taught the year before. I begin to read loudly from one student's piece, not remembering until too late, as the words pour from my heathen lips, that this particular piece is about Satan.

After the reading, one of the official Friends of the Library, a man hovering closer to grave than cradle, takes Paula and me to see the pride of Mount Pleasant. We follow him to a field and walk through the dead grass to the place it stands—ancient faded tombstone of Henry Clay Thurston, who, at seven-feet-seven-and-a-half, had been the tallest Confederate soldier. Some locals are trying to raise money to erect a fitting monument: a pillar the height of old Henry.

The Carrollton Public Library stop provides an unexpected drop of sunshine, a sort of corollary to the old bait and switch. Carrollton is a suburb of Dallas, and for a few years I was a regular reporter and columnist for the *Dallas Morning News*. Folks liked my column, and I grew a decent-sized reader following, and even though that ended years ago, I'm still sometimes recognized in the Metroplex area.

I walk into a big bright room—the library has been converted from a Food Lion and still has those high grocery store ceilings—filled with eager participants who know my work and are glad to see me. This is another workshop/reading combo, and the writing they produce makes me (and them) cry. They reveal beautifully rendered accounts of abusive pasts, secret hopes, and, in one instance, a deeply mourned and missed wife, recently deceased. They buy my books. They invite me back. After so many long drives to sell so few books, I now suddenly become falsely lulled into a big-budget-movie-plot mentality that the underdog actually can (and will) win in the end!

Which is why I need to travel to Odessa, to humble my badass self. Midland/Odessa, from whence the George Bushes hail, is a conservative hub and a cultural wasteland. When I mention to folks I am going to Odessa, a place I've never been before, I am only ever met with a cringe. *"Odessa?"* they say, and if looks could spit, the ground at my feet would be damp with saliva. Thus warned, I plan to make the eight-hundred-mile round trip inside of thirty-six hours. Get in. Read. Get out.

Despite fear of destination, the journey is pleasant. Cranked to its maximum, the Toyota enjoys cruising at a hundred along the long, flat, fast road. Getting to Odessa requires taking a right off of the main empty highway onto a smaller and even emptier highway that runs alongside the Giants, a herd of stupefying windmills that appear to be perpetually doing yoga, stretching their arms toward a sky that carries upward and onward for approximately three hundred thousand miles in any given direction.

This area is so sparsely populated, you thrill at the idea you might finally, actually, be entirely alone in this world. You also dread the thought of breaking down or having a blowout or wrecking your car running into a wild javelina. Because it's a really really long, damn hot walk to the next tiny town.

Staying at La Quinta Inn, I discover you can get soft porn movies in run-of-the-mill chain hotels. I guess I thought you had to go to certain particular seedy motels with burnt-out letters in their neon signs and broken-toothed drunks behind the counter. I didn't realize otherwise, because when I am alone in hotels, I use my time to read and rarely turn on the tube.

But for whatever reason, I turn it on this night and learn that "movie titles do NOT appear on your hotel bill." I also peruse synopses that promise me, "With no plot to follow, these actors can really concentrate on the action!" and "Enjoy this exciting twist: All the naughty girls in this movie are wearing GLASSES while they get what they deserve!"

Not one single child shows up for the AM poetry workshop, though one woman does. Krista is familiar with my work and, in an earlier email, had assured me Odessa possesses liberals, enough to make a trip here worth my while. Together we sit, and I knit while she breathlessly offers her dream of forming the next Bloomsbury group right here in Odessa. She admits her ex-military husband isn't into this highfalutin concept of hers, and, well, okay, he is sort of conservative, but she is an independent woman, just waiting for the Virginia Woolf of the West to appear and rescue her soul in all its literary longing.

Krista returns for the afternoon session, joining four or five others in a theater room made larger by its screaming lack of occupants. I sell about five books and am cornered by a woman who wants to tell me, in detail, how she is living off the grid and to show me, on the next floor down, a photograph of hers, matted and hanging on the wall. Before leaving, I help myself to some of the free DESIGN YOUR OWN JACKRABBIT! bookmarks at the front desk, commemorate the City of Odessa Jackrabbit Jamboree and include directions to local historical markers regarding jackrabbits, details of "Jack Ben Rabbit," the World's Largest Jackrabbit, and a recipe for rabbit stew.

In Denison, Texas, Laura the librarian offers to put me up in her mother's guesthouse. She meets me off the highway and leads me down a dirt road to a little cottage, clean and bright, warning me to watch out for scorpions in my bed and asking if I mind if she stays with me.

I sit listening to Laura tell me about her life. Like Krista in Odessa, she reveals enough details for me to piece together that her husband is probably controlling and conservative. He also might be agoraphobic and, perhaps, employaphobic, though Laura prefers to see him as a househusband, ever present for the kids.

I ask how she met him, and Laura's face lights up. She was a teenager, visiting a friend. There was a knock upon the door. Enter Larry. In a conspiratorial whisper when Larry's in the other room, the friend asks if Laura likes Larry. Yes, she says, but she has to go home now, to see a long-lost sister in town for a visit.

So Laura runs home and hastily prepares to meet her family at a restaurant. Then she runs to the car, not noticing her mother's toy poodle at her feet, and slams the car door on the dog's head. The dog wavers and crumples. Laura runs back to her friend's place, hysterical. Larry, tall and consoling, puts a strong arm around her frail, narrow shoulders and tells her he'll help.

Walking back to Laura's house, where Larry will bury the dog in a shoebox in the yard, he tells her he totally understands how she feels—why, just the week before, he himself had run over a puppy. They bond over shared dog tragedies. Not long after, they marry. One day, Larry thoughtfully buys Laura a toy poodle to replace the one she accidentally killed. Unfortunately, they leave the poodle unattended in a room with a Rottweiller. Suffice it to say, the family no longer gets poodles for pets.

Laura's stories go on late into the night, until finally I beg off, exhausted. The next morning, in the Denison Public Library, I sit and wait for an audience. Only one woman, a friend of Laura's, arrives. The two of them belong to a writing group, and so, rather than stand and read to them, we swap writing stories. I sell three books. Round trip drive: 535 miles.

With any shred of optimism beaten out of me entirely, I set out on a stormy morning late in April, six months after I began, for my final leg of this pathetic tour. What little comfort I conjure comes from knowing I am heading to another suburban Dallas library. Surely I'll sell some books at this event. Surely someone will recognize me. Plus, I know an added bonus awaits me.

Ten days prior, I received an email from Gwen, a Dallas reader who, two years before, had clipped a story I wrote about knitting. Now her sister had died, leaving Gwen a huge stash of expensive yarn, which she was hoping to sell for thirty-five dollars. Did I know anyone who might want to buy it?

My eyes bug out at the description of the Scottish wool and angora and alpaca. I am a yarn fiend, having taken up chain-knitting when I quit smoking. I write back, offer her forty, and ask if she can meet me at the library.

I also tell Gwen that her yarn will go to an excellent cause. I've recently started a knitting club at an alternative high school where I teach. Some of my students are high risk, a point I emphasize to make Gwen feel extra good knowing her sister's yarn is going to a good cause. Taking my bait, I believe Gwen interprets "high risk" to mean "mentally retarded" and/or "profoundly disabled." Duly impressed by my saintly volunteerism, Gwen tells her retirement community chums of my endeavors. Inspired, her friends gather together their spare yarn and needles to send to the crippled knitting children.

Driving north on this final leg, thinking about the yarn, my optimism void begins to fill with a sudden hopefulness. Not at the prospect of selling books. But at how life sometimes tosses us unexpected rewards. Like sixty skeins of yarn from a faraway stranger.

I whip my brain into movie-of-the-week triumph, telling myself what I want to hear—that this whole tour has been worth it after all, and look at all I've seen and done and everyone I've met. I gloss over the very many moments, driving alone on the highway, when I've questioned why I was writing at all, and when I was forced to face the truth: People wouldn't die if I stopped writing. In fact, they wouldn't even notice.

I fast-forward over other negative thoughts—how I've gotten too far away from writing for passion, how I've let money become the object. I block out the idea that this trip has been a waste of time and gas and money, and of how crass marketing is, and how it doesn't matter how good a writer you are, it's all about the stupid market. I cut off all the mean sentiments I've directed at more successful, less talented writers whom I detest for having the right combination of whatever to merit readings that involve more than two people sitting in a dingy basement in a town of two hundred and sales that get them big contracts.

I focus instead on the promise of Gwen and her yarn and how I'll share it with my students—after taking the good stuff for myself, of course. I think how wonderful it is to be alive and to have people contact you out of the blue with offers of kindness. I stop at my favorite truck stop, the Czech Stop, and buy Gwen and her friends a dozen *kolaches*, these delicious little fruit- and cream cheese–filled Czech pastries. I do not grow glum, despite the rain falling hard enough to limit my visibility to three inches. I even invent a slogan for myself—"Be Delightful!"—and imagine myself charming the hell out of Gwen and anyone who crosses my path from now on, for that matter. I swell up with joy that, even if I only sold around thirty books in six months, at least *I have a book to sell!* And isn't that everyone's dream?

I arrive at ten-thirty at the library and find other writers setting up. This is some authors' day event, word had been sent to the community, and all we have to do is stand around, bond, talk author talk, and wait for the cash-wielding patrons to descend upon us and pick our stockpiles clean like locusts on the crops.

I wait. And wait. I talk to an author about her book of morning meditations and her mission, with her husband, to bring the Lord to prisoners. I am blindsided by a juicy authoress who joyfully gushes about how she and her husband cowrite kids' books and cookbooks and inspirational romance and antique books, as if writing were as easy as crapping after a big bowl of chili—you're never sure what form it will take, but rest assured something will pop out.

I eavesdrop while this woman's husband tells another author the secret method he and his wife use. "She adds the sensory details and makes sure there's no redundancy. She makes the women sound like women." I sit, listening to these people blather on, secretly wishing they'd leave me alone to my knitting. In my heart I have already violated my vow to *Be Delightful!*

Gwen arrives. She's a pencil of a woman, and she drives some big American car, a Lincoln or a Cadillac—champagne or beige, depending on how you look at it. She heaps her yarn upon me, and in return, I hand her the *kolaches*, twenty bucks more than I originally offered, and a copy of my book—what the hell. Gwen, truly pleased with my gifts, hugs me, and I transfer the yarn to my car for the long drive home in the rain, my slogan transforming itself from *Be Delightful!* to *Be Relieved!* For at long last, the ordeal is finished, and I can return home to my keyboard and the joys of writing my next book, a task so all-consuming that, thankfully, I won't even have time to contemplate future promotions.

Souvenirs from Ecuador

Bethany Gumper

• • • • • • • • • • • • • • • • • • •

Despite my parents' pleading, I did not buy traveler insurance before going to Ecuador. It didn't occur to me that I'd regret my choice; in fact, I believed I was being *thrifty*. I was a rookie traveler, and the trip—a semester abroad during my junior year of college—was the first of my visits to another country. At the time, shelling out for hypothetical protection seemed extravagant.

My mother disagreed, worrying out loud as she helped me pack my bags at home, the night before my plane left for Quito. "Bethany, you're not going to Kansas, you know," she said. She tucked the Montana calendar and huckleberry chocolates she had picked out for my host family into a side pocket of my carry-on bag and listed the potential dangers that lay in wait: scorpion bites, bone breaks on treks through the Andes, malaria.

"Please, Mom," I interrupted. "I don't even like going on roller coasters. It's not like I'm going to be performing daredevil feats."

I was, of course, planning to try new things in Ecuador, but I expected to spend most of my time on tame pursuits: practicing my Spanish, sampling the cuisine, getting to know the local students at my school, and perfecting my salsa moves. Even my most extreme plans—taking a guided Amazon tour or snorkeling with sea lions off Ecuador's famous Galápagos Islands—did not exactly rank as high-risk activities.

"Six months is a long time," my mom answered, as she folded the three copies she had made of my passport, slipping one into my carry-on, tucking one into my backpack, and handing me the other. "Keep this in your bra at all times. It should be safe there."

"If there's *anyone* who doesn't need insurance when they're traveling, it's me," I said. I stuffed two rolls of toilet paper into the top compartment of my backpack; I'd heard a rumor that it was hard to find outside larger cities like Quito. "I'm a wimp. Plus, I'm living with a host family. How extreme can my Ecuadorian experience be if I'm living with kids?"

As I zipped my backpack shut, I figured, case closed.

FAST-FORWARD THREE months: The morning started like every other since I'd arrived, with a breakfast of *batido de naranjilla*—a tangy milk shake made from a small orange citrus fruit that's a cross between an orange and a tomato—and a cold shower. (My "sisters," Gabriela, fourteen, and Estefanía, seven, left for school before me, so by the time I got up, the hot water was gone.) As I was putting on my sneakers, I noticed a bump on the tip of my left middle toe but, after an inspection, decided the small bulge looked harmless, and ignored it.

A week later, the mystery bump was still there. It hurt a little, sort of like someone was pinching me, especially when I wore close-toed shoes. However, the fact that I hyperventilate when I see needles—even a tongue depressor gives me the willies—combined with the language barrier, made visiting a doctor seem less than appealing. I decided to let my bump be. I resolved to wear flip-flops for the next week or so to see if it would go away.

It didn't. And two weeks later, I drunkenly limped out of my favorite salsa club at three in the morning. I'd left Marco, my nimble-footed dance partner, confused—after he'd stepped on my now-quite-swollen toe, I'd almost passed out from the pain. (Probably my fault, because I'm *not* nimble-footed.) I resigned myself to visiting the doctor.

The next morning, my "Ecua-mom," Consuelo, drove me to the clinic, fretting over my toe and asking why I hadn't done anything about it. My real mother's final half-joking admonition as I prepared to board the plane echoed in my head: "Don't complain to your father and me when you're stuck in a clinic with malaria and have no insurance to pay for it!"

Despite Consuelo's fussing, I insisted I'd be fine on my own, and that I'd call her when I was done. I hobbled inside and looked around the empty waiting room in puzzlement. I scanned the sterile white walls, single row of blue plastic chairs, and counter, but there was no receptionist.

"*¿Sí?*" The sound, more of a loud croak than a friendly greeting, startled me. I leaned over the counter to see where the voice was coming from and saw a gnarled woman so tiny she couldn't even see over the counter. Aha—the receptionist! A formidable woman with her hair scraped back into an austere bun, she looked to be in her eighties. "*¿Sí?*" she repeated, annoyed.

I gave her my name and began explaining in halting Spanish, supplementing with charades, "*Algo le pasó a mi dedo del pie. Hay un* bump *en el.*" Impassive, she told me the doctor would be with me shortly.

I sat as other patients came and went, and then sat some more. Nearly four hours later, when the waiting room was empty again, the crabby receptionist turned to me. "*¿Señorita Gumper? El doctor la verá ahora.*" I'd learned a valuable lesson: When visiting the doctor in Ecuador, tell the receptionist you're on your deathbed.

After a five-second examination that consisted of pushing on my toe and gazing at the mystery bump, Dr. Zalles made his diagnosis. "Ahhh, *sí. Hay que amputarlo.*"

I hadn't learned the word *amputar* in Spanish 101, but it sounded suspiciously like "amputate." Call me crazy, but any diagnosis that included amputation seemed hasty after a five-second exam.

"*¡¿Qué?!*" I exclaimed. "*No comprendo. ¿Me va a cortar el dedo?*"

The doctor calmly explained that he had seen my condition many times: A bug had laid an egg under my skin, and he had to cut it out. Dr. Zalles chuckled at my horrified expression. "*No te preocupes. Podría ser una mariposa. Usted puede guardarlo como animal doméstico.*" What? Don't worry? If it turns out to be a butterfly I can keep it? Not funny.

Had I gone to the beach recently? he asked. Apparently, sand-living bugs find homes for their eggs in unsuspecting barefoot travelers' toes. I had indeed visited a beach in the coastal town of Atacames about three weeks prior, with Summer and Kurt, two fun-loving students on my abroad program. We'd gone despite Consuelo's suggestion that we go somewhere cleaner and less dangerous. Atacames was the closest beach town, a harrowing five-hour bus ride north. If the doctor asked, I thought I could even pinpoint the moment when that bug had started digging in: When José, my salsa partner at the time, noticed that my sandals were slowing me down during a dancing competition at the beach, so he told me to take them off. "*¡Quítatelas!*" he'd cried, and I'd obliged, kicking off my shoes to keep up with the racing tempo. We'd danced for hours, my bare toes digging into the sand again and again.

I told Dr. Zalles I needed to go home and think about what to do (really, this was a cover for the fact that I wanted to go home to do computer research on whether he was feeding me a line). Alas, I had no such opportunity: He told me he needed to remove the egg as soon as possible because apparently it could *hatch*. In my *toe*.

I agreed to let Dr. Zalles do the deed. Then, as best I could, I explained that I have a very low pain tolerance and asked if he could put me to sleep or something before he started cutting. Again, he laughed. Dr. Zalles was young and likable, with a better bedside manner than many doctors I had visited back home; despite the fact that he was about to cut open my toe, I liked him. When he laughed, his dark eyes crinkled up in a friendly way. I trusted he was doing the right thing.

He wiped my toes with a cold, wet liquid that he promised was an extremely strong anesthetic. Still, I screwed my eyes shut in terror as he approached with a sharp instrument.

"This won't hurt a bit!" he reassured me in Spanish.

To my surprise, he was right. The anesthesia worked, and I didn't even feel my toe, much less Dr. Zalles hacking away. I did, however, nearly throw up when I opened my eyes and saw my left foot covered in blood. Three minutes later, the surgery was done. The doctor stitched up my toe, asked if I wanted to see the egg (no!), and wrapped my foot in some gauze. He advised me to change the gauze and wash my toe daily and gave me a prescription for Cipro, an antibiotic to prevent infection. He also recommended investing in some aquasocks to protect my tootsies on future beach excursions.

I hobbled out to the ancient receptionist to settle my bill. I was a little nervous, given the expense of medical bills in the States. I remembered shelling out nearly a hundred dollars for a yellow fever immunization before my trip; surely a near–toe amputation would set me back far more. I waited for her to total my bill, biting my lip nervously, thinking of my parents and their good advice: I definitely should have bought travel insurance instead of new hiking boots. Or at least kept the hiking boots on my feet the whole trip.

She held out the itemized bill. I looked at the total on the bottom and gasped.

"*¿Es correcto?*" I asked in disbelief. She nodded, scowling. I was so relieved, I nearly climbed over the counter and kissed her wrinkled cheek. Apparently, in Ecuador, it costs $23.67 to get the tip of your toe amputated. My amazement didn't stop there: When I went to fill my prescription, ten days' worth of Cipro cost $2.43.

My mother, it seemed, was *wrong*—insurance hardly seemed necessary given the negligible cost of healthcare here. But despite this triumph, I had an odd, nagging worry: Perhaps I was tempting fate by traveling footloose and policy free; perhaps travel insurance was more of a karmic safeguard than a financial one.

When I arrived back at my host family's home, I called my friend, Courtney, whom I've been friends with since seventh grade. She was living in Quito, too, but on a different program, and I was glad to hear a familiar voice after my harrowing ordeal. "Are you serious? A bug laid an egg in your toe?" I explained that I couldn't wear a shoe on my left foot, much less salsa dance, and that I wouldn't be able to go with her to that night's concert by the Colombian singer Carlos Vives. I got the sympathy I wanted: She decided to skip the concert to keep me company.

While I didn't care about telling Courtney, I *was* embarrassed to tell my new Ecuadorian friends about my toe. But I told them anyway. Their reactions were quite the opposite of Courtney's astonishment.

"*Ohhhh, sí. Lo mismo le pasó a mi hermano,*" said María, the chatty girl who sat next to me in my Andean anthropology class, about the similar fate of her brother. Even my host family seemed unimpressed; apparently I wasn't the first family member to serve as a bug incubator. My host dad told me, "The same thing happened to me a year ago. But I didn't go to a doctor. The egg hatched inside my arm. I put a Band-Aid over it, suffocated the bug, and pulled it out with tweezers." It sounded just as bad in Spanish.

Two weeks later, Dr. Zalles took out my stitches. I was so grateful. I even hugged him goodbye.

The next few months were everything I had envisioned for my travels—devoid of weird medical situations and full of wonder. I visited the Galápagos Islands, six hundred miles off the coast, with a group of students, and island-hopped for ten days on a twelve-passenger boat. I snorkeled with sea lions every morning, feeling their long whiskers brush against my toes as they zipped by playing tag with each other. I sunbathed on the deck with Gabriel García Márquez novels in the afternoons, slathered in sunscreen to protect my skin from the hot equatorial sun. I ate fresh fish the crew caught each night and was rocked to sleep in a bunk bed inside a cabin so small I had to stoop when standing. I met giant tortoises that weighed six hundred pounds, marine iguanas that looked like miniature dinosaurs, blue- and red-footed boobies, tiny penguins at home in the tropics, and giant, graceful albatrosses made famous in *The Rime of the Ancient Mariner.*

By the time five months had elapsed, I had changed my mind back about the karmic necessity of travel insurance. Having spent just $26.10 on medical mishaps, I was convinced it was a *good* thing I had been thrifty. Then, halfway through a ten-hour bus ride back to Quito after a trip to the nearby town of Cuenca with a friend and fellow traveler, Laura, I experienced a strange throbbing pain in my back, at the very top of my coccyx bone.

At first I thought I was just sore from sitting for so long, but as it worsened, it soon became apparent that this was no normal bus-rider's backside. Although Laura and I had gotten to know each other pretty well when we'd bunked together on a trip through the Amazon, I felt strange telling her about my insane, pulsing butt pain. I squirmed around in my seat, trying to get comfortable. After about an hour of this, she asked, "Hey, are you okay? You seem really uncomfortable."

"My back is really hurting me," I fibbed. "Don't worry about it. I'm fine.

I think I'll try to sleep for a while." I closed my eyes and assumed a peaceful facial expression, hoping she would leave me alone. Forty-five minutes later, I couldn't bear it anymore. "It's not so much my back that hurts as the very top of my butt," I blurted out. "It is *killing* me."

"Maybe you could have broken your tailbone?"

"No way. I didn't fall." Yet it hurt so much that I didn't think I could survive the next three hours.

"Well, the bus has a bathroom," Laura said. "Although I would normally recommend *against* going there, maybe you could look in the mirror and see if your butt looks funny?"

I agreed and prepared to go assess my—well, my ass. Since it was the middle of the night, it was no easy task to make my way down the narrow aisle. I gingerly stepped over young travelers in bandanas sleeping on the grimy floor and tiny old women in traditional indigenous dress stretched out across the seats. Once I reached the bathroom, I returned quickly.

"Any luck?" said Laura.

I grimaced and shook my head.

"Well, this might help," she said. She pulled a small pillow out of her backpack. "Sit on this—maybe you'll be more comfortable."

Though the pillow had helped a little, as soon as I got off the bus, I went to see my old friend Dr. Zalles. I didn't want to have to explain the humiliating situation to my host family, so I didn't even stop to drop off my backpack. The pain was reminiscent of the throbbing in my toe just over a month ago, and truthfully, I was terrified that my butt was about to hatch.

The receptionist didn't seem to remember me. Intent on *not* waiting for four hours this time, I crossed my eyes a bit and swayed from side to side like I was about to pass out. She asked for my name and what was wrong with me. *"Ayyyyyyy,"* I groaned that I was going to die, *"Me duele la espalda.*

Creo que voy a morir. " This time, she looked worried. She ushered me into Dr. Zalles's office immediately.

"Hola, Bethany!" The doctor greeted me like an old friend and told me he had seen four unlucky travelers become human incubators since I had gotten my stitches removed. When he asked about my current ailment, I suddenly got sheepish. At first, I used the same routine I had with Laura on the bus.

"Me duele la espalda," I said. He asked where on my back it hurt, and I explained circuitously that it was very low on my back. Once said, however, I decided I was being stupid. How can Dr. Zalles figure out what's wrong with me if I don't tell the truth? Then I realized that I had no idea how to say butt in Spanish, except for *culo,* which is slang for "ass" and gets bleeped on the Latin music stations in the States. I decided it would be more respectful to moon Dr. Zalles than swear at him. I dropped my pants and hopped on the table, cheeks to the ceiling.

After inspecting my tush, he admitted he didn't know exactly what was wrong. He too saw nothing that looked particularly out of the ordinary. The only manifestation of my pain was a small bump at the top of my butt. He promised it wasn't a bug egg and wrote me a prescription for a strong painkiller (that only cost $3.45!). He told me to put a hot compress on the sore spot for thirty minutes twice a day and see if it would go away on its own. Since he had proven himself with his correct assessment of the toe-bug egg, I agreed to follow his orders.

Later that night, I lay down on my stomach and put a hot compress right on the sore spot. "Sweet Jesus!" I yelped. The weight of the compress pushing down on the spot was nearly unbearable.

The next morning when I woke up, I could barely walk. I told Consuelo my back was bothering me and asked if she could drive me to the clinic. When we got there, I tried to convince her that I'd be fine on my own, but she insisted on accompanying me inside. This time, I didn't even have to fake it with the receptionist. She took one look at me and ushered me straight into Dr. Zalles's office.

"*¿Qué pasó?*" He seemed obviously concerned at my inability to walk just twenty-four hours after he had last seen me.

I explained that his remedy was *not* working, and that the pain was much worse than before. I told him it felt different this morning: It was more of a stabbing pain than a dull ache. I assumed my position of humiliation—bare cheeks to the ceiling—so he could take another look.

Then Dr. Zalles did the unthinkable. He asked his nurse to come in, and she did . . . with three other doctors . . . and even the crabby receptionist! Clearly, he needed a second (or fifth) opinion, but it was more of an audience than I wanted for my exposed buns. As a quartet of Spanish-speaking doctors argued over my tush, I was happy at least not to have to look them in the eye. Is it solely an American practice, I wondered, to refrain from showing your patient's ass cheeks to other doctors without her permission?

"*¡Ayyyy! ¡Díos mío!*" exclaimed one of the doctors. "*¿Qué es?*" another one asked.

As each reacted with revulsion and disbelief, I started to freak. As alarming as it had been to discover the mystery bump on my toe, it was far more unsettling to *not* see the source of my butt pain, which was, apparently, hideous. Adding to my embarrassment, Consuelo heard the commotion and came in, too, and cried out in horror.

Dr. Zalles and the other three doctors decided it was some sort of a boil. Not exactly a glamorous affliction. They thought it could have been caused by my two ten-hour bus rides. Their diagnosis explained the excruciating pain I'd experienced with the hot water bottle and my inability to walk in the morning. According to Dr. Zalles, putting heat on a boil opens it up so it can drain on its own. Mine, however, was in an inconvenient spot. The doctor had to lance it.

"This won't hurt a bit!" he assured me in Spanish. This time he was lying. Forget childbirth—get a butt boil lanced in an Ecuadorian clinic if you want to feel some real pain. Consuelo soothed me as I gripped her hand to keep from screaming.

When Dr. Zalles was finished, he instructed me to keep the area clean and wash it with mild soap twice a day. The only problem with Dr. Zalles's recommendation was that I was supposed to accompany Courtney and some friends to Baños, a rustic village perched high in the Andes, for the annual Nuestra Señora de Agua Santa festival. Baños has lots to offer in the way of natural wonders—hot springs and an active volcano—but I doubted I'd find any creature comforts like a shower at my two-dollar-a-night hostel.

That night, as I packed for the weekend, I tried to figure out how I could possibly follow Dr. Zalles's instructions in Baños. Luckily, Consuelo had an idea. She went into the kitchen and came back with a stainless steel mixing bowl that, just a month ago, I had used to teach my new little sisters how to make chocolate-chip cookies. Consuelo instructed, *"Aquí, hija, tome este plato hondo. Puedes utilizarlo para lavar su fondo si no hay ducha."* I would definitely use the bowl if there was no shower. Unfortunately, it wouldn't fit in my backpack, and I had to secure it to the top with a bungee cord.

"Are you serious?" Courtney exclaimed when I called her with the news. "You got a boil on your butt?"

"I have to carry around this big bowl so I can wash my butt if there isn't a shower in our hostel," I said, humiliated. "What am I going to tell everyone?"

"Maybe you can tell them that you like a really big bowl of cereal in the mornings," she said helpfully. "Or that you brought it so you can take some of the mineral water from the hot springs home with you."

The next morning, five of us assembled at Quito's downtown bus station. I prayed no one would notice the adornment on my pack, but it was hard to miss. "Hey, Beth, what's up with the bowl?" asked Kurt, one of the friends I had gone to Atacames with several months before.

"You know how they sometimes don't have showers at hostels? Well, I want to be able to, um, wash my hair."

"Couldn't you just use the sink?" he said. Courtney tried not to smile.

AS A FOREIGNER, I was used to getting a lot of attention. It was impossible to blend in with my fair skin and light hair—especially in rural towns, like Baños, where there's a large indigenous population. During other trips to Andean towns, I had even been stopped by locals who wanted to touch my hair. I had grown accustomed to being hissed at (the equivalent of a wolf whistle) by Ecuadorian men and good at ignoring shouts of *"¡Rubia! ¡Rubia!"* (Blondie! Blondie!). But in Baños, wherever I went, they called, *"¡Oye, chica con el plato hondo!"* (Hey, girl with the bowl!) It was an original catcall, at least.

And besides, the bowl turned out to be a very good thing. The bathroom in our dirty hostel was about the size of the tiny bus bathroom where I had first looked at my rear in the mirror. And, just as expected, it had no shower. So twice a day, I crammed myself into the tiny bathroom with my bowl, some gauze Dr. Zalles had given me, and a bar of Dove soap. "Happy butt washing!" Courtney would call out when she saw me gathering my gear.

I'd never before understood the need for a bidet. In Baños, I would have killed for one.

Fortunately, nothing kept me from enjoying the trip. On Saturday night, Courtney and I and our friends mounted a double-decker bus, called a *chiva,* for a nighttime trip up Tungurahua volcano. Although the volcano was technically active, locals told us it had been for years and recommended we take a trip to the top for an unforgettable view. It was freezing outside and pouring rain. We stayed warm by sipping *canelazo,* a tasty beverage that some of the other bus riders had brought with them. It's a sweet Andean drink that tastes like a hot toddy, prepared by boiling water and adding sugarcane alcohol, lemon, sugar, and cinnamon. Two of those, and I forgot all about my butt boil. When we got to the top, we saw smoke billowing out of the tip of the volcano and ribbons of fluorescent orange lava jumping in the sky. I had never seen anything like it. The next day, we soaked in the hot springs, and I even sampled the local specialty: guinea pig.

THREE WEEKS LATER, my butt was entirely healed, and it was time to say *adiós* to Ecuador. When I returned to Montana, I stepped off the plane like any traveler coming home—excited to be back but disappointed to see the adventure end. And my backpack was bursting with souvenirs. I brought back paintings and pottery by local artists in Cuenca, handmade ponchos and scarves from Baños, and turquoise pendants and silver rings from craft stalls in downtown Quito. The two souvenirs *not* on every gringa's list? A lopsided middle toe and a sore derrière. Oh, and a lifelong commitment to travel insurance.

Heading South

Samantha Schoech

• • • • • • • • • • • • • • • • • • •

It's another Taco Tuesday at the Baja Cantina, and in addition to slogging Coronas and shots of Cuervo to a bunch of smug twenty-two-years-olds, I am being scowled at from the line, where Fernando, the cook I have just decided to stop sleeping with, is giving me the evil eye.

It's 1996, I am fresh out of graduate school and still reeling from the collapse of a four-year relationship that my fling with Fernando has done nothing to diminish. I'm working as a waitress in a part of San Francisco known as the Herpes Triangle. My coping mechanism involves a lot of margaritas and a few late-night sobbing phone calls to the ex, who lives three states away. It is not my proudest moment.

But this is all about to change. I am returning to Mexico—to the town where I spent much of my childhood—for a much-needed vacation, and this, I am convinced, will fix everything. The Cantina won't give me the time off, so the day before my departure I quit, say a final adios to Fernando, and don't look back. Those losers can keep their enchilada specials and their sticky strawberry daiquiris; I am going to the real thing. No more happy birthday sombrero bullshit for me.

In the glow of that warm tropical light, under the rustle of swaying palm trees, I will be revived. I will get over the ex, live cleanly, and prepare myself for the dazzling future that surely awaits anyone with a master's degree in English and an encyclopedic knowledge of tequila. Even my mother, with whom I will be staying, thinks it's a good idea. So on the Wednesday after my very last Taco Tuesday ever, I pack my bags—tank tops, pareos, flip-flops—and leave gloomy, noirish San Francisco for the warm, effervescent shores of Puerto Vallarta, where the Pacific Ocean will cure what ails me and wash away my sins. I will come home tanned, happy, and full of renewed career ambitions that have nothing to do with chimichangas.

THE PROBLEM WITH visiting my mother in a tropical paradise is that she lives there. This means that while I had envisioned sunsets and piña coladas, what I get are trips to the cable company where I stand in line with her while she waits to pay her bill. I go with her to Sam's Club to stock up on American batteries and Fruit of the Loom underwear. I take loud, stinky buses through industrial neighborhoods where skinny dogs sniff at piles of garbage. At night we watch Mexican TV. Except for the talavera tile, the telenovelas, and the traveling knife sharpener, who sings his services from the street each evening, we could be in Fresno or Salt Lake City or St. Louis.

After she goes to bed, I sit on the balcony mooning over my ex and tormenting myself with images of him in the arms of the massage therapist he started dating a mere ten days after we broke up. The lights of Puerto Vallarta twinkle and mock me and my pathetic, solitary vacation. A few bars of "Feelin' Hot, Hot, Hot" carry through the night.

I comfort myself with the fact that this is still vastly superior to replenishing trays of jalapeño poppers for the hordes of happy-hour yahoos in the Herpes Triangle, and with the knowledge that tomorrow I will leave Vallarta and all of its gaudy vacation trappings to catch the boat to Yelapa, where there is no electricity and no cars. Yelapa, where I spent fourth grade, and where every turn in the dirt path reminds me of childhood, of riding bareback upriver or of collecting empty Coke bottles for the five pesos they would fetch at Ana's. This is where my real renewal will begin, where the new me will emerge like a chrysalis. In Yelapa, the place I go to in my mind when I can't sleep, even the texture of the air—soft, salty feathers— makes me feel beautiful.

But first I will have just two fingers of tequila, just to, you know, take the edge off. I will sit on the balcony and enjoy the view. I will sip my drink and forget about the ex and his massage therapist. I will listen to the mingling of car horns and club music and the occasional joyous shout drifting up the ravine. I will relax and get into the rhythm of Mexico.

BY MIDNIGHT, THE two fingers of tequila have multiplied alarmingly. I have successfully opened the wound of my breakup, exposing it for the bloody mess it is. The lights of Vallarta pulse and blur below me. I pick up the phone.

As soon as I hear his voice, I start to cry. "Hello," I snivel. "I just wish, you know, that we could, oh God . . . this is so hard. How could you? What does she have? I just . . ." I can hear myself, but I can't make myself shut up. It's like an out-of-body experience. I am flying overhead, above the balcony and the lights of Vallarta, watching helplessly as I transform into the whining embodiment of every man's worst nightmare.

The next thing I know, it's bright outside, and I have ten minutes to get down to the pier and catch my boat to Yelapa. The tequila is punishing me: My mouth tastes like the floor of a bar, and my stomach lurches as snippets of the previous night's conversation float to the surface of my memory like bodies dumped in a river. My cheeks burn with shame. I gather what's left of my dignity and board the boat. Puerto Vallarta recedes behind us as we zoom out on the ocean. As the wind cools my face, I feel as if I am leaving the scene of my final heinous crime.

YELAPA BAY IS the shape of a bent horseshoe, and I feel better the minute the boat swings into it and heads toward the strip of steep white sand. I love this place. It is both familiar and exotic, filled with Mexican villagers and whacked-out expats who generally smoke a lot of pot. Though I have been coming here for twenty-five years, it still takes my breath away every time.

Some things have changed since I was little: They no longer slaughter pigs once a week by the side of the path near the pool hall; they get pork from Vallarta, wrapped in plastic. You don't have to boil your own drinking water anymore; it, too, comes in from Vallarta. Despite the fact that there is still no electricity, more people have TVs and VCRs, which they run off car batteries and play at maximum volume. There is a phone booth now, and a clinic, and a high school. But mostly things stay the same. Kids still gather every evening at the *cancha* to play basketball and flirt. The Yelapa Yacht Club, a cinder-block frame with a tin roof, still has a disco every Saturday night, and the same crazy old gringos still show up and do the hippie shuffle to Gloria Gaynor. The roosters and the dogs still start at dawn. And Diego, with his big mouth and his brown limbs, still loves me.

Like Yelapa itself, Diego is something I hold in my mind when everything else seems like shit. When I am lonely and awful, I comfort myself with the thought that in a small village in Mexico there is an undereducated married man with slightly buck teeth and a goatish mole who will always love me. It's not much, but there have been moments when this has been a tremendous help.

I run into him almost immediately. He's walking down the path, eating strawberry yogurt, and when we see one another, we both grin. Diego has loved me since I was ten years old. I sometimes believe that no man will ever love me like he does. He has written me love letters in impossible-to-understand Spanglish. He has called me and courted me and visited me in San Francisco. When I was seventeen, he took me out on the most spectacular date of my life, which was only slightly tarnished by the fact that he wore a *Saturday Night Fever* suit—white polyester (with vest) over a black shirt opened low enough to display an impressive collection of gold chains and Jesus medallions. We have kissed once, against the side of a building at the end of the spectacular date about ten years ago.

The fact that Diego is now married and the father of a beautiful little girl doesn't stop him from declaring his love for me each year when I show up in Yelapa. It does not stop him from asking me out and trying to plan a clandestine rendezvous with me in Puerto Vallarta, away from the suspicious gaze of his wife, a girl I have known since she was about three. A girl I have wronged a million times in my mind but never in real life.

We stop on the path and lean against an old stone wall. He continues licking the plastic spoon and grinning, a combination that produces a clear view of his yogurt-covered tongue and gold-filled teeth. My heart pounds a little. I am hugely glad to see him, and as we chitchat—how long am I staying, where is my boyfriend from last year, do I remember our date—I feel even better. It is not the yearned-for peace of mind I am getting. What I get from him is better: the pleasant, nervous buzz of an attraction. I tilt my face toward the sun and bask in his attentions. So I drank a cup and a half of tequila last night? So I made a fool of myself on the phone? So up until a few days ago, I was best described a slutty waitress with a moldering degree in English? At least Diego thinks I'm cool. He looks me up and down appreciatively, and I realize instantly that it is not Mexico that will make it all better, it is Diego.

We talk a bit more and then part before someone sees us. This is a place thick with gossip and grudges. Smile at the wrong man, and you may find yourself on the sorry end of a vendetta that will outlive your children.

I DON'T SEE DIEGO again, except from afar, until the day before I leave. He is busy working on his boat, taking tourists and locals back and forth between Yelapa and Vallarta. I spend my time lying on the beach and eating great quantities of rice and beans and guacamole and tortillas. I write in my journal. I go to the Yacht Club and hop around with the expats. I stroll along the sand at sunset. I relive the humiliating conversation with the ex-boyfriend (what little I can remember of it) and castigate myself. But mostly I fantasize about Diego, imagine that he might be watching me, that I might run into him in a dark corner of the path. By the end of seven days, I am dying to see him. I long for the respite of his attentions.

Which is why, when he approaches me on the beach and asks me to go out with him on my last night in Vallarta, I readily agree. He will stay over at his family's apartment, and we will go out. On a *date*. I say yes, despite the fact that this is a bad idea and that I know his wife and daughter. I say yes because this night with Diego seems like the inevitable conclusion of a nearly twenty-year crush and I am in Mexico and I am lonely and it now seems clear that the ex-boyfriend and I will never speak again. I say yes with a reckless, self-destructive urge. I am starting to suspect I enjoy making a mess of things.

BY THE NEXT evening, the magic of Yelapa is already being worn away. Puerto Vallarta is so noisy and hectic and choked with smog after Yelapa. It's a real bubble-burster of a town. Tomorrow I will return to California, where I will have to pay my rent and find a job and go about the business of getting a real boyfriend. Diego no longer shields me from these looming realities, and I await our meeting with a growing sense of apprehension. What was I thinking? He's married. He's macho. He's not at all what I'm looking for.

But when the sun finally goes down on my last night in Mexico, I put on a little eye makeup and meet him at the pier. I am still willing to be swept away.

We walk along the *malecón,* in the footsteps of a million lovers before us, and end up in some overpriced restaurant with creepily solicitous waiters and a strolling mariachi band. We begin awkward, halting conversations full of language barriers and misunderstandings. We play with our cutlery and smooth our napkins on our laps. Diego twists in his seat to admire the ocean view over his shoulder. I order a margarita because I have apparently failed to learn anything from my last experience with tequila, and because it is immediately clear that I am going to need to be a little tipsy to get through this night. He orders a glass of milk, maybe the least sexy choice of beverages available. The spark has gone out, and now that we are actually together it feels like having dinner with a distant cousin you haven't seen since the sandbox days.

I attempt to salvage the evening and my ego by flirting. I look at him over the salted rim of my glass and smile. "I've been waiting for this night," I say. And, "I'm glad we can finally be alone." I'm being cheesy in the extreme, but it's all I can manage. And he's not helping matters. In place of my grinning suitor is a distracted married man whose hair could use a good washing. He grimly digs into his rabbit *pibil,* holding his fork in a fist and hunching over his plate. His eyes flit around nervously, as if he is expecting at any moment to be found out. I order another margarita and continue my bad porn lines. "The air feels so sexy against my bare skin," I say, rubbing my shoulder. I am totally grossing myself out.

By the time dinner is over, this date has an inevitable feeling about it. Gone is our easy, playful relationship, and in its place is a grim march toward fate. Diego and I are going to finish what we started ten years ago, whether we like it or not. This is confirmed when, in the cab, he sits across from me in the back seat and says, "I need to know if you are going to sleep with me tonight, because if not . . ." he yawns, "I think I will go home early." I gape at him, blinking. Weaving in and out of the chaotic traffic, we are on our way to see *A Time to Kill* with Sandra Bullock. I laugh and playfully slap his leg. But he is not kidding. We are getting close to the theater, and he wants an answer. "I have the apartment to myself tonight," he says, as if my only hesitation were logistical. My mouth opens and shuts like a grouper's. Where is the renowned Latin romanticism? No language is better than Spanish for sweet nothings—*mi amor, mi vida, mi cielo*—and I was sort of hoping to be on the receiving end of a few of them. I am not naive; the thought that I would finally end up sleeping with Diego on this night did occur to me. But what I was looking forward to was not the act itself but the feeling of being helplessly swept up in the act. I wanted to be seduced, to surrender.

It was *Mexico,* I would tell myself by way of explanation. The warm nights, the romantic music, the language—*of course* I succumbed. But no. Instead, I am being romanced with all the finesse of a real estate transaction. It's about as passionate as standing in line at the cable company with my mother.

Outside the windows of the cab, groups of sunburned tourists walk slowly down the sidewalk, simultaneously wide-eyed and oblivious. I watch an old man with white knee socks buy a tamale from the lady on the corner while his wife crosses her arms and scowls.

Then I do an amazing thing. I say, "Sure," as if someone has just asked to borrow a stamp. "Good," Diego says before leaning forward and asking the cabbie to pull over in front of a convenience store.

He is gone only a few minutes, but it is enough time for me to twist his pathetic seduction into a helpless display of clumsy charm. He is flustered by the possibility of finally being with me, I decide. He is so turned on by me, he is beyond normal conversation. I smile. He may not have the smooth moves I was expecting, but no one can fault me for falling for that boyish eagerness.

He comes back to the cab with a few foil-wrapped condoms and a pack of spearmint Chiclets, and we continue on toward the movie theater. He is decidedly cheerier, now that he knows what's in store.

I hate the smell of spearmint. It reminds me of the dentist's office. When chewed too long, it starts to smell like metal and cabbage. As we sit and watch Sandra Bullock flounce and scowl, I listen to the sound of Diego smacking his gum and smell the wafting scent of spearmint. I stare straight ahead and try to muster some of my former enthusiasm for Diego's brown forearms. At some point my hand creeps over to his, begging to be held. Instead he lays a grandfatherly hand upon my arm and continues his chewing. He thinks this movie is riveting.

MEXICAN HOUSES generally do not have closets. People hang their clothes over nails or hooks coming straight out of the wall. Diego's apartment, a nefarious pied-à-terre he shares with his brothers and father, is almost completely decorated in clothes. Yellow golf shirts and pressed jeans and polyester suit jackets hang flat against the wall like tapestries. Diego takes my hand and leads me directly into the bedroom, which is dominated by a huge bed covered with a fuzzy blanket emblazoned with a snarling tiger's head. A beach towel bearing the likeness of the Virgin of Guadalupe hangs above the bed. This is our love nest, and our sins are about to be witnessed by the holy mother of God and a very angry tiger.

At first the cabbage smell of his gum overwhelms me, but then we roll onto the bed, and he kisses me. After a little warm-up, I forget about the grim setting and the awkward date and the wad of gum he's been chewing for three hours and manage to focus my attentions on the task at hand. He is not ungenerous and makes rather a big deal out of heading south. It's not great, but it's not completely awful. Mostly it's blurry and quick.

When it is over we stand up, put our clothes on, and go outside to hail me a cab. I am more than ready to go home, first to my mother's apartment and then, tomorrow, to San Francisco, where this night can be chalked up to that strange vacation logic in which everything is a whim or an adventure or a joke.

I LET MYSELF into the apartment quietly—my mother would disapprove—and go to the bathroom. I want a warm shower before bed; some soap and sleep are all I need.

I am lathering away any traces of Diego in a great spume of soap suds when my fingers pass over something unfamiliar. I feel it again, a big lumpy knob attached to my, um, delicates. It's obvious to me that it is one of two things: vagina cancer or a record-breaking labial wart. I imagine photographs of my genitalia in medical textbooks next to that guy in South Africa with elephantitis of the nuts. I tug gently on the lump. It pulls but doesn't budge. My heart is really going now. I cannot afford a strange gynecological condition; I don't even have health insurance. I wonder if I could get treatment in exchange for appearing in the textbooks, but I hate the idea of medical students making fun of my misfortune.

I turn off the water and sit on the edge of tub. Be brave, I tell myself, as I fold over and peer into my dimly lit crotch. I locate the lump with my fingers and then seek it out with my eyes. At first I can't make it out, but then the identity of the lump becomes breathtakingly clear. I am both relieved and horrified. Nestled contentedly in a tangle of pubic hair is Diego's spearmint gum.

My head whips around frantically. Who else knows about this? But the bathroom in my mother's apartment is mercifully empty at one in the morning. I tug again at the gum but stop when my entire vulva threatens to come away with it. I think of peanut butter or ice, the remedies my mother used when I got gum in my hair as a child. I can't do it. Spreading peanut butter on my delicates at my mother's house in the wee hours of the morning is a humiliation I still consider myself above.

I scrabble around in the medicine cabinet and find some fingernail scissors that I use to free the offending wad. Then I hold it in my hand, gaping at the lump of chewed spearmint gum sprouting a pelt of wiry hairs. Did he know? Was Diego at this very moment desperately pawing through the rumpled tiger blanket in search of his missing gum? Does he think he swallowed it? Is he embarrassed by his carelessness, or is he resting easy, knowing the gum is in a safe place, hidden out of harm's way?

I wad it up in some toilet paper like a hairy bug and flush it down the toilet. Then I dry off, slip on an old t-shirt, and climb into the chaste twin bed in my mother's guest room. I lie there, trying to imagine being the kind of girl I want to be, not one who works as a waitress and cries pitifully to an ex-boyfriend who has clearly moved on. Not a girl who spends her vacation shopping for necessities with her mother or mooning over the imagined fun of others. Certainly not one who has sex in grimy Mexican apartments of ill repute or finds used chewing gum attached to her vagina. The girl I think about wears a fluttery sundress and says the right thing. Her work is noble and free of refried beans. She elicits unasked for sweet nothings and handholdings. She has neither the need to flee nor the urge to scurry home. As I lie there on the edge of sleep, the girl comes into vivid focus and then fades. She is like the perfect, restorative Mexico of my dreams—beautiful, idealized, and utterly imagined.

Knocked off My High Horse in New Zealand

Catherine Giayvia

. . . .

I spent a few days in New Zealand wandering the streets of Auckland in a jet-lagged daze, dutifully reminding myself of my true purpose: to get out of the city and explore the countryside. All too easily, though, I slipped into a familiar pattern of window-shopping and café-hopping. Deep down, I knew I hadn't traveled all this way to do what I could do at home in Baltimore. On the cusp of turning thirty, I had decided I needed to shake things up in my safe, uncomplicated life; thus, New Zealand became the first scheduled stop on a six-month backpacking junket around the Pacific.

In preparation for this ultimate break from routine, I had spent the entire previous year devouring guidebooks filled with photos of sweeping vistas and breathtaking landscapes. New Zealand, renowned as home of the bungee jump, rugged terrain, and Hobbits, had struck me as an ideal jumping-off point for my half year of adventure. Finally away from my predictable world of rush-hour commutes and cocktail parties, I imagined myself roaming freely through the country's hills and valleys.

But staying in Auckland would bring me no such great adventure, so I tore myself away from its urban comforts and boarded a bus for the rural countryside of the North Island.

From my window seat, I drank in the views of verdant, rolling countryside, green hills dotted with sheep, and roadsides sprouting with white and pink wildflowers under sapphire South Pacific skies: The excitement I craved would soon be within reach. The other backpackers on the bus buzzed with excitement, and I fantasized wildly about learning to skydive, kayak, and mountain bike. In the moment, it didn't matter that I had never done these things at home, where adventure for me was bringing home a comedy *and* a drama from the video store, and where pushing the limits meant testing the boundaries of the office dress code. Not to mention that I was hardly an athlete; I routinely missed buses because I didn't want to *run* to catch one. But things were different here—I had come a long way to reach this adventure mecca, and I meant to make the most of it.

I unglued myself from the beautiful scenery framed by the bus window to flip through brochures for white-water rafting, bungee jumping, and horse trekking through the hills and started eliminating my options one by one. Diving from a bridge and swinging around like a sack of potatoes didn't appeal. And white-water rafting seemed not only dangerous, but really, really cold. Now, horseback riding—that seemed reasonable as an introductory adventure. Besides, I'd been horseback riding a few times as a teenager. I imagined myself blazing a trail through the jade-green headlands I'd been admiring from my bus window. I was in New Zealand, and therefore, I was sporty and adventurous! I was not content to sit idly on some bus!

Unfortunately, the docile old ponies I had ridden in high school were my main frame of reference—plodding, steady, happy to follow along in a train of horses, ambling nose to tail. I might have suspected something was amiss when I arrived at the corral the next morning to saddle up. I wondered where the trail ponies were kept as I sized up the towering equines roped around the perimeter of the corral.

Our trekking guide, a blond and athletic-looking Kiwi woman named Buffy, grinned and said, "Now, who here has got some riding experience?"

The other riders shifted from foot to foot, mute.

I raised my hand, tentatively, still anticipating the appearance of ponies.

"Ah, good on you, mate," grinned Buffy, approvingly. "We'll put you on Mick." She gestured proudly to a colossal bay horse on the far side of the ring. And this is where things started to go wrong. My ego took control of my brain and my fate. "I get the big horse. I'm the only one here that can handle it!" I smugly thought to myself, flush with conceit. Mick stared down his nose at me. The top of my head was barely level with his shoulders. I blithely dismissed a momentary misgiving and stepped forward.

After a few hoists from Buffy, I was sitting high astride big Mick, surveying the rest of the group getting paired up with comparatively smaller and daintier horses. "Say, fella," I said soothingly to the horse beneath me, "nice to meet you. Hope you're up for a good ride this morning."

Mick's ears twitched ambiguously.

Even though my perch felt rather precarious, I now had no feelings of foreboding. In fact, I fancied myself a modern Dale Evans, first in the saddle and ready to lead the way to happy, scenic trails. Buffy passed out helmets, and one by one, horses and riders ambled out of the corral.

Mick agreeably set out after the horse just to the right of him. A younger girl I had met on the bus was astride. It was her first time riding, and she cast a nervous look over her shoulder. I gave her an encouraging thumbs-up as if to say, *No worries, this is just a pleasant little trail ride.*

Our horses hoofed along the gravel country lane outside of the corral, which Buffy told us would lead to the actual trailhead. As we plodded forward, I fell into the easy rhythm of riding a horse on a warm, sunny day.

The New Zealand sun beat down on my bare shoulders, and I straightened my back and pointed my heels downward in the stirrups. I sat back in the saddle and enjoyed the scenery: a sweeping vista of a deep green valley, lush with pastureland and struck through with a crystal-clear river. Beautiful! I had made the right choice! This was grand, and neither dangerous nor wet nor cold. And that's when Mick stopped dead in his tracks. I looked down and saw his ears flick back and forth, like a cat switching its tail in displeasure.

"What's up, boy?" I cooed.

Mick's source of consternation rolled around a bend in the road a few seconds later: He'd heard the car coming before the rest of us did. It rattled by, kicking up some dust in its wake.

Mick stamped a hoof petulantly, shifting his massive horse bulk from side to side, and finally decided it was okay to keep walking.

"Good boy," I assured him in soothing tones. "Good gigantic horse. No need to worry about a tiny little car."

I hoped that we were close to the trailhead.

We had only gone a few steps when another car swerved around the bend ahead of us. Mick, seemingly taken by surprise this time, sidestepped a bit, thumping his burly neck into the flank of the horse ahead of us.

"Steady there," I muttered as both horses shook the ground with their stomps.

I gave the reins a gentle tug to pull Mick to a stop. I considered calling ahead to Buffy, who was still in sight, to explain that maybe Mick wasn't the right horse for me. I spent a few moments planning how I might voice my sudden dissatisfaction with Mick without harming my expert rider status. "Say, Buffy," I'd call, "Can we take a break? Mick's acting up a bit. Maybe you can reason with him?" I mulled this over, my intuition urging me to get off the horse. As I played out various scenarios in my head, I heard an alarming rumble approaching—and approaching quickly. I looked for Buffy, ready to cry out to her, but—too late!—she had already disappeared around the bend in the road. Just then, a hissing, grinding yellow tractor lurched into view, expelling plumes of smoke and coughing up a cloud of dust and gravel in its wake.

"Well," I thought to myself, "Mick certainly isn't going to like this."

I glanced down and saw his ears flattened against the top of his head and sensed a sudden stillness, like time stopping. Adrenaline surged through my system, and my heart beat faster—I knew this meant trouble. Mick had stopped walking and stood frozen in the road as if cast in bronze. A voice in my head warned me to find purchase and hold on for my life as my fingers slipped on the reins and scrabbled with the underside of the saddle. Then, in a lightning-quick move, Mick reared up and flung us a full 180 degrees in the opposite direction. I envisioned the Lone Ranger comfortably astride a rampant Silver—"Maybe I can pull this off," I thought desperately—but instantly understood that there was no way I could control this beast.

I felt my legs losing their grip around Mick's bucking body, and that was that: Mick made falling off easy by simply throwing himself to one side. I obligingly slid off the other, slamming into the ground with my right shoulder.

My relief at being off the possessed beast overrode the shock and pain of the fall. I lay still for just a second, eyes closed and heart beating fast, promising myself that the worst was over. And in the next moment, I realized in horror that Mick hadn't simply run away. He was dancing around wildly in the same spot, just an arm's length from where I had hit the ground. The sound of horse hooves pounding the road and my helmet scuffing the gravel as I tried in vain to slither away was pierced by a high, keening sound, like a siren. "That's *really* annoying," I thought, curling into a fetal position as Mick made another pass over me. Then I realized that the siren sound was coming from me—I was screaming, in the way of ladies trapped on step stools by rodents. And that's when I knew things were bad. I sensed a flurry of motion around me. Many horse bodies moved in different directions, dirt stirred around my face, and Mick's body blotted out the sun and cast my cowering body in shade for an endless moment. And then I rolled onto my back and squinted up at the faces looming over me. Rocks poked me through the back of my tank top.

"Ow," I moaned feebly.

Buffy leaned close over me. "You've had a fall," she said by way of explanation. "Would you like to try again?" I blinked up at her, speechless. "Would you like to get back on the horse?" she repeated.

I was certain that I had suffered some sort of hallucination-producing head trauma. Had this über-Kiwi really suggested that I remount a horse that had just tried to trample me? She smiled winningly, as if nothing unusual had happened.

"No!" I choked through the dirt and grit in my teeth. No more equine colossus for me, thank you very much. This adventure is over, I thought. I felt woozy and faint. Did no one care that I might have a concussion? I prayed that someone had dialed 911. Surely someone had a cell phone. From the stunned looks I saw on the faces of my fellow riders, I gathered that no one had leapt to action. Buffy encouraged me to try to sit up and check myself over.

Another car came along, and the driver pulled over to see if he could help.

I caught sight of the girl who was having her first horse ride today. She was crying. There was no sign of the phantom tractor or Mick, who had finally wised up and taken off across the fields.

I was dizzy, shaken, and sore, but miraculously, I seemed to be physically intact. I scanned my ankles and shins for broken skin and protruding bones. Nothing. No pools of blood. Good. The reality of what had happened washed over me in a scary wave. Big horse. Out of control. Me hurt and far away from home. I looked over my knees and my hips. Buffy prodded my back to see if anything seemed amiss. I drew my eyes along my arms, over my wrists, and down each finger. Everything seemed fine . . . a little blood rimmed the nail on that left pinky . . . and oh. . . .

And here, everything went all white and tunnel-visiony for me. My left ring finger was bent at a sharp ninety-degree angle at the top joint, in a very, very wrong direction. "That," I muttered, before passing out, "is all fucked up."

The stranger who had arrived on the scene minutes before caught me in his arms as I fainted dead away. I came to almost immediately and was suddenly very unhappy about being there. I wanted medical attention. I could hardly believe that an emergency rescue helicopter hadn't come to rescue me. A burning pain started to throb in a few key areas on my body, and tears welled in my eyes. I was about to learn an important lesson about small-town life and the way things are done in New Zealand.

"I can drive her over to your mum's place, love." Through my haze, I heard the stranger and Buffy discussing what to do with me. What? I was confused. I wanted to shout, "Why take me there? Take me to the emergency room, like the sensible people I know you are!"

The glorious New Zealand landscape swam before my eyes as I staggered to my feet. I felt like I might vomit. I wanted to lie down again as soon as my legs were under me, but neither of them would let me. The stranger led me to his makeshift ambulance—a bright orange Pacer—and we zipped away. I didn't know where he was taking me, and I didn't care. I was glad to be leaving Buffy, skittish horses, and life-endangering farm equipment behind.

After ten minutes of squealing tires and veering around sharp bends in the road, we pulled into the driveway of a modest house. A stout woman with black hair and thick glasses, wearing a red fuzzy bathrobe, appeared at the door. "Morning, Angela," yelled the stranger, coming around to help me out. "Backpacker here fell off one of your horses."

"Oh yeah?" Angela eyed me suspiciously. "Which horse'dja fall off?" I felt the need to explain how technically I didn't fall. I was thrown. There's a big difference. To say that I'd fallen suggested that it was my fault, that I was inept in some way—and clearly this was not the case.

"Mick," I mumbled, staggering towards her house. "Big, big horse."

"Oh?" she said, doubt evident in her tone. "We don't *have* a horse named Mick."

"Nope, no Mick that I can remember," seconded the stranger, smiling at me apologetically and ducking back into his car.

I was left alone with Angela. I explained that I needed a ride to the town doctor, and that I felt horribly woozy. By way of demonstration, I ungraciously pushed my way past her and into her kitchen. I collapsed into a chair and propped myself up on her kitchen table. The table was strewn with frosted flakes. In the room beyond, a couple of kids in footed pajamas watched Sunday morning cartoons. I planted my forehead on the cheery yellow table, no longer able to hold myself up.

"I'll just get dressed," said Angela curtly. She seemed understandably annoyed by my intrusion, but I no longer cared. My head was spinning, and I felt like it might separate from my body and float away. As soon as the bedroom door closed behind her, I slid off my chair and lay flat on the cool linoleum, crunching a few stray frosted flakes on my way down.

It felt cool and still down on the floor. I lay spread eagled, eyes closed, saying silent prayers of thanks that I was once again reunited with a still, flat place where there was minimal dizziness and no danger of falling. I was down as far as I was going to get, or so I thought. I wondered miserably to myself how I had gone from riding the most beautiful horse on the most beautiful morning to lying pitifully on a kitchen floor covered with cereal.

I heard a faint scuffle beside my left ear. Angela's two youngsters stood over me, peering down with a mix of suspicion and curiosity. "What are you doing here?" asked one. "Do you want to watch telly?" invited the other.

I groaned and closed my eyes. Now was not the time to pander to Kiwi tykes. Angela reappeared, looming above all of us, sporting cowboy boots and tight jeans. She shooed the kids away and lent me a hand.

"I think I might throw up," I confided, feeling my stomach lurch and my head start to spin again. Every time I accidentally nudged something with my twisted finger, the shakes started anew. "Well, best to wait before getting into the car, then," said Angela. "It's new."

Realizing that fear of soiling the car upholstery would further delay our trip, I put on a calm face and reassured her I was feeling better by the minute. She gave me a skeptical once-over and reluctantly opened the door to her hatchback. I piled in. My relief that we were finally on the way to the doctor's came out in a long, exhausted sigh. "Thank you so much for taking me to town," I gasped, rolling my head over to look at Angela, my eyes filled with sincerity and gratitude.

Angela glanced over, fiddling with the knobs on the radio. "We'll go straightaway," she replied.

I smiled. I felt so sleepy. I could easily take a quick nap on the way to town. Wake up feeling refreshed. The bright New Zealand sunshine started to burn away the edges of the windshield, washing the landscape away as if with a great paintbrush, dipped in bright white paint. I felt the dizziness overpower me again but minded it less because I was being transported to a place where qualified people would look after me, fix me up, and lend me a sympathetic ear. Angela was saying something, but I couldn't focus on her words. She spoke to me as if from the end of a long, echoing hallway. I mused about how people in movies who are about to lose consciousness are always dramatically slapped awake—for fear that they may never reawaken.

Words swirled up out of the blackness and emerged on my lips: "Don't let them fall asleep," I muttered, falling asleep.

"What?" Angela barked. "I was *saying*," she continued, unaware of the life-and-death struggle in her passenger seat, "that I need to stop by the farm to let my husband know I'm leaving the kids alone."

"And how far away is that?" I tried to make my voice grateful, understanding, even.

"About a half hour," she said.

"Toward town?" I was still hopeful.

"Other way," she replied curtly.

AT THE FAMILY FARM, Angela maneuvered the car alongside a corral full of fluffy white sheep and one man in rubber knee boots. She rolled down her window and leaned out, calling into the wind that she had to leave the children to take this unfortunate backpacker to the town doctor. She expressed it as if she had said, "I have to go pick up a dozen eggs," as if it were an everyday errand of little import.

I pressed my cheek against the passenger side window, feeling forsaken. I thought I heard the man in the boots and the sheep yell something in reply. I wanted to believe he said, "Will she be okay?" or "Would she like a glass of water?" Any scrap of concern or sympathy would have done at that point. The wind was blowing, so perhaps his real words were lost, but what I actually heard was, "What's for dinner?"

An hour later, we were finally headed toward town. I felt less shaken, possibly due to the promise that bona fide healthcare was on the way, and possibly because, two hours after the fact, I was in less of a state of shock.

At the doctor's office, I found myself in the hands of yet another hard-nosed Kiwi.

"What have you done to yourself?" Dr. Kelly demanded, brusquely.

"I fell off a horse," I grudgingly admitted, too defeated to explain what had *really* happened. He checked my back and prodded my lumbar region as I sat on a stool in the center of his examining room. A quick peek below the waistband at my posterior revealed that I'd developed some impressively lurid red and purple swellings.

"Hematomas," he explained. "You'll need some ice on those." He poked at the egglike protuberance erupting from my lower calf. "Might need some physio on this one." He scribbled a few notes on his clipboard. I sensed I was about to be dismissed.

"Um, about my finger," I said, holding it up without looking directly at the mangled digit. He stood over me and grasped my finger gently, manipulating it in a surprisingly pain-free way. I squirmed anyway and squinted my eyes so that I didn't have to see what he was doing. He secured my ring finger to my middle finger with surgical tape.

"This is called a buddy splint," he said. "You should be all right with this for now," he said with an air of finality.

"But is it broken?" I asked, wondering if this was all the care I was going to get. "How do you know it's not broken?"

"Well, I don't, really. Might be fractured, might be broken. If you want an x-ray, the x-ray machine comes through town once a week on Tuesdays."

It was Sunday. I tried to imagine staying another two nights in this godforsaken town. Sure, it was quaint, surrounded by breathtaking scenery, and everyone seemed to know everyone in a friendly, small-town way. It was just as I'd pictured life in the New Zealand countryside. But no one admitted to knowing my cantankerous equine—I was the outsider, and they were protecting their own. Clearly, this city girl would never receive a drop of sympathy from these Kiwis, toughened by life in their rugged, remote terrain. "Should I stay and ride it out?" I wondered. "No," I thought. "No way!"

That afternoon I was on a bus bound for the next big town—out of the country and back to the city life I had been so eager to escape—where I would lick my wounds, drink lattes, and seek out a sympathetic ear or two. I had been humbled by a horse, but I still had six months of adventuring to plan. Perhaps my luck with hang gliders would be better. As far as I knew, they came one size fits all.

The Lion Sleeps Tonight

Sarah Franklin

· · · · · · · · · · · · · · · · · · ·

Colin, our driver and guide in the South African outback, had pretty much guaranteed us an escape from death by stating categorically, ten minutes into that day's trip into the South African bush, that we wouldn't get to see a leopard.

My brand-new husband, Dave, and I did not feel as upset at the prospect of a wildlife-free safari as we perhaps should have been. After all, it was cocktail hour, twelve days into our honeymoon through Europe and Africa, and we had fine drinking company: six British honeymooners, none of us having guessed in advance that our choice of honeymoon was the current "unique" honeymoon destination fashionable in the U.K. Needless to say, champagne and great honeymoon sex (with our new spouses, not communally; we're British, after all) seemed more pressing than leopards. "Time for a sundowner?" I suggested.

Sundowners are an ex-colonial tradition, brought to Africa by borderline-alcoholic British military officers adept at finding any excuse for a snifter at sunset. The idea is simple. Find a good spot on a hillside, pour yourself a stiff gin and tonic, and watch the spectacular sunset slink over the horizon faster than you can say "loss of empire." Being honeymooners, and thus incapable of surviving without champagne in our bloodstreams, we had added two bottles of Bollinger to the stash. To accommodate us and provide the best view, Colin halted the truck on a ledge overlooking three hundred miles of African bush land and pointed it obligingly west.

"Anyone for biltong?" he asked, offering round the South African version of beef jerky. It didn't pay to be a snob about meat here; I'd learned to love biltong whether it was made of kudu, a huge moose-type animal, or as it was now, made of ostrich.

I inhaled the smoky scent of the meat as I chewed slowly, washing it down with a sip of bubbly. "Bolly and dried bird," I said. "Could life be any better?"

"Bugger," said Jack, a fellow honeymooner, wrestling the second champagne bottle to the ground. "I'm having real problems with the cork. And you'd have thought that I'd be an expert at this by now."

"Hey, Jack," said my husband, turning momentarily from the sunset he alone had been admiring and peering with concentration into the shadow behind the truck. "I don't think you need to worry about the champagne right now." Something in his tone made us all look up. "You know that elusive leopard? He's coming down the track towards us."

Colin had taught us some rules when we joined the safari two days previously:

1. Don't leave the truck in the presence of animals unless you are happy becoming part of the natural selection process.

2. Don't bait the animals or show them food.

3. And above all, don't run. If a predator sees prey in flight, its natural instincts are to catch it and kill it. "If I see you running," Colin had informed us, "I'll shoot you to stop you and save you from a far worse fate."

When Colin had delivered this advice, we had all nodded sagely—and tuned him out. We were all dewy eyed with anticipation at seeing little fluffy animals and fuzzy with the aforementioned honeymoon staples of sex and champagne. And after all, who really pays attention when flight attendants point out the emergency exits? Same thing in the bush, right?

While I was glad that my new husband was able to spot an animal in the middle of its hunt (more proof of his perfection), our lack of attention to the lecture became suddenly and dreadfully clear. With an actual, live animal bearing down on us, this is what we did:

1. Flung the biltong basket into the air and scattered small pieces of dried ostrich in our path, thoughtfully providing an appetizer for the leopard.

2. Ran like hell to the truck, whose comforting presence we had no idea why we'd left, hoping Colin wouldn't make good on his threat to shoot us.

3. Dove into the truck and started whimpering about loss of cocktails (typical Brits).

When he spoke, Colin's voice sounded unnaturally calm. "Move forward a seat so that the leopard can't reach the backs of your legs if she jumps into the open trunk." He was directing his comments to the couple in the very back of the Land Rover, but all six of us in the truck leaped forward two seats until we were huddled together near the front—and near Colin, who at this point was seeming almost godlike in his composure.

"Good," said Colin. "Now we just have to wait and see what the leopard chooses to do. We can't gun the engine because we might startle her, and after all, we're the ones trespassing, not her. And you're all safe now. In theory."

Yeah, right. *In theory*, we were safe once in the truck. *In theory*, bush animals are accustomed to guide trucks and treat them like another large wild animal—a particularly chunky rhino, say, or a trunkless elephant. At that moment, all the theories in the world gave no comfort. . . . Because in practice, let me tell you, there's nothing remotely safe-feeling about a leopard sniffing around the wheels of an open-topped, open-sided truck while you're huddled inside.

"Dave," I hissed.

"What, honey?" he hissed back.

"Next time we get married, let's go and lie on a beach for three weeks."

Forget the wedding kiss. We were fast perfecting spousal communication at its finest: the hiss.

IN FAIRNESS TO my adored new husband, our pre-leopard honeymoon stint had been picture-postcard dreamy. For us transplanted Brits now living in Seattle, even returning to the U.K. to get married had been an adventure, although I was a little peeved when my wedding dress got to fly first class and I was relegated to the back of the plane.

We'd spent the first few days as post-nuptials holed up in a three-hundred-year-old lock-keepers' cottage on the Grand Union Canal in Worcestershire, the heart of rural England, where we'd reveled in the best of all things British: bad food, bad weather, and great booze. We'd eaten fish and chips out of the paper by the banks of the canal, watching the fractious holidaymakers negotiate the eighteen locks in their fifty-eight-foot narrow boats. We'd toasted each other on a feast of Heinz baked beans on toast, washed down with Veuve Cliquot. And we'd splashed through the downpour and crossed the muddy fields by the thatch-roofed cottage to drink pints of lager shandy in the Hope and Anchor. Shandy—warm beer diluted with fizzy pop—is a uniquely English drink, palatable only to those brought up on lumpy mash and overboiled vegetables. With cuisine like ours, shandy's the ideal accompaniment.

Most of the time, we'd kept ourselves to ourselves. A great idea, because we'd been nauseating company, with much of our conversation reduced to exchanges like:

"More tea, Mrs. Franklin?" (Giggle.)

"Well, thank you, husband, I will." (Snigger.)

Indeed, a passing stranger would have felt the need to beat the living shit out of us. But we were oblivious newlyweds and felt heartily entitled to our mushiness.

After three days of this extreme behavior, we'd worked off the excesses and felt fit to be seen in public on the next leg of our honeymoon: a one-way trip on an original 1920s luxury train from London, through Paris, Zurich, and Innsbruck to Venice.

A plummy liveryman greeted us at track two at Victoria Station in London. "Welcome to the London–Venice Orient Express," he intoned with a suitably obsequious expression. If he'd been wearing a trilby, he'd have doffed it, no question.

Victoria Station had been an old stomping ground in my pre-Seattle life as a frantic London career woman, so I thought I knew it pretty well. And at first glance, it looked as I'd always remembered. Thrusting against each other like waves in a sea storm were throngs of gray commuters, buttoned up and anonymous in defiance of the April rain and the barrage of the city. Here were the newsagents, the tabloids' headlines proclaiming the latest David Beckham scandal and the (dis)approval ratings for Bush-loving Prime Minister Blair. So far, so normal. And here was the "scoreboard" showing the schedules for the thirteen commuter trains pouring into Victoria from Croydon, from Brixton, from Hayward's Heath, and points beyond. All delayed. So far, so normal.

Yet at our platform, everything was not so normal: Awaiting us on the track, as if sent in a luxury time capsule from the 1920s, was our temporary home, the Venice Orient Express, the train that would transport us through the lush French countryside, the Italian Dolomites, and the Swiss Alps to, of course, Venice.

To refer to a sojourn on the Venice Orient Express as a train journey is like describing the movie *Casablanca* as a film about a Moroccan nightclub. Strictly speaking, it relays the facts—but what it misses is the emotion, the sense of an epic, unforgettable experience never to be repeated. And the Venice Orient Express, much like *Casablanca*, is all about nostalgic romance.

Waking up on the train the next morning, I pushed aside the mounds of feather bedding and pulled up the blinds on our carriage window.

"Holy shit!" I exclaimed in a manner not entirely in keeping with the genteel grandeur of the voyage. "We're halfway up a mountain!"

We were indeed in the Alps, the train having swished through France and Italy as we slumbered, exhausted after the previous evening's indulgence in the dining car, complete with caviar and veal. From our vantage point—the very first sleeping car of the train—we gazed spellbound at the rest of the carriages snaking along the mountain track behind us as we took our morning tea and nibbled on freshly baked pastries. The snowcapped peaks shimmered in the spring sunshine.

Ten hours later, I skipped off the carriage steps into twenty-first-century Venice.

"A day in the 1920s should be mandatory for everyone," I said.

"True," said Dave, staggering behind with our beautiful (yet oh so impractical) leather luggage. "If you haven't seen a dinner-suited pianist tinkle 'Blue Moon' on a baby grand as Paris rolls by, then, quite frankly, you haven't lived."

I toddled happily after Dave, purse dangling from my wrist in an insouciant fashion. Oh, lordy, wifely subservience was already upon me—and worse, I *loved* it. No more carrying heavy bags! Yay for husbands!

"I'm not sure if I enjoyed the piano more or the sheer opulence of having the porter stoke the boiler before turning down the bedcovers," Dave expounded.

"Mind you," he added, "thinking about the bed thing, I'm not sure that bunk beds on our honeymoon was quite the plan."

"Thank the lord we'd worked the noisiest sex out of our systems in the cottage," I said. "At least out there only the horses could hear us."

Finally feeling bad about his labor, I caught up with him up and grabbed one of the bags off him, then immediately regretted it. Why can't I allow a little light bag-carrying, for pity's sake?

"Out of our systems? Speak for yourself," he said, giving me a lascivious wink. He turned eagerly down a narrow, canal-lined street. "C'mon, let's hurry up and find our hotel."

Venice was magical, but then, at the risk of sounding like the original spoiled brat, we'd expected that. Venice was where we'd spent our first weekend as a newly engaged couple, simpering pathetically and feeding gelato to each other at the Gran' Caffe in Piazza San Marco. Of course, that was the first flush of romance. But hey, this was the second flush of romance. So we spent our visit, well, simpering pathetically and feeding gelato to each other at the Gran' Caffe in Piazza San Marco.

Maybe when we're eighty and the many flushes of love's young dream have faded like the frescoes on the Venetian walls, we'll hobble to Venice on a bus tour with forty other wizened crones and their equally wizened spouses. On that trip, I'm sure we'll bitch about the stench of the canals (such stagnant water, riddled with disease!), the winding cobbled streets (so difficult to negotiate on walkers), and the language (how dare the Italians not speak English!). But these pleasures await us. For now, as we floated in our love-bubble, Venice was as romantic as a whisper, from the gondolier singing "O Sole Mio" on the canal outside our bedroom window to the single red rose awaiting us at dinner.

However, as is the wont of bubbles, the Venetian one had to burst eventually.

"I can't believe we have to leave already," I sniffled the next day, craning past Dave to get a good look out of the plane window at the waterways fanning out beneath us.

"You poor thing," he teased. "You really are the world's most deprived wife, aren't you? Four days in Merrie Olde England, the train journey of a lifetime, yet another slushy sojourn in Venice, and now we're en route for the *Out of Africa* part of the trip. How will you ever cope with such slumming?"

Slumming, it turned out, was hardly the word for it. After landing in Cape Town, we took an internal flight to the town of Port Elizabeth on the Eastern Cape. From there, a chauffeur brought us to a luxury game reserve in the African bush. Dave's stock as World's Coolest Husband continued to soar when I discovered he'd booked us the honeymoon suite on the first floor of a gorgeously restored Edwardian manor that served as the main game lodge. A four-poster bed faced floor-to-ceiling windows, giving us the spectacle of zebra crossing the plains without so much as a need to plump up the pillows for a clearer view.

I tossed my fashionable-yet-functional wide-brimmed safari hat onto the rattan chaise longue and fondly pictured myself sipping martinis by the pool after a gentle jaunt to take soft-focus close-ups of me with the zebra.

How wrong could I be? The reserve owners took the not-unreasonable view that, since you were paying for a safari, a safari is what you got. Five-star luxury it undoubtedly was, but only for the few precious hours in between game drives. From 6:30 until noon, and again from 3:30 until seven at night, we were to be out in the bush, jammed into a juddering Land Rover as we pushed through brush and forded water holes in search of the Big Five: elephant, leopard, rhino, buffalo, and, of course, the king of the jungle himself, the lion.

In terms of customer satisfaction, the owners were dead on, of course. The bush was enthralling, despite my fears that having my period would turn me into a bull's eye for predators. Yes, terrific timing—a period on honeymoon. The ultimate in romance. Still, it gave me an excuse to look sexy in black, I suppose.

And fortunately, it turned out that the African veldt holds far more alluring victims than a wussy Englishwoman with the odd drop of menstrual blood. Praise the lord for wart hogs! Far smaller and uglier than your average woman, they were also a much more appealing entrée, it seemed.

This knowledge freed me to venture merrily on a night drive to watch a pride of lions stalk and hunt their prey, feeling like nothing so much as a girl in a Tampax ad. "Be as active as you like, all month long," said the imaginary soundtrack in my head, "without fear of being eaten."

However, we hadn't counted on Colin, our previously noted guide and driver, who regarded safari as an extreme sport, rather than a road trip with sun and optional hippopotami. The cocktail hour with the leopard, which we'd found intensely memorable to say the least, had, as it turned out, been only mildly diverting to him.

Which is why, several days later, he brought all of us within five feet of the starving and hunting male lion. Once there, he insisted that we wait until it killed something. Us, presumably, if it didn't find anything else to its taste.

Never have I wanted a wart hog to die more in my life.

"Stay put," Colin warned us (somewhat unnecessarily). Then he switched off all the lights on the truck to let the animals continue their hunt undisturbed.

All went dark, and when I say that, it's not a figure of speech. The dark on the African plains eliminates any suspicion of light. I couldn't see my hand in front of my face, even if I squinted. I reached for Dave's hand for reassurance.

"There's a lion right next to the truck," I whispered.

I wasn't sure why I was whispering. Did I think the lion was going to overhear me and realize with a shock that it was crouching next to a truckload of honeymooners? Did I honestly think I was tastier than a wart hog? Maybe I did.

Dave, forgoing the whispering, said, "It's like Mount Rainier."

"Huh?"

"It's like driving over Lake Washington in November, when there's no sign of Mount Rainier. There's not even a hint of mountain. Not a hillock in sight."

As he spoke, I could picture Seattle's steely gray sky, the one that tourists always stare at, wishing they could see through the cloud cover to spot the vast snowcapped glaciers.

"That's like being out here, right now," he continues. "You know that ten paces away there's a hungry lion practicing his kill moves. You know that if you as much as step out of the truck, you enter the food chain and become fair game, pun intended. When it's light and you can see the lion, you can't do anything except stare at it, because it's so amazing to coexist with such a huge force of nature. But now, when it's dark, there may as well be no lion. It's impossible to imagine there ever was such a thing."

"True. But you know what, honey? Given the choice of meeting either of them in the dark, I think I'd pick the mountain."

Even without this comparison, our fellow honeymooners agreed that one "big cat" adventure was more than enough. Colin turned the truck around and took us back to the lodge, where we feasted on the game we'd been admiring earlier that day and bored the other residents stupid with our tales of derring-do (or derring-don't in our case).

A week later we returned to Seattle, to weather so clear that the mountain came out. In the comfort of our own cozy apartment, I wondered if we'd made the whole thing up—lions, leopards! But then we got the pictures back, and there was the leopard, larger than life, with its head back. Enjoying my gin and tonic.

No Strings Attached

Paige Porter

. . . .

I've never owned a wet suit. Let's face it: Wearing a neoprene body-suit is about as appealing an idea to most women as wearing a string bikini. I'd rather be caught dead than caught in either one, but on assignment in Santa Catalina, I ended up wearing both.

I've come to the conclusion that the laws of economics don't necessarily apply to my field of journalism—or at least not to me as a journalist. As the supply of my embarrassing moments on the road increases, so does the demand. Acquaintances often assume I have a dream job: writing features on food, travel, and lifestyle for a glossy publication. My close friends know, however, that glamour isn't an indigenous part of my job. Sure, there are the perks: the occasional complimentary bottle of pricey champagne, the upgrades to ocean-view corner suites, the frequent flyer miles. But the moment I begin to feel like a VIP, the reality call of public humiliation brings me back to my humble senses.

I could mention a night at Delta baggage claim when I thought I saw some familiar undergarments riding the carousel, independent of any luggage; how moments later I discovered, upon seeing my bag ripped at the seams, that it was in fact my black lace bra and purple thong riding alongside someone's Louis Vuitton; how I raced between complete strangers to scavenge for my underwear.

I could mention a crazy afternoon in Newfoundland when, desperate to check my email, I took the grocery store manager up on an offer to use her son's computer; how, in the Playboy model–plastered bedroom of that teenage boy, who happened to have the only Internet connection in town, I raced through my correspondence as he strummed his guitar and sang eighties love songs in my ear.

I could mention the day my rental car had a blowout on the west side of Kaua'i; how I'd neglected to put on sunscreen that morning, thinking I was only going for a quick jaunt to the bakery for granola; how, walking down the highway in my bathing suit, searching for help, I fried my fair skin into something resembling smoked salmon.

These are the moments when I covet cube life, a business suit over a bathing one. Most women would consider it torture to roam the office in a two-piece. It isn't part of the job, they would argue. But on the road for *Coastal Living*, it was my duty to study the beach. And that requires a whole different dress code.

I'd bought my first string bikini during a previous vacation in Ireland. The diminutive number cost me just four Irish pounds, an appropriate price considering the minimal amount of material used in its design. That cobalt-blue bikini enjoyed a lengthy hibernation in my trusty Samsonite suitcase. After all, I had never actually planned on wearing the get-up in front of anyone other than the girlfriend who'd dared me, in Dublin, to buy it in the first place. But on that fateful day on Catalina Island, I was forced to awaken it—crumpled into a ball the size of an apricot—from its two-year slumber.

I was traveling solo, staying in a rustic, one-room cabin at Catalina Island Camps. My assignment: to spend some time with the lovely Kern family, who live year-round on the west side of the island and run the adventure camps there. This trip was a reprieve from my relationship woes. In fact, it was a gift to my then-boyfriend, who'd recently requested a bit of space. I thought seventeen hundred miles was generous.

After retrieving me from the harbor, my gracious hosts, Tom and Holly Kern, walked me toward my weekend abode. Both were tan, well-groomed, and very blond—the kind of people who appear in a J. Crew catalog. You know the ones: Perfectly photogenic, perfectly fit, they relax in khakis and white t-shirts, enjoying the good life. I quickly learned the Kerns didn't come to look like models without a bit of work.

Holly soon suggested a change of clothes and some exercise. "Why don't you get unpacked, put on something comfortable, and join us up at the house?" she said, pointing toward their home at the top of a rather steep hill and mentioning an early afternoon hike.

I fancy myself in fairly good physical shape. I force myself to take the stairs rather than the elevator, provided the destination is no more than two stories away. I carry my own groceries to the car, giving the bag boys a deserved break. I refuse rides on airport trams and opt instead for moving sidewalks. I even belong to a gym: I did my research, and joining a health club was cheaper than getting cable in my apartment. So I organize my workouts around my favorite television shows—typically sitcoms that last no more than thirty minutes—as half an hour is my cardiovascular cutoff. Still: I lift seven-and-a-half-pound dumbbells, not fifty-pound backpacks. So the thought of a weekend spent hiking Catalina's west side did bring to mind a certain conversation I once had with a dear friend who, in an apparent moment of insanity, suggested that we spend our spring break hiking the Grand Canyon rim to rim. "On foot?" I replied.

I'll admit it: When I accepted this assignment, I had imagined profiling a family whose days revolved around long hours of lounging by the water, drinking iced tea with lemon, and falling asleep under beach umbrellas. I'd recently visited the north shore of Kaua'i, where a family I met confessed they spent almost every afternoon of the year tanning themselves in the sand on a nearby beach, going barefoot to the grocery store, taking outdoor showers at night. To my mind, the beach provides an escape from all tasks involving energy expenditures. People move to islands to remain horizontal, right? But the Kerns exploded all the clichés about island life.

I thought it a good idea to do a bit of preliminary stretching. While on the floor, I checked under the bed for the snakes, rats, and stray cats I tend to associate with camp cabins. Finding the room clear of unwanted enemies, I performed a reconnaissance mission on my temporary wardrobe, sorting through the duds I'd deemed suitable for this trip.

I walked out of the cabin in my favorite khaki capris to face the looming incline in my most comfortable shoe option: black wedges. Ten minutes later, I was out of breath and working on a few impressive blisters when Holly came to the door to greet me. She took one look at my shoes and gingerly suggested that I borrow her more sturdy Tevas for the long walk—all of it uphill—to Emerald Bay. I was putting on her shoes when Holly asked me, "You don't, by any chance, have a pair of shorts with you?" Of course I didn't have any shorts with me. I haven't worn shorts since I was in sixth grade. All women know that shorts belong in the same family of unflattering apparel as overalls, muumuus, and high-waisted jeans. How many times have you seen Nicole Kidman or Cameron Diaz photographed in a pair of khaki shorts?

"It's okay, you can borrow some of mine," she suggested. I knew immediately that wouldn't ever work, as Holly's petite frame hadn't known the dubious honor of meeting those unmistakable twins, the Hips. I, however, knew them on a first-name basis. And so it happened that her husband's swimming trunks fit me perfectly. Now I know that some men get turned on by the idea of women wearing their clothes. But believe me, there is nothing sexy about a white-legged woman in a man's swimsuit.

We were soon on our way. The Kerns' energetic daughters, two-year-old Hannah and her older sister, Haley, were ten paces ahead, so I lagged behind, pretending to take scouting shots. It was a legitimate excuse, a real part of my job, as the pictures always stir my imagination when I'm in front of my laptop weeks later, searching for words to describe the experience. Not that I could ever have forgotten this one. "I'm just going to hang back a bit, take a few shots from this angle. The perspective is great," I said. "I can get the whole family in the frame."

I could almost hear my quads begging, pleading for mercy. I alternated deep breaths with staccato conversation, wondering why I had never considered challenging myself with the incline buttons on the treadmill at the gym. When we made it to the top of the hill, I took in the view—diamond-laced waters caressing amber cliffs—and declared it well worth the arduous climb. "It's like looking at a newborn baby and forgetting all about the twenty-four hours of hellish labor required to meet her," I said, panting.

"Pardon?" Holly turned to me, her sweat-free brow furrowed, her blond hair so straight and shiny you'd have thought she'd just had it blown out by a stylist.

"Nothing," I said. "It's exquisite. I've never seen water this emerald green." Except, I thought, from the comfort of a hammock outside my *palapa* in Tulum, Mexico.

"Just wait till we go kayaking after this," said Holly. My stomach sank to my knees when I realized she viewed this hike as a warm-up. "You won't believe how clear the water is. You can see forty feet down. You did bring a bathing suit, didn't you?"

Enter, stage left, that teeny-weeny blue bikini. It qualified, certainly, but I'd already deemed it unsuitable for public viewing. I gave myself a pep talk: This was an assignment, and my job was to get up close and personal with the Kerns. Duty called. If daily kayaking was part of their life, well, a bikini would have to be part of mine. This job, however, would be a little more intimate than I'd expected. Little did this innocent family know they'd be getting so up close and personal with me.

I hated to disturb it, slumbering there in my suitcase. I sighed and pulled out the fragments of fabric; the bathing suit was even smaller than I remembered. I avoided contact with the one mirror in my cabin, thereby evading the truth—for fear of total breakdown and the exorbitant cost of future therapy. But I did give myself a once-over and immediately regretted my decision not to purchase self-tanning cream. Thank Hawaii for sarongs, I thought, as I wrapped mine around me like a bandage.

Slapping sunscreen on my face as I walked, I made my way down to the beach, where Holly was waiting with life vests in hand. "Tom's going to keep the kids while I take you out in the ocean," she said. "Have you done much kayaking?"

"No, not really," I said, as I was more comfortable pitching stories on spas and five-star resorts than those travel adventure stories other editors coveted. I'd always thought of it as a kindly gesture—to leave the biking, surfing, kiteboarding, and kayaking stories to other writers, alleviating both the threat of story envy and the promise of workers' compensation.

"Well, it's not that difficult, really, once you get the hang of it," she said. "You look pretty coordinated, and that's all it takes."

Little did she know I secretly wondered why grown-up bikes don't come with training wheels. I'm the kind of person who has excellent coordination when it comes to my ten fingers and the keyboard, but that's the extent of my dexterity. I trip on flat surfaces with alarming regularity. I stub my toes on pebbles. I get my curly hair caught in tree branches.

Still, I succumbed. We carried our kayak to the water, and Holly explained that we'd be paddling out of the safety of the cove and into the ocean.

"Oh, where the big waves are," I said. My palms were sweating. She put me in the front seat of the kayak, explaining, as she pushed us out to sea, what I'd need to do if the kayak flipped over in the water.

"Does that, uh, happen very often?" I asked.

"Don't worry," she replied. But it was too late. Fear had invaded my bones. I'm not the kind of person who deals well with panic situations, and I always feel a twinge of guilt when I answer yes to the flight attendants who ask me if I'm comfortable with the responsibilities inherent in occupying an exit-row seat. I know full well the only comfort I feel in an exit row comes from having a bit of extra leg room.

"The ocean here is so cold, it'll shock you into a strong reaction," Holly said.

I remember the moment well. I was getting acclimated to paddling when the ice-cold water first touched my derrière. The shiver up my spine was so intense, I thought I'd been stabbed.

"You mean people actually swim in this water?" I asked in disbelief.

"Of course," she said, smiling. "You'll see how fast you get used to it when we go snorkeling later."

Surely I hadn't heard her right.

Oh, but I had.

After a few hours of boot camp–worthy sea kayaking, when the first signs of soreness were showing up in arm muscles I never knew I had, we were heading back to the beach. There, Tom was waiting with a huge red wagon filled with wet suits, diving masks, and flippers. "How was the tour?" he asked.

My upper arms were rebelling with spasms as I answered, "Oh, it was fantastic. I guess I know why you two are without body fat."

Holly was surveying the wagon, combing through beach bags in search of something that I hoped was food. I was wrong. "Here it is!" she said, pulling out a plastic bag. Holly, who's grown so accustomed to the frigid waters off her front yard that she never uses a wet suit, announced she was lending me hers—a flesh-toned neoprene bodysuit. I took one look at the outfit and had just one thought: This was it, the solution for actresses who refuse to do nude scenes.

Before I could put it on, I had to remove the sarong and life jacket. I felt like Eve in the Garden of Eden. Someone was stealing my leaves, and all that was left was a barely-there bikini and a whole lot of pale skin. Holly's little girls, as golden brown as their parents, watched me, wide-eyed, as I stared at the cruel costume. I will not be humiliated in front of children, I told myself, carrying the beige wet suit toward an enormous rock. Behind the boulder, I struggled to get one leg of the rubbery material over my foot. Ten minutes later, completely out of breath, I'd conquered the knee. My short-term goal was getting the wet suit up to my waist. "Why does everything have to be so difficult?" I asked myself. While I worked, the Kerns waited patiently by the water.

"Did you just get this thing out of the dryer?" I called from behind the boulder, attempting to lessen the awkwardness.

"It can be a challenge," Holly replied. "Take your time, Paige."

With one leg in, I set out to conquer the other. I thought putting on control-top pantyhose was a pain. Imagine pulling them up to your neck. Every inch of my skin was being lifted and tucked, lifted and tucked. I suspected my thighs were nearing my waistline one inch at a time. And there just wasn't enough room for all of me in that size 2 neoprene suit. I expected a triple chin by the time it was over.

After I shoved both my arms into sleeves the width of a cardboard toilet paper tube, I took the deepest breath of my life and tugged the zipper all the way up. By the time I was tucked securely in its packaging, I was so shaken and warm I was ready to dive into the frigid waters for some relief. The wet suit was so tight, inhaling oxygen was a challenge. I sat on a rock for a moment or two, attempting to recapture my breath. "Here goes nothing," I said to myself. Feeling a bit like a hot dog too big for its bun, I emerged from behind the rock and declared myself ready to go.

Holly and the girls looked at me with curious eyes and apologetic grins. "Oh, Paige, you put it on backwards," Holly said, muffling a quiet laugh and shaking her head in disbelief. "I thought you could tell from the built-in bra."

I looked over my shoulder and saw the two breast-size cubbyholes.

"Oh, those," I replied. "Well, ahem, you see, I have really big shoulder blades."

I went right back to the rock. After several ill-fated attempts at removal, I humbled myself and asked for help. With my back in the sand and my feet raised high in the air, I tried to relax as Holly and Tom tugged at the wet suit, one leg at a time, until they had successfully removed it. I've blocked out most of the details. I don't remember how long it took, whether I kept the bikini in place, or what I said to make light of this mortifying situation. I do, however, remember the way those two precious girls were staring at me, their heads tilted slightly, their tan brows furrowed, as if they had no idea what to make of this girl from the mainland.

Seventeen minutes later, I emerged from behind the boulder with cubbyholes aligned. The Kern family clapped. Haley—a virtual amphibian who lives as comfortably in the water as she does on land—grabbed my hand. "Don't be scared," she said.

I said prayers for a sabbatical from clumsiness and put on my flippers. "I grew up swimming in Miami," I said, suppressing shivers up my spine, as my feet hit the water. Holly smiled and handed me a mask and snorkel, and under her gaze, I inched—literally—my way into that ice chest called the Pacific.

My head might have been throbbing, and my body may have been in shock, but my eyes were working just fine, and what I saw made every bit of physical pain and public humiliation worth it. The kelp beds off Catalina teem with some of the world's most stunning underwater wildlife—including schools of golden garibaldi. The angels of this ocean, they swim together and glow like giant amber brooches floating in the sea.

In this exquisite, silent underworld, I quickly forgot about my tired limbs, my new rubber suit, my skimpy blue bikini. But an hour or so later, in the confines of a narrow camp shower, when I struggled to remove the dreadful apparel, I contemplated an evening campfire—a ceremonial good-bye, as it were, to the wet suit and the two-piece.

A few weeks later, at the camera store near my apartment, the Kodak moments came back to haunt me. Gone were the recurring dreams of giving speeches in my birthday suit. My subconscious had supplanted those with a nightly rerun featuring yours truly, outfitted in a blue bikini whose triangles seemed to shrink with each nightmare. It was with great joy and anticipation that I planned a special field trip to the nearest Goodwill store, wishing only, well, good will to any woman who dared to adopt the last string bikini I will ever own.

Y2K in Kandahar

Hannah Bloch

. . . .

ew Year's Eve in Islamabad was usually disappointing and
tedious, but in 1999, it threatened to be even more so.
I'd been living in Pakistan for a couple of years by then,
working as a journalist, so the initial excitement of being in
a brand-new place was over. And the man I'd recently broken up with had told me he would be entertaining a lady friend who was
coming in from Europe. I could imagine her all too well—a soignée Parisian
whose appeal lay as much in her charming mispronunciation of English as
in her habit of pooching out her lips (a supersexy habit all Frenchwomen
seem to inherit) as she spoke of her fabulous Frenchified life. As for me,
dishevelment was more my natural state, and around that time, it was a state
of dishevelment augmented by sleep deprivation, relentless work, and the
knowledge that a chic Parisian had usurped me.

I was still feeling a bit raw about it all and had no desire to be in the same
city with the two of them. In Islamabad, which is less a city than a small
village, it seemed inevitable that we'd run in to one another on the street or
at the same party. In part to avoid such an encounter, I'd fantasized about

fleeing to Delhi to visit a friend. But no: Just as I was really latching on to the idea, the editors at the magazine I worked for instructed us to stay put to produce special coverage of the new millennium.

As the final week of December approached, I found myself wishing for something—anything—to save me from a millennial New Year's Eve avoiding my ex while simultaneously watching for Pakistani Y2K glitches, which (if they happened) would run as a paragraph or two in a worldwide roundup. I couldn't imagine a more depressing or futile way to usher in the next thousand years.

In the end, I got my wish to flee Islamabad—and then some. Deliverance came in the form of a Christmas Eve hijacking. An Indian Airlines jet carrying 178 passengers was seized by five grenade-wielding terrorists forty-five minutes after taking off from Kathmandu. The flight was diverted from New Delhi, its intended destination, to Amritsar, Lahore, Dubai, and finally Kandahar—then home base for Afghanistan's Taliban rulers. The only international traffic at the Kandahar airport in those days usually came in the form of United Nations and Red Cross flights, and the sudden crisis gave the pariah Taliban regime a chance to shine—if the hijacking was resolved peacefully.

At first, the Indian government refused to negotiate with the hijackers—Kashmir separatists who demanded the release of terrorists from Indian jails—but then changed its mind and sent a team of negotiators to Kandahar. The Taliban played the role of mediators. Soon it became obvious that the crisis was going to drag on, and I saw my window for a New Year's escape from Islamabad: I began to push for a visa from the Taliban embassy so I could cover the story from Kandahar.

Oh, sure, most people might balk at celebrating New Year's Eve in a place ruled by fundamentalist zealots who banned alcohol and music, held public executions, ordered women to cover themselves from head to toe, and forbade them from venturing outside alone. This was not exactly the Vegas of Central Asia. But me? I was frantic to get there.

For an American, obtaining a visa from the Taliban was not a straightforward process. Sometimes you got one quickly, other times it took weeks. Sometimes your application was denied. Relations between the United States and the Taliban were terrible. It was 1999, and Afghanistan was struggling under heavy United Nations sanctions for harboring Osama bin Laden (who lived in a Kandahar compound). The visa application was a one-page form that asked for basic information including who you were "son of." I crossed out "son" and wrote in "daughter."

Even though the Taliban forbade photography of all living things as un-Islamic, they required a photo with the application, along with a thirty-dollar fee, paid in cash. After I handed everything in, I was advised to return the next day. When I did, there was bad news.

"Actually," the turbaned, bearded male receptionist informed me politely, "we have lost your application." He was completely unapologetic, and I requested that he double-check. Somehow, eventually, my application was located. But then there was a hitch: He told me the ambassador himself would have to make the final decision about my visa. He asked me to wait while the application was delivered to the ambassador. Then he told me to come back the next day.

I left, passing the ladies' visa section, where a few Afghan women, identical and anonymous in their light-blue burqas, sat outside on benches, cordoned off from the rest of the embassy. (As a foreigner, I wasn't technically exempt from this gender segregation, but I managed to dodge it simply by ignoring it.)

When I came back the following day, I was accompanied by a kind Pakistani journalist who had offered to help me. When I asked the receptionist what my status was, he told me the ambassador was very busy. So I waited. And then I waited some more. My Pakistani colleague excused himself.

After an hour went by, I asked whether the ambassador had made a decision.

The receptionist looked embarrassed.

"Actually," he said, "the ambassador has gone to the bathroom."

"Oh!" I said, startled by this revelation. I tried to banish the image the receptionist had just conjured. How on earth, I wondered, could he have known the ambassador's bathroom timetable? Was this just another delay tactic?

After a decent interval, I screwed up the courage to ask again.

Nothing.

It turned out my Pakistani colleague had been pleading my case with the ambassador. When he came back with my visa, he told me the ambassador had agonized over my application. "He was pacing back and forth, wondering out loud whether to give it to you or not," said my friend.

I DIDN'T ASK how my Pakistani friend convinced the ambassador to take a chance on me, but I knew immediately that it was only because of his intervention that I got the visa. I gazed at it adoringly, a purple stamp on page "S" of my passport, allowing me a single entry to Afghanistan for a visit lasting up to two weeks. The date, December 29, 1999, was inscribed according to the Muslim calendar as well: the twenty-first day of the ninth month in the year 1420.

I thanked my friend profusely, sprinted over to the United Nations flight office to reserve a spot on the next plane, and went home to throw some stuff into a bag.

I arrived in Kandahar early the next morning, carrying my PowerBook and a couple of changes of clothes, along with two clanking bottles of French champagne that my friend Gretchen, an American TV producer based in London, had handed off to me right before I boarded the UN flight in Islamabad. ("We want to make sure Miss Hannah has a happy new year, don't we?" she'd said to the UN flight official in charge of weighing the bags, implicitly daring him to forbid me to carry the bottles into dry Afghanistan. He stared at her, smiling in awe: Gretchen is six feet tall and blond. Since she fully intended to come to Kandahar as soon as her own visa came through, her insistence was partly self-interested; the champagne would help ensure her happy new year as well.)

I was also bearing several changes of underwear for a British correspondent, sent by devoted friends of hers in Islamabad, responding to her SOS "It's always nice to have a fresh pair of knickers," she said, snatching the bundle away the instant I'd stepped off the UN propeller plane.

She didn't have to tell me that very few of the usual Taliban rules were in force—I could see it for myself instantly. Normally the Taliban assigned a "minder" to every foreign journalist, but not here. I'd braced myself for a thorough Customs search, but no one even glanced at my bag. The champagne was safe. The only obvious concession to prevailing custom seemed to be the head scarves with which she and I covered our hair. Mine was a too-big black wool shawl I was constantly wrestling with. When it wasn't slipping off the back of my head, it was blocking my line of vision or getting tangled with the pen in my right hand or the notebook I held in my left. The damn thing seemed to have a life of its own.

As a Pakistani photographer greeted me and showed me the airport waiting lounge that had become the journalists' dorm room, I felt almost giddy. With its hectic informality, it looked like the site of a huge slumber party with sleeping bags and bedrolls everywhere. I was welcomed by friends and colleagues, most from Pakistan, who had preceded me in Kandahar by several days. Everyone fiddled with laptops and satellite phones, comparing notes, chattering, and laughing.

Across the way, UN officials and diplomats were hunkered down in the airport's VIP lounge. Some of them had been yanked away from Christmas celebrations with their families in Islamabad to try to ensure the welfare of their compatriots on the hijacked flight. I'd imagined they'd feel awkward accepting the hospitality of the Taliban, since the diplomats all represented countries that refused to recognize the regime as an official Afghan government, but they seemed right at home. I peered into the room, which had the air of a gentlemen's club or a quiet hotel lobby. Envoys from half a dozen countries were lounging on sofas and plump chairs, reading newspapers a few days old, conferring in hushed tones with each other and sipping green tea. Some of them looked up in curiosity or irritation when I opened the door. The Frenchman was grumpy, the Australian chummy, the Swiss chatty. A young Afghan attendant was waiting on them. I learned that the British reporter who needed underwear had been camping out with them, and I was invited to do the same, though in truth, the other room looked like more fun.

But it was agreed that as the two "lady reporters," we should stay in these plusher digs. The flip side of the region's chauvinism was its chivalry, and I was fine with that.

Having situated myself, I went out to find my old friend Phil, a British cameraman who had been covering the region far longer than I had. I found him positioned behind a massive zoom lens on a long walkway adjacent to the tarmac. The walkway afforded a good view of the hijacked plane, and Phil and a long line of other photographers and video cameramen had parked themselves there, cameras trained on the aircraft waiting for any flicker of movement. We all stared at the red-and-white Indian Airlines jet as if we were tourists at a wildlife preserve waiting for a shy animal to make a split-second move.

The plane sat on the runway, its shades drawn and auxiliary engines running. Strewn to the sides of the tarmac were old tanks and rusted-out fighter planes, remnants of Afghanistan's twenty years of war and civil war. The chilly, vacant terminal was a multidomed cement structure plunked down in a flat, dusty, brown landscape surrounded by jagged mountains. It was hardly a New Year's Eve pleasure dome. Turbaned Taliban guards milled about with automatic rifles. Not far away were two deserts, one known as "Desert of Hell" and the other, "Desert of Death." But it still looked like a fabulous venue to me, and by God, nothing was going to get in the way of my celebrating. I felt relieved—and then guilty—after learning the negotiating deadlock over the hostages hadn't ended and we'd all definitely be staying on for the big night.

As harsh as the surroundings were, and despite the story's seriousness, the atmosphere at the airport was convivial. Even though it was the middle of the Muslim holy month of Ramadan, journalists and diplomats were eating, smoking, and chugging down water right in front of the Taliban officials and guards, who were fasting at the airport from sunup to sundown. They seemed completely unfazed by our rudeness—and by the cameras, which the regime officially forbade.

"They have gone out of their way to be hospitable!" an Indian negotiator marveled to me. He and the other negotiators were staying on their own plane, parked some distance away, and in general they didn't like to talk much. But since everyone had to use the same airport bathrooms during the day—the same one for everybody, no men's room or women's room—they couldn't help having some contact with the rest of us. Unfortunately for them, that usually meant being ambushed by reporters casually lying in wait near the heavily trafficked bathroom entrance.

At night, the plane was surrounded by Taliban guards sitting cross-legged at campfires on the tarmac. The Taliban had promised to storm the plane at the first sign of violence by the hijackers. The plane's shades stayed drawn, and only a few pinpoints of light broke through where they didn't reach completely to the bottom of the windowframes. The continuous roar of the plane's auxiliary power system competed with the calls to prayer that echoed from Kandahar's mosques. I tried hard to imagine how miserable conditions must be for the hostages on the Airbus 300. At one point in the afternoon, Phil and I had seen a hatch open abruptly and some stuff slopped out of the bottom of the plane.

I looked at Phil and raised my eyebrows. "Oh my God," he said. "It's the shite!"

Some of the Taliban guards at the airport were eager to look through the cameras. In the photos I took from that time, I see them smiling in the background. Most of them didn't speak English, but they were not unfriendly. I owned a Pashto language instruction book, the only one I could ever find, but in these circumstances it was useless. In fact, I couldn't imagine any circumstances in which it would be practical. Compiled in 1867 by a British army surgeon, it provided a disconcerting and contradictory glimpse into Pashtun society:

"What has become of my sword?"

"Take the bread from these deaf women and give it to these weary men."

"The woman is stouter than the man."

"The man killed his own wife."

"Those women first abused me, and then they threw earth upon me."

"Women are weaker than men."

There were quite a few phrases about clouds and rain ("the clouds are dark and dense" and "this rain is very good for the crops"), but these were especially useless. Kandahar was in the midst of its worst drought in decades. The weather was cool, but the sun shone mercilessly all day, not a cloud in the sky. When I woke up on the morning of New Year's Eve, my lips cracked from dehydration, I realized I hadn't peed in twenty-four hours. I confided this bit of information to the Australian consul from Islamabad. He handed me a 1.5-liter bottle of Nestlé Pure Life water, which I gulped down in one go.

Later that day, the hijacking was resolved peacefully. The airport was by now overrun with journalists from all over the world who had come in, like me, to cover the endgame. Gretchen had arrived that morning with her crew, and other friends of mine had flown in from Islamabad, including one who had cut short her Christmas vacation with her family in the United States.

The Indian foreign minister flew in at 3:45 PM on a chartered jet with three terrorists his government had agreed to liberate in exchange for the passengers' release. Amazingly, the terrorists and the five hijackers were allowed to speed away into the Kandahar sunset, free men all.

I went back to the VIP lounge to sit on the carpet with my laptop and file an update. The Indian Airlines hijacking was one of the strangest stories I had ever covered, and it wouldn't be the last word from these terrorists. But my work at the time was finished.

I was ready to celebrate. I wandered out of the lounge to join the festivities and found Phil and Gretchen huddled on a blanket with a cameraman friend in the airport's empty luggage area. It was freezing. I brought out the two bottles of champagne, and we cut makeshift glasses from the bottoms of plastic water bottles. Fleetingly, I thought of my old boyfriend and his pouty French girlfriend, and how they would be at some bad New Year's party right about now, maybe even having a fight! (I could hope.) I took a seat between Gretchen and Phil, and bundled in coats, scarves, and hats, we clinked plastic and toasted the new millennium. The floor was cement, the glasses were jagged plastic, and our surroundings were relentlessly bleak. But it was the best time we could possibly imagine—a happy and unlikely reunion made possible by the Taliban and a rotten gang of terrorists.

Back in the VIP lounge, diplomats and journalists were hugging and kissing and saying "Happy New Year!" in half a dozen different languages. I doubted if Kandahar had ever seen anything like it. The young Afghan attendants were goggle eyed. "You mean you kiss women?" one of them asked a diplomat. "That's disgusting. We don't do that."

On New Year's Day, it was all about getting out of there. The airport was like a stage set being struck after a performance. The TV folks did their final standups and packed up their gear; diplomats and hacks disassembled satellite phones; we put our laptops away and stuffed our clothes in bags and backpacks.

The evacuated Indian Airlines jet rested silent and alone on the tarmac, no longer surrounded by guards. Gretchen, two Pakistani friends, and I posed in front of it and had our pictures taken.

A series of UN flights was scheduled to ferry journalists and diplomats back to Islamabad. My flight didn't leave till the early afternoon, so when an Italian diplomat invited me to join him and the other envoys on a quickie bus tour of Kandahar city, I didn't think twice. This up-and-coming diplomat's friends affectionately nicknamed him "Ambasciatore," in anticipation of the ambassadorial position they expected him to hold someday. In the midst of all the disorder and dust, he was beautifully dressed and somehow managed to look dapper, refined, and refreshed. I was enjoying his company and the ebullient way he said my name—"Annnnn-ah!"—smiling, with arms outstretched. Besides, I'd never seen the city of Kandahar before. We piled on the bus and were driven forty-five minutes along the desolate, dusty highway into the center of town.

I started feeling a bit queasy by the time we stopped in the Charsuq, the Kandahar bazaar, and reacted badly when a Belgian diplomat admonished me to cover my head more conscientiously while I was still sitting in the bus.

"These people are not used to seeing hair!" he scolded me. He had lived in Saudi Arabia and fancied himself a bit of an expert on devout Muslims. Now he was out-Talibaning the Taliban, none of whom had ever ordered me to be more attentive in my head-covering.

"They're not used to seeing cameras, either!" I shot back, angrily pushing loose wisps of hair under the wool shawl covering my head. He had been snapping away blatantly ever since we got on the damn bus, disregarding the Taliban rules.

I realized I was very ready to get home to Islamabad. But by the time we arrived back at the nearly deserted Kandahar airport, I had missed my flight. The journalists had all taken off, and the only plane coming back was reserved for the diplomats. There was no room for me on their tiny aircraft.

The UN flight coordinator was not sympathetic.

"You should have been here when you were supposed to," he said.

"I'm sorry," I said. I truly was.

"You might have to stay overnight till tomorrow's flight," he said, motioning at the airport.

"I am not staying here!" I said.

"You may not have a choice."

"I am *not* staying here." (What has become of my sword?)

I was dehydrated again and feeling like I might throw up. I withdrew to the shade, muttering curses to myself. Where was that famous chivalry now, when I most needed it, huh? Hypocrites. I was covered in a layer of grime, and with my black head scarf flapping about in the blowing dust, I felt like a bag lady. I resigned myself to the possibility of staying on in Kandahar. It wouldn't be too bad, aside from the fact that it was almost the worst thing I could imagine. For a number of years, its own residents had been only too happy to get the hell out of Kandahar, even if that meant living an awful refugee life. Now all I wanted was to get out, too.

Ambasciatore, ever cheerful and chivalrous, somehow came up with two bottles of water. "Don't worry, we'll find room for you," he said, sitting down next to me. "Or you can take my place. I'll stay behind." *(No, wait!* I thought, suddenly brightening up. *I'll stay behind with you!)*

We looked around and agreed the Kandahar airport had transformed into a different place. The Taliban guards, so hospitable and gracious earlier, now glowered at us as we swigged the water. They didn't want to chat and showed no interest in anything other than our leaving. They kept their distance and stared at us in what we took to be a hostile way—and who could blame them? We'd been their guests, but now we were close to overstaying our welcome. The party was over. Life was back to normal in Kandahar.

I ended up traveling as baggage. My name never appeared on the flight manifest. The diplomats agreed to leave 110 pounds of their luggage behind for one more day so I could fit on the plane. I sat on the floor most of the way and was seat-belted onto the lap of a Japanese diplomat during takeoff and landing. He laughed rather hysterically each time but sent me a beautiful card later that week saying, "I will not forget friends like you from Kandahar."

Prada on the Plaka

Michele Peterson

. . . .

hen I embarked with my two daughters on our first trip to Europe together, I was filled with romantic visions. I imagined us transported to that gilded era when every young woman's education included the grand European tour. Yet the fantasies swirling in my mind's eye like scenes from the film *A Room with a View* came to an abrupt halt as a diligent Customs official at Athens International Airport pulled my oldest daughter aside to inspect her bag. The moment he unzipped the suitcase, everything popped out like a jack-in-the-box. A long feather boa, two oversize coffee-table books on Greece, and a jumbo box of condoms that rendered me speechless. Heather looked unfazed and just twirled one of her corkscrew curls with fingers encased in full-length snakeskin gloves.

My youngest, Hayley, who was sixteen, adopted her best I've-seen-it-all-before look. "She *is* twenty-three years old. You should be proud that she is so responsible," she said, tossing her long blond hair over her shoulder. Intergenerational travel—it's never what you expect it to be.

The trip had started innocently enough. I'd vetoed their suggestion of the island of Ios—known as "the island where spring break lasts all summer"—opting instead to tour places that I thought might be slightly more stimulating for all of us. Although I knew that it was unlikely that the girls would be spending their spare time studying the myths of the ancient Greeks, I was hoping for more than total debauchery. Since this was to be the girls' first trip abroad, I wanted to give them a balance of fun and culture. We finally agreed upon an itinerary that included Mýkonos with a cruise of the islands of Santoríni, Rhodes, Pátmos, and Crete.

I tried to ignore the fact that among the three of us, we had one reluctant traveler. Hayley would gladly have chosen a few more weeks hanging out with her friends over spending time with her sister, who had been living on her own and working as an Internet programmer in Vancouver for the past three years. My secret hope was that the trip would be more than an introduction to Europe. With Heather living in Vancouver, and Hayley and I living more than 4,500 kilometers away from her in Toronto, a vacation seemed just the thing to help us reconnect.

Seeing the sprawling contents of my daughter's suitcase at the airport was a dubious beginning, but we recovered quickly enough. On our first day in Athens, we explored the cobblestone streets in the Pláka area at the foot of the Acropolis and, shaded under a massive platano tree, snacked on *mezethes* (Greek appetizers) while facing the marble ruins of the Roman Agora, which turned rosy red and then golden as our dinner progressed.

The next day, after a visit to the National Archaeological Museum, we headed to Akra Sounion, just thirty minutes east down the coast from Athens. There, at the Temple of Poseidon, fifteen marble columns provided a perfect frame for the sunset. An orange and violet sky hung over the limestone peninsula. I recounted the legend of the site to my youngest daughter, describing how Theseus forgot to switch his sails from black to white—the signal that he was alive—in his haste to return after successfully slaying the Minotaur on Crete. And how King Aegeus saw the black sails and took his own life by throwing himself into the sea below.

Hayley seemed unmoved by the tragedy.

"Perfect example of parental overreaction," she said. Seeing I wasn't going to be able to continue my cultural history lesson, we descended to retrieve Heather, who was recovering in the restaurant below.

Earlier, in the heat of the day, she'd climbed to the top of the Acropolis—wearing patent-leather Prada boots and what seemed to be a high-tech dress made entirely of plastic. Eventually, she'd hit the sandy trail—headfirst—a victim of the 104-degree heat. Fortunately, the owner of the restaurant had three sons, all of whom seemed very solicitous of her health. They created, near the kitchen, a special spot that was protected from the sun but just right to catch the evening breeze—unlike the tourist section where the rest of us sweltered. We could see the young men offering her cool cloths, icy lemon drinks, and later, crispy calamari. Soon enough, their friends pulled up on Honda motorbikes, and it turned into a party. Her recovery was remarkably speedy.

After a few days in Athens, we headed to the port of Pireás to board our ship, the *Aegean II*, for a one-week stopover in Mýkonos. It would be followed by a four-day cruise to Turkey and the Greek islands. As we perched on our bunk beds trying to free up floor space in our cabin, our luggage arrived. Six Russian porters carried in bags that stacked nearly to the ceiling of the small berth.

"Maybe I shouldn't have bought that bongo drum at the street market last night," said Heather. She didn't mention the *bouzouki,* the traditional guitarlike instrument that she'd also picked up, but I couldn't blame her alone. I suspected that part of the problem was Hayley's two large bags pulled from her suitcase that were filled to overflowing with platform shoes the size of butcher blocks.

As for me, I had packed light but was now toting a ten-pound bag of Meow Mix. Our first night in Athens, the girls had spotted several scrawny cats prowling the streets. Determined to save as many as possible during our stay, they had insisted on purchasing a large bag of cat food. Then, like feline versions of Johnny Appleseed, we'd strolled the historic streets of Athens, scattering handfuls of kitty kibble along the way. Somehow I'd ended up carrying the bag, and now what remained of our lifesaving mission rested on my pillow.

The ship's approach to Mýkonos was picture-postcard pretty. Bathed in dazzling sunlight, the crosses on the domed churches soared over white houses stacked like sugar cubes. Our destination was Petasos Bay Hotel in the village of Platý Yialós, a quiet corner. Most of the island's sheltered coves and protected beaches cater to families, scuba divers, and the occasional topless German ladies trying to suntan, but I was well aware (thanks to Internet sources) that this island also harbored some of the best party beaches in Greece, complete with famous DJs and all-night dancing.

It wasn't long before Heather discovered the discos and the nightlife at Paradise and Super Paradise beaches. She'd return to the hotel late at night full of stories of young men with long eyelashes and of heartfelt conversations under star-filled skies.

"Spyro . . . he's so innocent!" she'd sigh, flopping herself across the bed with sand flying from every crease in her clothing.

"But how did you understand him?" mumbled ever-practical Hayley from her pillow. "I thought you said he spoke only Greek."

"We didn't need words to communicate," said Heather as she rolled over to catch just enough sleep before heading out to Sunrise Bar, where party-goers welcomed the rising sun each morning. Heather even admitted that she was seriously considering staying on the island as a go-go dancer. She seemed to like the idea that a cabin bed and all the ouzo she could drink would be provided free, courtesy of Paradise Bar. Although she'd been capably living on her own for several years, this whole development made me worry. I took little comfort in the fact that her relationship with Spyro had not progressed beyond gazing. Yet.

"But what would you do in the winter?" asked Hayley. Although she'd been invited to join in the fun, she already had a busy schedule trying to catch the eye of Kostas, the hotel's young Greek porter. At various times of the day I'd spot her lurking at strategic locations—near the luggage racks, beside the shady tree where he could occasionally be spied puffing on a quick cigarette. But despite her best efforts, she always seemed to miss him. I was thankful that the amount of time she spent primping in the hotel room's bathroom for potential sightings, was, at least, keeping her out of trouble. For now.

Privately, Hayley and I worried that Heather might get into trouble. We didn't have to worry for long.

The party bubble was set to burst the morning that Heather had headed off wearing a bright red metallic fishnet halter top, red vinyl shoes à la Judy Jetson, and a short black miniskirt. Hidden underneath it all, she wore a pair of my Fruit of the Loom briefs—in a pattern best described as faded Holly Hobbie floral. Heather's busy party schedule left no time for laundry, so she had pilfered clean undies from me.

"After all," she admitted later, "I didn't think anyone would ever see them."

Later that night, when she flopped on the bed, I looked at the clock. It was suspiciously early. After some urging by her younger sister, she spilled the story.

"Well, I was dancing on the pedestal platform as usual and just getting into the music," she began. "As I got more into the rhythm, I began to feel a cool breeze gusting from below."

"I glanced down and was horrified to see that a guy in a gold lamé bodysuit had whisked up my skirt and was filming my every dance move," she said. "What could I do?"

Hayley and I just stared in fascination.

"I was wearing Mom's granny panties," she said with a groan. Hayley looked horrified. Although I wasn't particularly happy that my gitch had been out for a night on the town without me, I was secretly pleased that she'd been wearing modest attire.

"The guy was filming me like it was a documentary," she continued.

My mind leaped to what I'd heard about websites, and I wondered if the Holly Hobbies were gyrating on some far-off computer screen right now.

"What did you do?" asked Hayley. She was clearly horrified by the idea of being seen in Mom's underwear.

"I decided to go with it and keep dancing," said Heather "I pretended I wasn't wearing the damned granny panties and tried to incorporate pulling down my skirt into my dance moves."

"How can I ever go back?" she moaned. Indeed, I thought, feeling a welcome sense of relief that she wasn't going to cast aside her future to dance on tabletops in Mýkonos.

"But what about Spyro?" asked her sister.

"He's so nice," Heather said. Then she paused. "But so short."

Once Heather's partying scheduled had slowed down, the remainder of the week fell into a predictable pattern. We found time to rendezvous for dinner in our favorite open-air restaurant overlooking the water, where we joined the regulars for the nightly sunset display. Hayley would calculate the tip, Heather would flirt with guests at neighboring tables, and, thanks to a chivalrous waiter, I got introduced to Metaxa brandy. At midnight the girls and I would enjoy long chats in the hot tub. Mornings we floated together in clear, cool water that swirled over flat, smooth rocks. Colored fish darted between our toes. In the days that passed, I visited Delos, the birthplace of

Apollo, while my youngest took scuba diving lessons from a tattooed instructor at Psaroú Beach. Heather found new, safer dance spots and gave up her go-go-dancing aspirations.

On one of our last nights, local Greek men danced an impromptu dance until the moon was high in the sky. The aroma of oregano, crushed by their heels on the wooden floor, filled the air with bursts of its spicy fragrance.

The next morning, we woke up early because time was running out for Heather to fulfill her promise to join her sister for a banana boat ride in Petasos Bay. Wearing what Hayley and I had dubbed the "naughty nurse" outfit (a form-fitting white skirt and collared blouse combo) and sporting bushy armpits and a strong odor, Heather was a pretty picture, but we didn't argue, as she was surprisingly agreeable given the early hour. She barely even grumbled as she strapped on her life jacket. Meanwhile, Hayley was busy fending off the attentions of the boat staff.

"How about a date?" asked one fellow with a hairy chest and tiny Speedo bathing trunks.

"I'm only sixteen, and I already have a boyfriend," said Hayley. I could tell from her expression that she hoped, like I did, that this bit of information might dissuade further attentions, since the guy was at least thirty-five years old. But he didn't mind.

"That's okay. How about midnight tonight?" he asked pointing to some nearby bushes.

Just as I was ready to jump in and express some maternal indignation, he turned to the business at hand, attaching the ropes to the inner tubes to connect them to the towboat. I waded into the cool water, carrying my camera up high. As I tried to wrestle my way up and into the boat, a muscular arm reached out to help me over the gunwale. I looked up and saw the Greek dancer from the previous night. With his hair slicked back with salt water and his muscular thighs planted firmly in front of the boat's steering column, he put Anthony Quinn to shame as a candidate for Zorba the Greek. I had to admit that the day had begun most auspiciously. I flopped myself over the gunwale and landed like a hooked tuna amid the water at the bottom of the boat.

At the shore's edge, Heather was extinguishing her final cigarette, and Hayley was swatting off the attentions of her mature admirer when the boat captain gave the signal to lift off. We pulled away from the shore with the two girls bobbing behind like apples in a barrel.

The smug grin that Heather gave her younger sister as the boat started up was soon replaced by a look of concentration as she grabbed for the inner tube's handles. As we cleared the edge of the bay, the captain opened the engine's throttle, and we took off with a roar. My camera was soaked with spray, and my glasses were askew, but even so, I could see the girls hanging on for dear life. Heather's usual flirtatious insouciance had been replaced with a look of grim determination. Meanwhile, Hayley laughed wildly, reveling in the revenge she'd managed to exert on her sister. By some stroke of good fortune, she seemed to be riding the quiet side of the boat's wake and was barely experiencing a ripple.

The boat captain, his bare chest glistening with sea spray, roared back and forth across the bay with ferocious speed. Even Hayley looked concerned about the beating her sister was taking. The bumping and twisting had twirled Heather's hair into a Hershey's Kiss on top of her head, and even at a distance, I could see that she had a distinctly greenish tinge. Just when I thought I'd have to tap the captain on his powerful thigh as a sign to stop—and I wouldn't have minded—it was over. With one final roar and a quick turn, both girls landed with a splash in the water. They were towed back to shore to a welcome cocktail of ouzo and orange juice. Hayley extended her cocktail, the larger of the two, to her sister as a peace offering.

"How was it?" I asked.

"Pretty tame," responded Heather, giving a nonchalant shrug.

We left the next day for Santoríni, Rhodes, Pátmos, and Crete. Beforehand, Hayley finally had a conversation with Kostas, the porter. Due to language barriers, it was rather brief, but she managed to find out that he missed his mother in Athens, and she seemed satisfied with that. Box of condoms still unopened but bonds of friendship forged, Heather predictably cried saying goodbye to all her party friends. I packed a bottle of Metaxa in my hand luggage.

After our week of unbridled and unscheduled island life, our first few days back on the cruise ship were a challenge. The scheduled side trips and mealtimes were an unwelcome adjustment. But I knew we were back in the swing when the boat made its first stop in Turkey and Hayley and I were running after Heather, who had gone ashore in an eye-popping, fitted black satin cocktail dress, teetering black sandals, and a matching wide straw hat. "A classic outfit for a piece of classical history," she said.

A few hours later, after going our separate ways to explore and shop, Hayley and I met up at our rendezvous spot at the dock. We waited. No Heather. With only a few moments remaining before departure, we decided that she must have already boarded and climbed aboard the transfer dinghy to the cruise ship.

Fifteen minutes later, a commotion ensued. Heather was racing down the dock, heels clacking against the wooden slats of the dock. She was clutching a newly purchased hookah pipe in one hand, its hose flapping dangerously behind her. In her other hand, she held a rug with a psychedelic depiction of the Virgin of Guadalupe. Behind her, like a frenzied crowd of paparazzi who'd just spotted Sophia Loren, a posse of Turkish border agents pursued her, yelling, "Stop! Stop!"

A dinghy bobbed in the water at the end of the dock, piloted by a handful of stragglers.

"You can make it!" I heard one of them yell.

She leapt aboard.

"My savior, the *Aegean II!*" she said, referring to our cruise ship by name.

"No, no! This is the *Princessa!* We're going to Italy!" screamed one of the passengers, pushing her back onto the dock.

Fortunately, the real *Aegean II* had sent a sailor out to retrieve her. The Turkish guards were left shaking their fists from the dock.

Meanwhile, on board, the intercom intoned, "Miss Hayley Koroluk, please report to the purser's station."

"Isn't that you?" our lounge-chair mates asked. Hayley tried to be as inconspicuous as possible under a beach towel by the pool. It turned out, of course, that Heather had grabbed Hayley's ID card in order to sneak one of her cocktail allotments (her own having been exhausted after the first night). The authorities were paging the wrong sister—believing her to be the missing person in the head count.

I stayed right on my lounge chair. I'd reached the end of my maternal rope. We'd already racked up enormous bills using the ship-to-shore radio to make emergency bank transfers so Heather's rent check didn't bounce. Hayley had done calculator duty—standing by the phone and figuring out the exchange rate and the implications in drachmas. It was all too stressful.

So now, I took a sip of my cocktail and resigned myself to the fact that, at twenty-three years old, if Heather got stranded, she was resilient enough to be able to figure out a way back to Athens to meet us for the flight home. I had, after all, pinned the hotel's address to her purse. Plus, as she said, she could always get work as a go-go dancer.

Honeymoon in Hell

Marrit Ingman

• • • • • • • • • • • • • • • • • •

The pillow was too small, too oddly shaped, too flat. The blankets were too thin and too heavy. The air was too recycled, the passengers too numerous. The cabin seemed at once too loud and too quiet. I looked out my window at the wing of the 747, which had just taken off from LAX. Destination: Maui. Some kind of rubberized wing part seemed to be flapping ominously in time with my menstrual contractions.

I do not enjoy travel.

Yet, like legions of honeymooners before and since, I felt compelled to have fun. Thus I and Jim, my partner of many years and husband of two months, were beginning our lifetime of officially sanctioned matrimony with a perfect, photogenic Hawaiian vacation. Jim loved Maui and regaled me with tales of the delights awaiting us. Of course we'd drive the road to Hana and bicycle down Haleakala at sunrise. Of course we'd drink Kona blend while waves lapped our toes, followed by volcanic sex in the condo. We'd ride the Sugar Cane Train and swim with turtles. We'd eat seared opah with guava. Jim made it sound impossible not to enjoy the trip. The only dangers in this Pacific paradise were swimmer's ear and a touch of the trots from eating too much pineapple.

I AM NOT an enthusiastic traveler. Trouble follows me. I am the one who loses her luggage (Madison, Wisconsin). I get airsick (Laramie, Wyoming) and carsick (Cheyenne, Wyoming). I jackknife trailers (Pine Valley, California, and Kerrville, Texas) and lose maps (Peekskill, New York). Once I blew the fuse to my car stereo and air conditioning during an interminable trip through the Mojave (Gila Bend, Arizona). I can't make it from the ticketing counter to the terminal without losing my credit card and ID (Houston, Texas).

Now I was on the trip that would set the tone for the rest of my marriage, and I was hungry, hung over, anxious, and bleeding. My period, which is as unpredictable as I am not, arrived during liftoff, as if it were eager to accompany me on my first-ever trip off the North American landmass. Caught unprepared, I had to stuff a freebie maxi from the lav—some kind of supersize Beltless Freedom Monolith for Her—into my traveling pants for the flight.

The wreckage of the USS *Arizona* loomed beneath the clear water as we landed at Honolulu International, where we would be stranded for an eight-hour layover. Though flights to Maui departed every hour, we weren't able to leave until that afternoon, for some inexplicable reason. My hormones were at high tide. Jim sat me down in the airport's restaurant, a nauseating tropical-themed diner. An artificial parrot perched on a swing by my head; steel drums over a loudspeaker hammered me. Other flights to Maui came and went as we sagged in whimsical too-tall chairs that left my swollen ankles dangling girlishly.

"Just try this." Jim passed me his iced tea. I glared at him. By now I was soaking a fauxpon made of rolled-up toilet paper. "The lemon is great."

It was. It was the single greatest lemon of my life. I sighed and drank and felt buoyed. It was piquant and sweet and fresh. My mood swung violently in the opposite direction, and I dissolved into grateful tears. We were in the islands at last. There was ground beneath my feet. The crowds around us had abated. I could eat a square meal—albeit a kitschy one— and breathe unrecycled air.

I sat, and Jim patted my hand, and I was reminded of the purpose of marriage, ideally: helping two people in love stick together through the shit. We would travel together. If I jacknifed a trailer somehow, we'd straighten it out. If I blew out a fuse, we'd replace it. If I became violently ill, Jim would bring me Gatorade and, if necessary, the paramedics. Perhaps we'd even have fun.

Both our moods lifted. By the time we trundled our gear into the trunk of our rental car and were skimming along the Maui coastline, we were both giddy. We laughed our way through the supermarket, where we bought a seven-dollar box of tampons and fixings for cocktails. We laughed our way into the condo, occupied during the off-season by friends of Jim's parents, whose jovial voices sang "Mahalo!" on the answering machine whenever the phone rang. We laughed our way through piña coladas and sex on a towel on Jim's parents' friends' couch. We laughed our way out to the pool and splashed around drunkenly. Then we laughed our way into a Vietnamese restaurant next door.

"Does it smell off in here to you?" Jim asked.

I shrugged, as my sense of smell is extremely weak. My olfactory deficiency is partly to blame for my apprehension in the world. I can't smell fear or trouble or danger, nor apple pie or *yakitori* or dirty diapers. "You think something's wrong with the restaurant?"

"I don't know. Maybe it's us." We dissolved into giggles. Just the same, I ordered vegetables.

I felt the motion of the sea around two o'clock that morning in Jim's parents' friends' creaky rattan bed. Too many drinks? I staggered into the little pink bathroom, waiting for relief. I shat. And shat. And shat. And shat blistering lava with volcanic force. Tears sprang to my eyes. Saliva sprang to my mouth. And I sprang to my knees in front of Jim's parents' friends' toilet. Up came the mung beans and curry, the piña coladas, the sassy, piquant, locally grown lemon in fiery torrents.

When Jim staggered in just before sunrise, I waved to him. "Hi, honey." Then I turned back to the basin and projected a stream of something green and watery. "How did you sleep?"

"How long have you been in here, doing . . . that?" he squeaked.

"All night, I guess. What time is it?"

"I don't know."

I vomited again.

"I've never seen you puke before."

It's true. Like Jerry Seinfeld, I'm not a puker. Allow me to recall an instance in particular from my flaming youth, when we all drank assy keg beer and party punch and smoked tainted pot until no one was standing except for me. I curled up in a corner and moaned for hours, but I did not vomit.

Jim was saying something unintelligible. I pulled my head out of the toilet. "Did you say something else?"

"Yeah, I said if you're puking it has to be serious."

We ticked off the culprits. Sun poisoning? Food poisoning? Traveler's sickness? "I think the islands are rejecting me," I whispered, then gagged.

"I feel okay," he said.

We sat for a minute. What did I have that Jim didn't? Alarm pricked my queasy stomach. "Oh, no. It's toxic shock!"

"What's that?"

"An infection from tampons or sponges that takes over your body," I said. I was doomed.

"Is it serious? I've never heard of that."

"Nan Robertson, the writer, had it! They had to amputate her fingertips!"

"How likely is that?"

"They're going to have to amputate my fingers, Jim."

"Really?" We looked at my fingers and at each other.

He sighed. "Okay. I'm calling."

In fact, paramedics were not an unusual sight at this building, populated as it is by elderly retirees. Jim's mother later had a heart attack there. And I'm happy to report that the Maui emergency response team is just as polite and efficient as can be.

One suntanned tech took my blood pressure while another took my temperature. "Where you folks from?"

"San Diego," I mumbled, for that was our residence at the time.

"So your weather is probably a lot like ours, huh?"

I nodded weakly. So why, exactly, had we left?

"Okay, your pressure's fine, and your temp's a little elevated. Just keep pounding the water, and let's hope some of it stays put so you don't get dehydrated."

"Mahalo," Jim said. Then he went back to the store to get Gatorade. He said the same clerk from yesterday had checked him out and remembered us. "Whoa, man," he'd said. "Today's not as good?"

Indeed, today was not as good. I sipped and vomited various colors of Gatorade. I tried to focus on the book of crossword puzzles Jim had brought. I watched a *Dragonball Z* marathon on the Cartoon Network. I moaned and slipped in and out of consciousness in a high-backed rattan chair. At one point Jim materialized, wet and smiling, in front of me, wearing a mask, snorkel, and fins. I blinked, but he didn't disappear.

"I found all this stuff in the closet, and it fits! So I went out to the cove. It was pretty murky, but I saw this one huge thing that was, like, a grouper or something, and it swam right up to me and looked me in the face. Man, I almost shit myself!" He paused. "Um, sorry."

"No, it's okay. You had fun. That's good."

"Yeah. And I saw turtles. Little baby turtles! They were cruising around like *this!*" Jim approximated a drunken, shambling swim stroke with the arms and legs unsynchronized. "It was wicked."

"Wicked, yes." I nodded.

"Are you hungry?"

"How can you even ask that?"

"Yeah, right. I, uh, think I'm going to go get some dinner."

"Uh huh."

I watched the American Music Awards almost in their entirety before he returned, hiding plastic takeout bags behind his back. He clattered around in his parents' friends' kitchen.

"You can bring that out here," I said. "I'm feeling better." It was true. I hadn't excreted anything violently for a few hours.

"Good, okay." He plunked down with a steaming plate of rice and orange chicken. "You would have loved this place. I sat at the bar while they were making my order, and the owner is this guy from the Bay Area or something, and he's been out here for fifteen years. 'I'm living my dream,' he told me. He gave me free drinks while we were talking, and—"

"Oh, that looks good."

We paused.

"Do you want some rice?"

"No, I want *that.*" Suddenly I did. And just as suddenly as I'd eaten some, it came right back up.

BY THE NEXT MORNING, I felt better, if tired. (Our upstairs neighbors, who turned out to be the septuagenarians in Speedos at the pool, had kept us awake with noisy, grunting sex.) After I kept down a glass of pineapple-orange-guava juice and a plain waffle, we decided to rent snorkeling gear for me and go to the beaches.

First was Ulua, a snorkeling spot surrounded by resort hotels and noted for its gentle slope. All of Hawaii's beaches are public, so we were able to march right up in our Target swimwear and borrowed towels and plunk down next to the beautiful people.

I'm conspicuous at the beach because I'm a shade shy of albinism and I swim like a rock. But once I'd put on my flippers and waddled down to the water, Jim was able to tow me around while I took pictures of needle-fish, humuhumunukunukuapua'a, and myself. ("Look! I'm underwater somehow!") The current was slow enough that my stomach stayed steady.

In the afternoon, after lunch at a fish shack and some shave ice, I felt confident enough to swim at Olowalu, a popular beachfront with moderate reef coverage and stronger tides. The payoff was better snorkeling; I was still envious of Jim's turtle sighting. I reattired myself in my flippers and mask and slopped down to the waves, only to be swept out on my ass.

"Dude, did you get tossed?" Jim righted me. "You're gonna have road rash for sure."

The other problem was my mercurial period. I'd slowed to a trickle over the course of the morning. I spent the first half of the day wincing and tiptoeing around with a junior Tampax, which seemed too absorbent, as if my eyeballs and nose were drying out. Then I'd had to decide whether to let myself go free. Maybe I'd get a tiny brown spot on my suit. If I ran around with an overabsorbent tampon when I didn't actually need one, maybe I *would* get TSS and have my fingers amputated.

"Hey, I just thought of something," I called to Jim. "What if my period starts up again in the water? Don't people get bitten by sharks here?" In fact, they do. There are shark populations throughout the Hawaiian waters, but

Olowalu has a particular reputation for attacks, including a fatal one in 1991. Signs advising that SHARKS MAY BE PRESENT were posted on the site in 2002, four years after our trip.

I envisioned the headline in the *Maui News:* PALE, DYSPEPTIC TOURIST SAVES FINGER, LOSES LEG TO TIGER SHARK. As I pondered, I failed to realize that the current was sweeping me toward a pointy reef. I was starting to get too tired to fight it.

"Let me pull you back in," Jim suggested. "You're not full strength. You should hang out for a while."

Jim is a burly guy and a former water polo player, meaning that he can tread water for hours while batting a ball around and wearing funny little cups on his ears. He is as aquatic as I am terrestrial. He can swim while punching jocks from Irvine in the face. So once again he enjoyed the island's choicest snorkeling while I lay on the sand—in the shade, sipping water—like a tenderized chop.

I struggled out of my wet t-shirt and stood in my suit. I shook the sand off my shirt and let the wind blow it dry in my hands. In minutes my shirt was dry and warm and clean but suffused with the pleasant saline stiffness of seawater; it crackled over my head as I pulled it back on. I sat in its embrace and closed my eyes, actually starting to feel contented for a change. When would I learn to inhabit the moment, to free myself of my expectations? Surely, the objective of a honeymoon wasn't *really* to have a perfect beginning, but to throw couples into a torrent of chaos away from home and let them reel themselves in. It was a walkabout or what a more adventurous friend of mine, a Peace Corps volunteer working in Mali, calls a *yalla yalla—a* journey to test your mettle. It was and it wasn't paradise, just as any day of your life is or isn't.

Jim materialized, and we packed up the car to go back. While he chattered at the wheel about his underwater discoveries (more turtles, a steep drop-off in the ocean floor that scared him so much he turned back), I felt my head sag against the window of the car. The cadence of the coastal high-way underneath our wheels lulled me half to sleep in the glow of the setting sun, and we swept along through Lahaina and the resorts of Ka'anapali.

As we rounded a sharp curve to Honokeana, a chartered tour bus veered into our lane. Jim laid on the horn and ground our wheels into the dirt. The bus plowed on.

"Shit!" he yelled.

I laughed.

He was trembling behind the wheel. "What's so funny?"

"Dude, we almost went out like Falco! That'd be perfect."

Jim paused, distracted. "Are you telling me Falco is dead?"

"Yep. Taken out by a tour bus in the Dominican Republic. He was planning his comeback."

"Really? Was it good, you think?"

"I guess the world will never know."

He laughed too. As he put the car back in gear and pulled onto the road, I felt emboldened by danger. Maybe I'd learn to face the unknown—the unforeseen delays, the buses bearing down around every corner. Maybe someday I'd even apply for a passport.

As OUR WEEK went on, I became more stable and less wan, though the community *pu pu* party on our condo's lanai almost did me in, and we didn't drive to Hana after all. ("Dude, there're too many switchbacks. You'd totally barf.") Even I was disappointed not to see the legendary black sands of Wai'anapanapa and the Seven Sacred Pools. We didn't bike Haleakala, but we drove to the top and ate a picnic, mystified by the sight of cows grazing above the clouds. I loved the mountainous and verdant upcountry, the cool wetness of the air. We hiked around the crater long enough for me to get vertigo, fall off the trail, and squash a silversword plant.

On the shores I had felt as if I were teetering on the edge of nothingness. Inland, in the upcountry, I felt more centered, more in *place*, less like I was bobbing on a cork formed by volcanic extrusion in the middle of the Pacific. Instead of beach bums and tourists, I saw farmers—much like my own people back home in Texas. I gazed at the homesteads terraced into the mountains. I felt as if I could lie in the grass and stare at the sky and truly give myself over to being in another place.

We went back to the condo reluctantly. Jim grilled pineapple and sweet Maui onions with our neighbors, and we ate them with fresh fish on the patio, watching the sunset. Jim moved the tiki glasses—the ones we'd had our piña coladas in—to the back of his parents' friends' cupboard, since the sight of them made me gag.

On our last night, we had a final farewell dinner in an upscale Lahaina restaurant, with a bottle of local wine and opah, and even though I could complain—at one table next to us a couple was having a noisy, tearful breakup, and at another, a titan gastronome was belching unabashedly, hands spread wide and his mouth raised to the sky in gratitude—I didn't.

And I slept all the way home.

The Occidental Tourist

Judy Wolf

• • • • • • • • • • • • • • • • • • •

veryone raised their metal tumblers and bellowed a word I didn't understand. "Drink up," said Martin, my motorbike-taxi-driver-turned-host, leaning toward me. Not wanting to be rude, I took a sip of the harsh rice whiskey, most likely distilled in the dark, soot-stained interior of a village hut.

"All of it," he said. I grimaced and threw back the rest of the drink. My glass was immediately refilled, I looked at him and he shrugged, grinning.

I had met Martin the afternoon before in Phnom Penh and, charmed by his easy smile, accepted an invitation to step off the beaten tourist track for a visit to his home village. I'd been traveling solo for several months, having escaped from home shortly after tying the knot to wander the world on my own, a devoted vagabond adjusting to this startling concept of myself as *married*.

My trip through Cambodia had started off normally enough: a visit to Siem Reap and the ancient ruins of Angkor Wat, followed by a slow boat ride south to Phnom Penh, where I thought I'd spend a couple of days doing the usual tourist things—seeing museums, visiting pagodas, contemplating monuments, getting a massage, firing an AK-47 at a range outside town. Martin had driven me to my hotel, then (as savvy motorbike drivers do) said, "I wait here. You see your room to decide if you like it. If it's not okay, I take you to another place." He'd settled himself in a wooden chair on the sidewalk while I went inside. The room had been fine, but (as per his cunning plan) I felt obligated to go down and tell him so.

When I'd stepped onto the sidewalk, Martin was napping in the dusty late morning sun, his chair leaned nonchalantly back against the wall. He was a handsome guy, striking in his simple, slightly oversize white button-down, jean-clad legs stretched in front of him, black army boots casually crossed, like a man with all the confidence in the world.

I cleared my throat, and Martin peered up at me from beneath his lowered eyelids, a mischievous boy about to share his next idea for getting into trouble. "Want to go to a wedding?" he said, his tone seductive.

He's a swinger! I thought. *Austin Powers incarnate!* "I'm married," I said. "I'd love to go, but if you want to ask some other single tourist, I totally understand."

He'd looked me up and down, his expression inscrutable, then given an offhand shrug. "It's okay. I pick you up in twenty minutes."

That night, we went to a wedding near the Killing Fields. The dramatic monument to wrongful death that marks the site sat two hundred yards away from the flamboyant celebration of life we then joined. *This,* I thought, pleased as only a tourist can be by my accidental good fortune, *is a true introduction to Cambodia.* Afterwards, Martin asked me if I'd like to go to another wedding, this one near his village the following day. *What an opportunity,* I thought, remembering an anthropology professor's advice never to turn down an invitation to someone's home while traveling.

And so I found myself sitting cross-legged on a low bamboo platform in the raked dirt yard of his family's hut, drinking rice whiskey. His mother had made a special dinner of seasoned fish, tender field greens cooked in a spicy sauce, and the ubiquitous sticky white rice of Southeast Asia. The scent of seasoning mingled in the warm evening air with the tang of our bodies. Seven of us were seated around the platform, eating, drinking, talking, and laughing. One of us (that would be me) hadn't a clue what was being said. I relied on body language and Martin's occasional translations.

"Where is your family?"

"In the United States." They discussed this amongst themselves.

"Are you married?"

"Yes." They looked at me in mild surprise.

"Where is your husband?"

"He is at home." *Watering the plants,* I thought. *Minding the homestead. Can you imagine?*

"Do you have any children?" *Ah, the inevitable question.*

"No."

"Why not?"

There is no answer to this question in many countries. *Because I don't want any* is inconceivable—preposterous, even. What kind of freakish woman travels alone and doesn't want kids? And—I could see this in their sly smiles—what fool leaves a husband at home on his own? I was obviously touched in the head, but I was a guest. Despite what I had already come to think of as his usual candor, Martin didn't translate the majority of the banter. From the nonverbal exchanges, it seemed that much of it was sexual innuendo—and a good deal of it appeared to involve him.

As if to confirm their teasing, Martin reached over to pile more fernlike greens and spicy fish onto my tin plate, then picked up a wad of the greens, which tangled together like weeds, with his chopsticks. He held this offering to my mouth, and his family giggled as he fed me. "Just like newlyweds," he translated for me. *Great,* I thought, sauce dripping down my chin.

The conversation wound its way like a jungle snake through the undergrowth of daily gossip, occasionally slithering back toward me. "How long have you been away from home?" "Where have you been?"

"Show them your pants," said Martin, indicating my convertible cargo pants, which unzipped into baggy shorts.

"It's okay to show my legs?"

I wasn't sure of cultural expectations of modesty but wasn't feeling particularly shy after my pre-dinner bathing experience in the family's back yard. We'd rinsed the road dirt from each other, Martin ordering me to squat down in my thin, borrowed sarong while he scooped water over my head from a large bucket. This might have been a sensual, affirming experience—handsome man scoops water over exotic, sparsely clad woman—but the sarong had been designed to fit his minuscule mother, not an overfed foreigner. In addition, the back yard was surrounded by other huts on stilts, each of which (I was certain of this) had rows of hidden eyes peering at our farcical display. I'd concentrated on holding my sarong together, desperately trying to avoid that oh-so-attractive hospital gown effect, as I squatted beneath his ministrations.

"Yes, yes. Show them. It's okay."

I wasn't surprised by his answer, especially considering that, after our very public bath, I'd spent the afternoon being poked, prodded, and ordered to exhibit for villagers the pale flesh beneath my long-sleeved shirt. As Martin paraded me around his village for an afternoon tour, I'd quickly realized that the object wasn't to show the village to me, but rather, to show *me* to the village. My height, brawn, freckled skin, khaki pants, and lack of jewelry had drawn a crowd at every hut. "She looks like a man!" had been exclaimed so many times that Martin finally got sick of translating it and opted instead for, "She says you look like a movie star."

So I unzipped the leg of my pants, to the great amusement of Martin's family. One of the older men reached over and slapped my bare inner thigh with a sharp, resounding smack.

"Ow!" I cried.

The man laughed.

"Want me to do that to *you?*" I threatened.

"Go ahead," translated Martin.

My hand made a sharp crack as it slapped the man's bare thigh in return, a gesture that was followed by uproarious laughter. Martin nodded his approval as I replaced my pant leg, then climbed down from the platform and gestured for me to follow him.

We climbed onto his motorbike, referred to throughout Cambodia as a "moto," and followed a winding dirt road through the darkened village. Without artificial light, the open yards of huts we'd visited that afternoon were now cocooned in a shadowy privacy. My sense of space constricted to the width of a dim headlight.

We emerged into a bright circle of revelry and clamor: music, conversation, laughter, the clang of metal dishes, the smell of warm bodies. A wedding was under way. Martin climbed off his moto and walked over to greet his childhood friend.

"We're invited to eat with the family," he said, indicating that I should follow him.

Up a wooden stepladder and into a bamboo hut on stilts, we joined a circle of cross-legged friends and family for a candlelit dinner. Sweet delicacies wrapped in banana leaf were passed from hand to hand; more tumblers of hard alcohol were raised in toast to the happy couple.

Forty minutes later, some unspoken group consensus inspired us all to rise, protesting that we couldn't eat another bite as more tidbits of mango and sticky rice were pressed upon us. Our unsteady line of revelers moved to the ladder and descended to join the party.

The world wobbled as my vision struggled to keep up with my movements. Before me, a grassy square was lit with lanterns and filled with people. Martin led me into the circling crowd of dancers and began to show me the steps and arm motions. My attempts at grace drew good-humored attention, and I soon had a number of men endeavoring to teach me the "right" way while plying me with drinks. Within a few minutes, the playful contest over who would demand my attention had deteriorated into a tug of war. A hand on my elbow pulled me one way to show me a movement. A heave on my other arm spun me to view an alternative and far superior explanation. Back and forth I was hauled. The smell of the crowd changed, and a deep, animal instinct stirred in me. The men were drunk, and their quarrel was spreading to include others, taking on an edge of realism that jarred me out of the dreamlike setting.

A strong and athletic woman, I stood at least a head taller than the men demanding my attention, so I had trouble finding the experience immediately threatening—but at the edge of my consciousness, a thought nagged. *Should I be taking this more seriously?* I became acutely aware of the ebb and flow of the crowd, the abrupt change of mood, and was relieved to see Martin when he broke in and herded me out of the dance area. He pulled me aside and told me to stay put while he consulted with a huddle of men whom he described as the village leaders. I stood as ordered, inhaling the sweet scent of earth, candles, and trampled grass, listening to the music and revelry from the outskirts of the gathering.

"It's okay now," said Martin, returning to my side. "I tell them your country is very strong. If there's trouble for you, it's trouble for me. If there's trouble for me, it's trouble for the village. If there's trouble for the village, it's trouble for Cambodia. Not trouble with you, but trouble with your government. They will put an end to it." *An end to what?* I wondered. *What did I just miss?*

He led me to his moto and indicated that I should get on. "We're leaving?"

"I have another friend's wedding I want to visit. Is that okay with you?"

I shrugged and swung my leg over the seat. "Are you okay to drive?"

"Yes, yes," he said. "I will always tell you if I'm not okay to drive. You believe me?" He smiled at me, charming and earnest.

I had a fleeting moment of worry before the alcohol swept away any notion of concern. "Okay," I said.

The bike's engine roared to life between our legs, and he maneuvered through the crowd. A few hundred yards down the road, he stopped at a darkened hut and began to yell at it. From my increasingly drunken stupor, it seemed patently absurd.

"Why do you wake them up? They're sleeping."

"That's okay, they come with us." He called out again.

"But what if they don't want to come?"

"That's okay, it's what I pay them for."

Two sleepy men emerged from the hut and came over to talk with Martin, then disappeared again.

"You pay them?"

He nodded. "Yes yes. For protection. That's what they do. They are the strong men of the village. I think you say mafia? It's a good idea. My friend wedding is outside my village. They come with us."

A few minutes later, they had climbed onto another moto and were following us through the village. We zipped through the darkness, past murky forest and what, in daylight, had been flat expanses of hand-plowed rice fields but now seemed sinister. A narrow track off the main dirt road took several forks through thickening underbrush, then surfaced into an open clearing: another village, lit for a wedding celebration.

Martin rode his bike into the midst of the crowd, taking up space, as I'd noticed he liked to do. We made our way into the dancing throng, but this time, I was watched by my personal bodyguards. When men approached to press me with drinks, I didn't have to figure out how to politely refuse: my bodyguards materialized by my side and skillfully deflected the proffered intoxicants and excessive attention. I found I was free to smile and laugh, dance and joke, clowning good naturedly as travelers do when they don't speak the language.

Then, with the belated urgency of one who has imbibed too much rice whiskey, I realized I had to relieve my bladder. I worked my way to the edge of the crowd and looked for an opening between huts. Under cover of darkness, modesty in this part of the world dictated only that one move out of sight and into the shadows for bladder relief. As I made my way along a fence line beside a nearby hut, I noticed that one of my bodyguards was following me.

I acknowledged him with an inquiring nod, and he pointed a few yards in front of me, saying something that I took to mean, "This looks like an excellent substitute for a lavatory." Then he turned his back, folded his arms, and stood with his feet solidly apart while I squatted behind him, stifling my giggles.

Martin was right. I am like a movie star, I thought, trying not to topple over or pee on my pant legs.

Having made our appearance, we soon climbed back onto Martin's moto and roared through the crowd to retrace our route home. My bodyguards had already gone ahead, for reasons I never clearly understood. Martin and I wobbled unsteadily down the dirt path until we reached a particularly sharp left bend, whereupon we tilted into a slow-motion plunge that came to rest in a pile of underbrush.

"Are you okay?" exclaimed Martin, struggling to extricate himself from the foliage. His eyelids gave the impression of being too heavy to lift properly. I laughed.

"I don't think I can drive," he said, sounding serious in his effort to speak coherently. "Can you drive?"

"Me?" I laughed again. My world was a woozy place that couldn't seem to keep itself properly in focus.

"I say I tell you if I am not okay to drive. I am not okay to drive."

He must be joking, I thought. For someone who typically volunteered to be the designated driver, the situation was comical in its incongruity. My limbs seemed to be controlled by an unseen puppeteer. Rather than being directly manipulated by my brain, they moved in a strange sort of slow motion.

Taxi! I thought and giggled. *Oh, wait, he is my taxi.*

We eventually disentangled ourselves, floundered to our feet, and righted the moto, then switched places. I felt around for the starter and switched on the dim headlamp. Concentrating hard, I picked a slow, blind path through the ruts and potholes. "Which way?" I asked, as we reached a fork in the road.

Martin looked blurrily around us and pointed left. I jerked the bike forward, bouncing through unseen humps and hollows. I wasn't giggling anymore. All my powers of concentration came to bear on keeping the moto upright and following the pale circle of light from its feeble headlight. The road to his village began to appear in my mind as a long and arduous minefield of potholes and treachery. *We'll never get home at this rate,* I thought. Bouncing behind me, Martin must have been forming the same opinion, because he tapped me on the shoulder and said into my ear, "I'll drive. I'm okay now to drive."

Forty minutes later, we were back at his mother's hut. He called out to let them know we were there, and received a sluggish response that must have meant "Sleep on the platform under the house where we keep the chickens," because that's what we did. I fell into an exhausted sleep, thinking our adventure was essentially over. Little did I know.

The next morning I awoke with the sun, as usual. Martin was decidedly less lively, and it wasn't until his family was up making breakfast around us that he raised a groggy head. "You drive," he said.

The family gathered around to witness our exit, and Martin grinned with what I hoped was pride as I managed to pull smoothly forward through the village. Children flocked along the side of the path and called after us. Martin waved to his mother as we turned a corner and made our way to the main road—a narrow and lumpy dirt lane no less treacherous by daylight.

I spent the next three hours with my hands gripped tight to the handlebars, the road vibrating up through my arms and shoulders as I zigzagged the moto over and around potholes, rocks, and patches of deep sand. Martin's head lolled against my shoulder, and I struggled to keep us both upright, half expecting him to vomit in my ear at any moment.

As if this rural road weren't challenging enough, we occasionally had to navigate oncoming obstacles such as ox carts, herds of ducks, bicyclists, and other moto drivers. Then came the greatest challenge of all—ahead of us loomed a trio of motos, toddling along at a slow speed that not even a hangover could justify. As we approached, I saw that what had appeared to be long bundles strapped to the back of each vehicle were, in fact, the stiff bodies of huge, dead hogs. Not only did I have to pass them, I had to do so without falling into a pothole or causing a pileup of dead pig flesh.

Swiveling up beside the motos along the narrow section of road left open by their wide loads—cloven hooves tied with twine and outstretched like pleading hands—I saw that a hulking ox cart was approaching from the other direction. It was too late: I was committed. I tried not to look at the bouncing pigs as we passed. I could feel the sweat trickling down my spine as I tightened my grasp on the handlebars and twisted the throttle to pull ahead of the trio. The ox cart was closing on me. Holding my breath, I swerved to the right, only to discover that an especially large mud hole had been crossed by a narrow plank.

And then we were through. The ox cart and limp pigs were lumbering along behind me. I exhaled, and Martin clapped me on the back. "You sure you never drive one of these before?" he laughed. "You a fast learner!"

Back in Phnom Penh, he dropped me at my hotel, indicating he would be back to pick me up in an hour for some sightseeing. I went inside to shower and wash the dust out of my clothes. I sighed as I towel-dried my hair and said to my reflection, "Oh, well; back to being a tourist."

Or so I thought. What I didn't know was that it was wedding season in Cambodia: About 80 percent of marriages occur within a two-month period. When I walked back outside at the appointed time, there was Martin, looking much recovered and leaning on the seat of his moto. He glanced up as I walked toward him, gave me a sly grin, and said, "Want to go to a wedding?"

Acknowledgments

First of all, if I could buy around-the-world plane tickets for every one of the writers herein, I would. Each of these funny, revealing, and unexpected journeys invites another one—if only to result in more essays as fun and surprising as those in these pages. Thanks to all of you for traveling so far and writing so well.

Special appreciation goes to the inimitable Leslie Miller, who made good on her promise to edit this book; she did so with her characteristic wit, curiosity, wisdom, and charm. Thanks also to the Twilight Exit bar on Madison Avenue in Seattle, which provided a happy spot for myself and the former ladies of Seal Press—Leslie Miller, Ingrid Emerick, and Jenna Land Free—to enjoy loud jukebox rock, cough-strong cocktails, and a fine conversation about this book-to-be.

For transforming this dog-eared collection of essays into a polished book, thanks to the book's Avalon team players: Marisa Solís, as well as copy editor Cynthia Rubin, proofreader Annie Tucker, and designer Gia Giasullo.

Thanks also to my supportive family—especially to my brother, Gray, whose ridiculous road trip behavior would be immortalized in this book if I wasn't concerned about his eventual run for office. A special shout out to my youngest brother, Peter, too, whose best travels are still ahead of him—sure to start soon, sometime after middle school graduation.

Finally, thanks to Dave for saving us both from that enormous hairy spider in our bedroom in Baja, and for endless other reasons.

Contributor Biographies

C. LILL AHRENS was an artist all her life until a sojourn on the edge of Seoul made her a writer. Excerpts from her memoir in progress, *Seoul Survivor: A Humorous Memoir of Serious Culture Shock*, have won several contests and are published in literary journals, including *Calyx: A Journal of Art and Literature by Women*, and anthologies such as *Scent of Cedars: Promising Writers of the Pacific Northwest*. Lill is a contest coordinator and judge for the Oregon Writers Colony and teaches memoir and fiction writing in Corvallis, Oregon. She belongs to three long-standing critique groups: one monthly, one weekly, and one emergency.

HANNAH BLOCH is a writer based in Washington, D.C. She was a *Time* magazine reporter for twelve years and covered Pakistan and Afghanistan for the magazine from 1996 to 2002. She was CNN's first bureau chief in Islamabad, from 2000 to 2001. She earned two master's degrees from Columbia University, in journalism and international affairs, and studied at the University of Hawaii as a Freedom Forum Asian Studies Fellow and at Stanford University as a John S. Knight Professional Journalism Fellow. She speaks Urdu and Mongrel Dog.

British born and bred, **SARAH FRANKLIN** lived in Austria, Germany, and London before moving with her English husband to Seattle. Alongside her career in publishing, she's an avid freelance writer, and she moonlights as a performer—the English accent being suitably snooty for classical music stations, as well as international enough for the Seattle International Film Festival. Her humor writing has appeared in the *Seattle Times*, and her performances have been heard on NPR affiliates and seen on dimly lit stages throughout Europe and the United States.

CATHERINE GIAIVIA earns her keep producing and designing websites, but her true passion lies in part-time pursuit of two other pleasures: travel writing and cheese. She recently celebrated the one-year anniversary of her move to San Francisco, and the relocation has continued to provide a wealth of new material and unexpected adventures. Her local travel writers' group has trouble maintaining membership because everyone keeps leaving the country. This is her debut publication.

SPIKE GILLESPIE shares her home in Austin, Texas, with her son, Henry, as well as two cats, three dogs, a one-footed yellow bird, and five chickens. Spike has been inching her way toward overnight success for over twenty years, and her work has been published everywhere from *Veterinary Practice Management* to the *New York Times Magazine*. She is the author of *All the Wrong Men and One Perfect Boy: A Memoir* and *Surrender (But Don't Give Yourself Away): Old Cars, Found Hope, and Other Cheap Tricks*. Her next book, *Quilty as Charged: Undercover in a Material World*, in which she explores the wacky subculture of quilting, will be out in 2006. Spike's website is www.spikeg.com.

Montana-born **BETHANY GUMPER** just can't settle down. Her long-held theory that travel insurance karmically wards off medical mishaps was recently disproved when she wound up, fully insured, in a Parisian hospital for gastrointestinal testing. She travels whenever she can save up the cash, which she accomplishes by editing and writing for *Shape* magazine, brown-bagging her lunch, and forgoing lattes. She has lived in three cities in as many years and is currently based in Los Angeles.

After a memorable stint of living in Belfast, Northern Ireland, **ERICA J. GREEN** is now settled in Washington, D.C., where she is the director of publishing for Discovery Communications. While much of her time is spent creating artful books about shows like *Monster Garage,* she still finds time to travel from Turkey to Tipperary to Timbuktu and many places in between. Born and raised in Los Angeles, she graduated with a degree in English from UC Berkeley and has worked in book publishing and media for more than ten years. She is currently working on a novel.

AYUN HALLIDAY is the sole staff member of the quarterly zine the *East Village Inky* and the author of *Job Hopper, No Touch Monkey! And Other Travelers' Lessons Learned Too Late,* and *The Big Rumpus: A Mother's Tale from the Trenches.* She is *BUST* magazine's Mother Superior columnist and contributes to NPR, *Hipmama,* and more anthologies than you can shake a stick at without dangling a participle. She lives in a very small apartment in Brooklyn. More at www.ayunhalliday.com.

MARRIT INGMAN is a freelance writer, film critic, and reluctant traveler. She is a regular contributor to the *Austin Chronicle, Mamalicious,* and www.austin mama.com. Her writing has also appeared in *Brain, Child; Isthmus;* the *Coast Weekly; Alter Net;* the *Anchorage Press,* and other publications. She has taught writing at Boston University and Springfield College. She lives with her husband and son in Austin, Texas. She has still never applied for a passport.

BUZZY JACKSON is the author of the book *A Bad Woman Feeling Good: Blues and the Women Who Sing Them.* She recently received her PhD in American History from UC Berkeley. In the course of her travels she has worked as a radio DJ in Los Angeles and Bozeman, in television in Barcelona, as a tennis hostess in Lake Tahoe, as a tour guide at NATO headquarters in Brussels, and in publishing in New York City. She currently divides her time between Boulder, Colorado, and the rest of the world.

JUDITH LEVIN is a children's librarian and freelance writer living in New York City. She has published plenty of work-for-hire children's nonfiction, professional articles, and random book introductions: Her favorite assignment memo stated, "This collection of stories doesn't make any sense. Please write an introduction for the collection that makes it sound as though it does." The essay in this collection is her first work-for-fun publication.

ANN LOMBARDI is a twenty-one year veteran travel consultant, born-again athlete, and former ESL teacher with a knack for misadventure. She has been heard on Fox, NPR, and Clark Howard's nationally syndicated "Friday Flyer" radio travel show and is often quoted in the *Atlanta Journal-Constitution* and travel industry magazines. Ann's zest for globetrotting has led her all over Europe, the Americas, Asia, and the Caribbean. She hangs her backpack in Atlanta, Georgia, where she is writing her first travel book. Check out her company's website at www.thetripchicks.com.

LESLIE MILLER is the editor of the anthology *Women Who Eat: A New Generation on the Glory of Food* and has published essays in various collections and magazines, including *Far From Home: Father-Daughter Adventure Travel* and *The Unsavvy Traveler.* She is currently at work on a book about Vegas weddings. Rather unbelievably, Adventure Pete came to be only one of three dogs residing in her Seattle home, including another beagle.

KARIN PALMQUIST is a Washington, D.C.–based freelance writer. She's written for the two Washington newspapers, the *Times* and now the *Post,* for the last five years. The job keeps her out of the country for six months a year, in godforsaken places that few people can spell. She passes her tips from the road on to NPR's "The Savvy Traveler," and she's a contributing editor to two guidebooks by Fodor's on her native Sweden and Scandinavia.

Born in Canada's north, **MICHELE PETERSON,** a former financial executive, now works as an international consultant with clients in Canada, Bolivia, Honduras, and Guatemala. She is also a freelance writer and columnist who has published essays on family, travel, culture, and shopping for publications such as *Homemakers, Globe and Mail, Christian Science Monitor,* the *National Post,* and magazines from Guatemala to South Africa. She is a contributor to *Sand in My Bra: Funny Women Write from the Road.* She lives in Greektown in Toronto, which is as close as she can get to Mýkonos.

PAIGE PORTER entered journalism Southern-style: through the back door. After receiving her master's degree, she interned with *Southern Living* and realized that writing stories about pound cakes was actually more fun—and a lot more filling—than writing a dissertation. Then, as features writer for *Coastal Living,* she wrote about the beaches of North America, Mexico, and the Caribbean while practicing the art of solo sunscreen application. Her humor column, nationally syndicated by Knight Ridder News Service, chronicled her misadventures on the road. Wishing to sleep more often in her own bed, she gave up the gypsy life and joined *Better Homes & Gardens* as West Coast editor. She lives in San Francisco.

SAMANTHA SCHOECH spent portions of her childhood in a fishing village in Mexico, at a Buddhist meditation center in Vermont, and in a leafy suburb north of the Golden Gate Bridge. She now lives and writes in San Francisco—fiction when possible, but also travel stories on Mexico and California and snappy copy about clothing. Her short stories have appeared in *Glimmer Train,* the *Gettysburg Review, The Sun, Seventeen,* and other journals and magazines.

KAY SEXTON's short and short-short stories have been honored in various contests, most recently in the *Guardian* fiction contest. She writes two online columns, which can be linked to through her website at www.charybdis.freeserve.co.uk. Her essays appear in numerous anthologies, including *France, A Love Story*. She currently lives in Sussex, England but has moved house twenty-seven times in thirty years, so she's not promising to stay there long.

As a senior travel writer at *Sunset* magazine for the last seven years, **LISA TAGGART** has ridden camels in the Moab desert, sailed a J-24 in San Francisco Bay, and dug her station wagon out of High Sierra snow with a croquet mallet and a hairbrush. She lives in Santa Clara, California.

MARA VORHEES has been working, traveling, and attracting stares by going jogging in the former Soviet Union since 1990. She notes the striking similarity between living in Russia and competing in triathlons: Both are grueling experiences that somehow seem fun after they are done. A freelance writer based in Somerville, Massachusetts, Mara has coauthored Lonely Planet guidebooks to Moscow, Russia & Belarus, and the Trans-Siberian Railroad, as well as to more mainstream destinations like Washington, D.C. and Morocco; her travel stories have appeared in the *Boston Globe* and *Roll Call*. Mara participates in sprint and Olympic-distance triathlons around New England.

JUDY WOLF is a freelance writer, speaker, mountaineer, and whitewater kayak instructor. She's taken numerous extended solo journeys around the globe, traveling by foot, bus, jeep, camel, truck, boat, train, plane, elephant, and bicycle to more than thirty countries on five continents. Her work has appeared in *Alpinist*, *Adirondack Explorer*, and numerous other magazines and journals, including the anthologies *Far From Home* and *A Woman's Europe*. She lives in upstate New York and is currently working on a book of travel essays. More at www.judywolf.com.

About the Editor

A few years after Seattle-based freelancer **KATE CHYNOWETH** stumbled into travel writing, she realized that she preferred disastrous trips to successful ones. This only occasionally gets in the way of her writing and editing for the *Best Places to Kiss* guidebooks. Her work is published in *Sunset, Seattle,* and *Real Simple,* as well as in the Seal Press anthology *Women Who Eat.* She is also the author of *The Bridesmaid Guide: Etiquette, Parties, and Being Fabulous.*

Selected Titles from Seal Press

For more than twenty-five years, Seal Press has published groundbreaking books. By women. For women. Visit our website at www.sealpress.com.

No Touch Monkey! And Other Travel Lessons Learned Too Late by Ayun Halliday. $14.95. 1-58005-097-2. A self-admittedly bumbling vacationer, Halliday shares—with razor-sharp wit and to hilarious effect—the travel stories most are too self-conscious to tell.

Solo: On Her Own Adventure edited by Susan Fox Rogers. $15.95, 1-58005-137-5. The second edition of this collection describes the inspiring challenges and exhilarating rewards of going it alone.

Italy, A Love Story: Women Write about the Italian Experience edited by Camille Cusumano. $15.95, 1-58005-143-x. Two dozen women describe the country they love and why they fell under its spell.

The Moment of Truth: Women's Funniest Romantic Catastrophes edited by Kristin Beck. $14.95, 1-58005-069-7. This anthology dispatches from the nasty but hilarious underbelly of relationships gone sour.

I'll Know It When I See It: A Daughter's Search for Home In Ireland by Alice Carey. $14.95, 1-58005-132-4. This lyrically written memoir explores the life of a young New Yorker, her ties to Ireland, and her eventual move to the country as an adult.

Lost on Purpose edited by Amy Prior. $13.95, 1-58005-120-0. Female characters held in thrall by an urban existence fill this vibrant collection of short fiction.